The **Graphic Designer's** Guide to
Portfolio Design

Debbie Rose Myers

WILEY

John Wiley & Sons, Inc.

Copyright © 2005 by John Wiley & Sons. All rights reserved

Published by John Wiley & Sons, Inc., Hoboken, New Jersey
Published simultaneously in Canada

For general information on our other products and services or for technical support, please contact our
Customer Care Department within the United States at (800) 762-2974, outside the United States at (317)
572-3993 or fax (317) 572-4002.

Wiley also publishes its books in a variety of electronic formats. Some content that appears in print may not be
available in electronic books. For more information about Wiley products, visit our website at www.wiley.com.

Library of Congress Cataloging-in-Publication Data

Myers, Debbie Rose.
   The graphic designer's guide to portfolio design / Debbie Rose Myers.
       p. cm.
   Includes index.
   ISBN 0-471-56925-9
   1. Art portfolios--Design. 2. Design services--Marketing. 3. Graphic
arts--Vocational guidance. 4. Computer graphics. I. Title.
   NC1001.M94 2005
   741.6'068'8--dc22
2004013111

Printed in the United States of America

10 9 8 7 6 5 4 3 2

● contents ●

This book would not have been possible without the support and inspiration of many people. I would like to take a moment to acknowledge these wonderful friends and colleagues.

You will see art by many of my most talented students throughout this book. I thank them all! I especially want to express gratitude to Julie Ruiz and Ryan Skinner for their insights and artwork.

I also extend special thanks go to Linda Weeks, Frank Balzano, Steven Bleicher, Karen Sanok, Christine David, Randy Gossman, Howard T. Katz, Valen Evers, Karen Sanok, and Carrie Cochran. These fabulous friends willingly donated their art for this project. This book presents compelling and dazzling art as a result of their contributions. A special thanks to Paul Kane, the designer who lent his considerable artistic talents to the project by giving me great art for the interior and designing the cover as well.

William Kalaboke, President of the Art Institute of Fort Lauderdale, Florida, and Arene Wites were also instrumental in the creation of this book. They offered their time (a precious commodity) and support.

I am most grateful for the encouragement I received from both Margaret Cummins, Senior Editor, Michael Olivo, Senior Production Editor, and Rosanne Koneval, Senior Editorial Assistant at John Wiley & Sons, as well as the copy editor Janice Borzendowski. They all knew when to support me and when to push me!

To M. Kathleen Colussy, who endlessly listened to my day-to-day traumas while working on the book. She is a wise and dear friend.

To my beloved husband, Glenn, who always knew when to hug me, when to leave me alone with my laptop computer, and when to bring me chocolates!

If you are looking for inspiration, please visit my website at www.debbierosemyers.com. There you will find examples of digital portfolios and tons of student websites. I will be happy to answer your questions.

1

The Portfolio Process— Start to Finish

"Can you start on Wednesday?" The words floated across the table. I paused for a moment before answering. "I believe I can free up the remainder of the week." (Not that I had had anything lined up.) The dean of education handed me a completed teaching schedule, shook my hand, and said, "The meetings are all day Wednesday. You start teaching on the following Monday. I'll need all of your syllabi by next week." I nodded and mumbled, " No problem." As I stood up, the dean spoke once more. "We're taking a chance on you, so don't let us down." Taking a slow breath so as not to hyperventilate, I said, "I'll do my best." I picked up my portfolio, walked out of the office, and headed to back to my car.

This certainly wasn't my first job interview. I had completed the interviewing process many times before. What made this interview so nerve-wracking was that I wanted the job so desperately. The expression, "Never let them see you sweat" came to my mind as the adrenaline finally gave out. Then it hit me: "I'm teaching college!" I hurried to the nearest phone to call home. I couldn't wait to break the news of my new position.

So how did I get that job? Was it my interview skills? My interview attire? Might I have been offered the job because of my positive attitude? Nope! It was my portfolio—plain and simple. I had come to the interview with a portfolio of design projects that I had completed in college, plus a number of pieces that I had created in my freelance business. They, plus my ability to discuss the portfolio projects and what they represented, were what got me the job.

The process of building a portfolio and conducting interviews for jobs is, possibly, the most intense you will ever undertake as you advance your career. Your portfolio must reflect the very best of what you can contribute as an artist/designer to a potential employer. And the pivotal moment in your interview process begins as the employer slowly opens your portfolio to reveal the best of what you have to offer.

You Need a Portfolio

As you arrive for your job interview, you notice that another applicant is leaving. And when your interview concludes and you are departing, you see that yet another applicant is waiting. Assume these three people have equal qualifications for this job, and that each candidate has a similar college degree, and had an excellent interview. How does the company make a decision?

No doubt about it, the competition is tough in today's job market. So you cannot just say you are an

above • **Preparation is the key to a successful portfolio.**
below • **Here is a beautiful display that really showcases the artwork.**

get a job. Not anymore. Today, portfolios are used to secure jobs in many different areas. Architects, interior designers, multimedia and Web designers, engineers, journalists, and teachers can all use a professional portfolio to advance their careers. A portfolio for these professionals will be unique to their field of specialization; however, the overall purpose is to present a unified body of work that represents what the designer can offer. Thus, regardless of your design background, you can develop a portfolio that highlights your accomplishments and shows off your talent. Portfolios are especially necessary for people seeking a new job, changing career fields, or negotiating for a promotion or raise.

It's one thing to say, "I have great organizational skills," but when you can give examples of that statement, you're demonstrating that you can do the job. It's the difference between saying, "I can do it . . . really!" and showing you can—the difference between talk and action.

If you look up the definition of "portfolio" in a dictionary, you're likely to read something like: "a portable collection of paper and artifacts that demonstrates one's experience and skills." That's pretty vague, considering that these papers can be made up of almost anything— artwork, writing samples, award certificates, even performance reviews. Other samples might include customer satisfaction surveys or graphs that chart improvements in products or services based on your contributions. The point is, the artifacts you include in your portfolio should always be chosen carefully to highlight your most relevant skills and achievements.

A Portfolio Has to Stand Alone

Suppose for a moment that your portfolio is being viewed by a potential employer but that you are not allowed to in the room while this is going on. Will he or she be able to understand the pieces, or your participation in the projects it contains? The point is, once you have selected what to include in your portfolio, organize them in a logical manner. You may choose to arrange you work by strengths, or chronologically. Whichever way you choose, document your involvement with the project. For instance, if you include a brochure from a training program, make sure the interviewer knows whether you designed the brochure, attended the class, or organized the event. Add a simple caption to clarify your connection to the piece.

extraordinary designer; you must provide the evidence. That's the purpose of your portfolio: it demonstrates the proof of your skills and abilities. Instead of just talking during a job interview about what you have done or can do, you can show samples of your work. Your professional portfolio showcases your talents. In this way, a well-designed portfolio can help you stand out from the other candidates. It gives you the edge.

It was once thought that only fine artists, graphic designers, and fashion designers needed a portfolio to

Building Your Portfolio

The hardest part about building a portfolio is deciding where to begin. You know that you must include your best art in the "port," but just how do you go about organizing the presentation? You may have several dozen pieces of your work or just a few. As you begin to develop your portfolio, you must first think about which pieces are worthy of inclusion. Your design background and history will most certainly influence this process. If you are still in college, your portfolio will more than likely contain a collection of projects that reflect the classes you have completed. In contrast, a professional in the field will exhibit a different set of layouts based, at least in part, on completed client jobs. Consider the following situations for which it makes sense to develop a portfolio.

You Are a Professional in a Related Field

You have been working in advertising, but want to move into the area of graphic design. You are a fine artist who illustrates or paints, and you have a number of finished pieces, but you don't feel that they best reflect your current design sensibilities. In this case, consider taking one of your illustrations or other arts piece and placing it in a layout. Show the application of the piece. A good illustration will look even better as an editorial spread.

Perhaps you have worked in a related field but want to change the direction of your career. In this case, consider displaying early versions of any client-based projects. You may have lots of sketches for ideas that were eliminated from final use. Many of my initial concepts were actually better than the ones eventually selected by the client.

Or perhaps as part of your job, you were part of several design-related workgroups. Why not display the art developed by the group, then clearly define your involvement with the project? Including these concept designs in the portfolio shows your range of design abilities and the thought process involved, and it freshens up the look of your port.

Demonstrate expertise and technical skills. Demonstrate that you are a problem solver. Employers want to know not only what work experience you have had, but what skills you gained. Give explanations of your involvement with a project and how you contributed to the overall success of the project. You want to be able to demonstrate that you are a top-notch designer who is both creative and self-disciplined.

You Are a Student Still in College

Much of the design work you complete in college or a technical school can be considered for inclusion in your portfolio. You may, for example, have recently finished a series of design-based classes, in which your professors challenged you to create a variety of creative pieces to fit the design criteria they established. Take a good look at these projects. Many of them demonstrate your style of design. And because student portfolios tend to be general in nature, be especially aware of projects that show your area of expertise. If you are an excellent illustrator or photographer, make sure your portfolio reflects that special talent. (You'll find additional discussion on the selection of appropriate projects a little later on.)

Was this project completed in college or in the field? A truly professional piece simply shows off your art skills and abilities.

Computers are an integral part of today's design environment. Most disciplines utilize technology to complete work.

You Are Searching for New Ways to Develop Artwork

Completing your basic studies is important, but you might also want to consider these additional options:

- Think about joining an advanced design group in your area.
- Consider participating in any design honor's groups or industry organizations.
- Investigate applying for an internship?
- Enter a community-based contest.

Each of these venues provides an excellent opportunity to show what you can do. And the best part is that you could end up with a printed piece that shows real-world experience. The point is, don't be afraid to show off.

You Participate in a Summer Program or Attend a Special Workshop

Special seminars in design are offered in most major cities throughout the year. And Companies such as Adobe and Macromedia regularly offer free demonstrations of their best-selling software. Companies that specialize in training frequently give one-day workshops in design-related areas. For example, as part of my master of fine arts program, I studied Native American culture and art for two summers in Santa Fe, New Mexico. During those months, I created a number of artistic pieces during week-long workshops. I highly recommend that you explore any opportunity to advance your design skills.

You Design for Family and Friend.

Never miss an opportunity to generate artwork that you might be able to include in your portfolio. Perhaps your aunt is starting her own business. Offer to design her business card and stationery package. Maybe she could use some interior design advice for her new building or home office. And designing a professional-looking Web site would most certainly make you her favorite relative. Likewise, your friends (especially the noncreative types) will appreciate you for designing creative resumes for them. And why not create original holiday or birthday cards? In short, keep your eyes open for project opportunities will help you to build up a body of work.

You Take Advantage of Freelance Opportunities

Don't overlook the chance to take on some freelance work. Most design schools feature a freelance bulletin board where local companies post their need for design assistance. Check out this board on a regular basis and contact any company of interest and offer your services. It may sound a little intimidating to do while you're still a student, but the rewards are many. You'll generate some artwork and collect a little cash as well. If you are unsure about what to charge, there are a number of ways to research the going rates. Books such as *Artist's & Graphic Designer's Market* (Cox, 2004), *Starting Your Career as a Freelance Illustrator or Graphic Designer* (Fleishman, 2001), and *Pricing Photography: The Complete Guide to Assignment & Stock Prices* (Heron & McTavish, 1997) will help you determine your costs and profits.

You Advance Your Design Skills Using the Barter System

In addition to freelancing, another viable way of marketing your design expertise is via the barter system. The benefits here are twofold: You get some valuable design experience and you get compensation (though not monetary) as well. I once had a student who went to restaurants in the local area and offered to redesign their menus. In return, he received a voucher for food from the establishments. Not only did he generate some great art, he got to sample some terrific food. What a deal!

You Design for Yourself

If you don't already have a personal identity package, design one. Create your own business card, resume, and stationery. You might also design an invoice for billing freelance clients. Additionally, you might create a self-promotional package (see color insert for some examples).

You Compile Examples of Improvements You've Made to Bad Design

You've seen them: those horrible ads in the back of magazines and newspapers. Find a particularly bad one and create a series of interpretations to improve on it. The same goes for all of the design majors. Bad design is everywhere! If you're an interior designer, find a less-than-effective interior space and show how good design can improve the environment. Likewise, industrial designers can demonstrate how home appliances, children's toys, and computers can be effectively designed.

Focus Your Portfolio

The second step is the most important in the portfolio process: to decide on the particular type of job you want. There are many different areas of specialization within each of the design disciplines, and you will want to tailor your portfolio to the job you want. For example, consider the field of architecture. Within this discipline are a vast variety of jobs available, including: corporate architects, building contractors, architectural engineers, civil and industrial engineers, marine architects, draftspeople, and even architectural journalists and historians. If interior design is your specialty, you'll find jobs as interior design stylists, manufacturers' representatives, sales associates, renovation specialists, draftspeople, facility and space planners, lighting consultants, and set designers. Graphic designers will be able to choose from such diverse careers as art director, production assistant, layout specialist, prepress specialist, illustrator, or production artist. Although every portfolio will look different for each field, the objective is the same: to create a design portfolio that demonstrates ability.

Identify Your Strengths

In order to develop a portfolio that highlights your accomplishments and shows off your skills, you must blend two different concepts. First, your portfolio must give a snapshot of your creative talents and imagination. Second, and more important, your "port" must represent your ability to communicate design concepts and ideas. As such, your portfolio must be an effective tool to

This beautiful display clearly shows the designer's range of style. The model stand to the right is an eye-catching way to attract viewers.

promote you. So, regardless of the job you're applying for—illustrator, photographer, or interior designer—place in your portfolio only those samples that match the job you're applying for. Beautifully designed greeting cards will not make an impression if the job calls for a space planner. Remember, you can always add samples of other work you have created in the back of your portfolio. Label it and include it in a separate section. Or you can create a second portfolio just to show how versatile you are.

The most important thing to remember when creating a portfolio is to ensure that your work always represents your best efforts. *Never* include a weak piece in your port even if it demonstrates the skills that a particular job requests. If you're not sure what to include, ask for advice. Consult with professionals and professors. Allow them to critique your work. It may make you a little uncomfortable, but it will help you to focus on your strengths. And don't forget to replace older design work with newer, fresher designs; and, whenever possible, use professional work.

Diversify or Focus Your Portfolio

There are a number of differing viewpoints on this topic. Many companies feel that you should diversify and show a wide range of pieces. Other companies believe that the portfolio should highlight a well-defined style by displaying art created within that narrow range. The problem with a narrowly focused port is that it can exclude you from a number of different jobs. As an example, a fashion port that focuses exclusively on, say, bathing suit and outdoor attire, may not get you an interview in a company that's looking for someone to design evening wear. Or a graphic designer who creates art with an urban approach might be excluded from a design firm that caters to a corporate clientele. Simply put, a diversified portfolio opens you up to a wider range of job opportunities.

left • Always be prepared to discuss your art. Expect to be asked to explain why you created a piece in a certain way. Your ability to articulate an answer can influence how you are perceived as an artist.

below • Make eye contact and demonstrate your confidence. You would be amazed how many people cannot look others in the eye when talking to them. If this is a problem for you, practice in front of a mirror or with family and friends, if necessary.

So do you diversify or focus your portfolio? The answer is . . . it depends! If the description of a particular job appears to ask for specific skills, you should tailor your work for the position you are applying for. However, if you are just starting out, it is best to have a portfolio that showcases the many different types and styles of work you can offer as a designer.

Some companies recommend taking a common-sense approach. Every potential employer has an idea of what should be in a portfolio, and most agree that the selection of pieces in a portfolio should be based on what the designer wants to say about him- or herself. If possible have a couple of extra pieces on hand. Perhaps the best advice is to research each company and determine what they might be looking for in a designer. Then rotate your design work in and out as the job indicates.

This much is clear: the portfolio you present should reflect your best examples of your designs and concepts. The pieces you ultimately choose for your portfolio will stand as an indication of your ability to organize, conceptualize, and to present. Whatever artwork you decide to show, make sure that each piece represents the best of what you offer as a designer. Keep the goal in mind: You want your potential employer to decide that they must hire you and have access to your unique design ability!

Be Prepared

Once you have created a portfolio, you will always have it at the ready. You never know when an opportunity to interview for a new job (or for a promotion) will come along. And when opportunity does knock, you will be ready to answer the inevitable question about your qualifications by opening your port and showing them. "I designed a new clothing line that would really enhance your product line—here let me show it to you." This book will show you how to be always prepared. ■

2

Planning Your Portfolio

If the portfolio functions as an evaluation tool for identifying the best applicant for a given position, then the way it is designed and arranged serves as a model for the organizational skills of the designer. The initial layout and overall display of the work in your portfolio should be the focus of your first attempts at its creation. You want to make it as easy as possible for a perspective employer to examine your work. To help you in that effort, this chapter begins with a discussion of the planning process for the portfolio and concludes with an examination of layout styles for the portfolio. (Note that this book is written to include many different design disciplines, so many of the concepts presented here reach across the arts.)

It is best to start considering your portfolio as soon as you determine that you will need one. For many of you, that will be when you enter college or technical school. By creating the portfolio as you advance your education you have the best opportunity to create top-quality pieces. Think about it this way: As each class assignment is given, you create a new piece to satisfy the requirements of that class. Thus, in time, you are able to build up a body of art. These pieces become the basis of your first developmental portfolio. Although this is an exciting process, at times it can also be overwhelming. Sometimes it seems that there is just too

much to organize and no easy way to carry out the work. Don't worry about where to start; just jump right in.

How do you recognize when you have professional-quality work? What should stay? What should go? What should the portfolio reflect? By answering these questions you will be able to develop a strong, creative set of visual solutions. A good rule of thumb is to never include a piece of art in your portfolio unless you are prepared to discuss it in detail.

To assist in the design process, consider these three rationales:

1. Concept
2. Content
3. Follow-through

Let's examine them one at a time.

Concept

Regardless of your creative background, you can develop a portfolio that highlights your accomplishments and shows off your skills. The first step is to define the objectives for each of the pieces that you will include. Ask yourself questions such as: What was the overall purpose or target audience of the art or design? Why did

Encourage your friends to critique your work. By doing so, you may gain some valuable insights as well as different points of view.

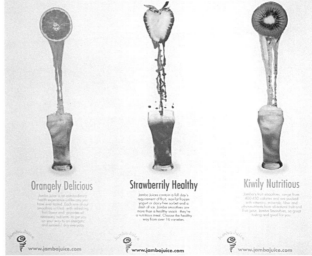

above • **Ad series that use a consistent style to promote a product are difficult to create. Here is a successful example.**

below • **This wonderful fashion illustration shows off the talent of the designer through the use of both style and attention to deatil.**

you pick the particular colors and the layout of the piece that you used? Was a particular age or gender targeted? The following is a sampling of the types of questions that might be asked about a magazine advertisement that is to be included in the graphic design portfolio:

- What kind of company or organization would request the ad?
- What was the purpose of the ad?
- Who was the target audience for the ad?
- What was the page size (full page, half page, quarter page, etc.)?
- What images were included and where did they come from?
- What was the message of the ad?
- Where does the client want the ad to be run?

Content

What do you want to say about yourself as a designer? Do you specialize in specific areas of design, or are you a generalist? Do you have a well-defined style? The work

you select for your portfolio will speak volumes about your art and design skills. Here are some guidelines to help you get started identifying content.

Don't Throw Away Good Ideas

Too often, students come to my port class and inform me that they are "throwing out every piece they've made because they just aren't good enough." In fact, that's not the case. Most of their projects incorporate some wonderful concepts that just didn't quite work out. You need

A versatile portfolio case is one that can hold a lot of work, yet is easy to manipulate during an interview.

to learn to recognize when a project contains a good idea, even if the result is not all that you had hoped. And when you find such a situation, redesign and refine the piece. A good idea is always a good idea worth developing. Building a portfolio doesn't mean you have to start completely from scratch. If you have doubts about the quality of a project, seek other opinions. Professors, industry professionals, and friends can often offer a valuable fresh perspective.

Chapter 1 discussed some of the many other ways in which pieces might be created for a portfolio for those no longer in school. Freelance work, workshops, redeveloping related art into new pieces, and designing

for family and friends all are ways to generate portfolio work. For the working professional, the portfolio process is exactly the same. Look for ways to utilize existing art. Keep in mind, your port exhibits the growth of your, the designer's, talent.

Keep Every Successful Piece

In fact, keep every unsuccessful piece. Do not discard even preliminary sketches. You never know when inspiration will hit and you'll think of a better solution or a new way to handle the project. Your portfolio is more than just a case filled with work; it is a collection of work gathered over time that reflects your visual approach to design.

Identify Your Format

Before you assemble all of your design work, you must decide on a display format. How you organize and present your concepts speak volumes about you as a designer. Your portfolio display case can be traditional, elaborate, or even wild in the extreme. Whether you display work on loose boards or on CDs, keep in mind that the presentation must not overshadow the work. Its purpose is to serve to enhance the design examples. Let's begin by taking a look at the traditional method of display—the portfolio case.

The Portfolio Case: Functionality versus Appearance

As you begin assembling your work, you must think about the presentation methods that are available. One of the most popular display methods is the traditional portfolio book or case. A variety of sizes and styles can be found in art supply stores and at numerous Web sites. A typical portfolio case consists of a bound set of pages with a coiled edge, although some cases feature a ring binder and sheet protectors, which allow you to add and remove pages as you need them. Work is then slipped into the sleeves. Traditionally, black pages have been the color of choice, although gray and white pages are sometimes used to display work as well.

Some portfolios feature a permanently bound case without the inside spiral binding. As with most cases, you simply insert your artwork into the sleeves. The difference is that the portfolio has a finite number of pages, which may be a problem for someone who wishes to display a large number of pieces. However, these types of

cases tend to be a bit sturdier than others, and you don't run the risk of your pages getting mangled from constant changing.

When deciding on a case, look for those that allow the pages to turn easily. The portfolio should be easy for you to handle. Look for a quality case that has comfortable handles. (I once went on an interview where I had to drag my portfolio around an office building for an hour as part of the interview process!) The case should be big enough to give your art some "breathing room." Buy one that is at least a couple inches larger than the biggest piece you intend to showcase. Most artists choose 11 by 14 inches or 18 by 24 inches (a more in-depth discussion of portfolio case sizes is included in Chapter 4). And if you can afford it, buy a case that has a nice cover. Leather (or simulated leather) makes the most professional-looking presentation, although recently I've seen some high-tech metal cases that look pretty sharp. A good case will help you to keep your work in a logical sequence and well protected.

Frayed and ripped cases, pages that fail to turn properly, and ripped sleeves make a poor showing and imply that you do not care about your work. The care you take in displaying your work says a lot about how you feel about yourself as an artist.

Another important criterion for deciding on the right case is to keep in mind that you may have to open the case on someone's desk. So don't buy one that is cumbersome or difficult to work with. You don't want to fumble around with it during the interview. You may find that a letter-size case is more convenient to carry and can more easily present smaller works such as logos, business cards, and postcards.

In contrast, if you are a fine artist and your work is too large for a portfolio, you may choose to display in an altogether different manner. Since much of your work may be large, you might choose a case that allows for slide displays as well as several small works. Yet another option is a colored box, which might be plain or embellished. This innovative style of case can easily accommodate loose pieces and 3-D works.

Many artists feel that more than one type of case may be necessary. They bring both small and large portfolios to a job interview. In conclusion, the size of the portfolio case you select should be dictated by the size of pieces that you will be displaying.

The Digital Portfolio

Digital portfolios have become very popular in recent years. They are small, easy to carry, and can be left with the potential employer as a reminder of your skills and

● ● ● Take a Walk on the Wild Side: The Concept Portfolio

What if you're an individualist and want to set yourself apart from the crowd? A practical portfolio is not for you! You want a different kind of portfolio. You want to display your work in a creative and original way. You want a *concept portfolio*. A concept portfolio thematically ties together both the art and the presentation. This unique system, usually created from scratch, allows you the freedom to fully exhibit your creative vision. What you are trying to achieve is an entire identity system that begins from the moment you produce the portfolio to the perspective employee. A concept portfolio goes far beyond the traditional port. It may feature a case created from thin sheets of steel bolted together with small rivets, or introduce unusual colors to offset the art. A series of dazzling layouts may be applied to show off the contents. Whatever methods are applied, the concept portfolio will not look like any others.

As you probably can tell, deciding to use a concept portfolio usually involves taking some risks. So before you go full speed ahead, sketch some ideas and try them out on your friends and family. Make sure you get the response you desire. A comment like, "Oh, man, that's weird" is not necessarily what you want to hear. Make sure the portfolio does not overwhelm the work it displays. The following describes two examples of well-designed, single-theme concept portfolios, by Ryan Skinner and Julie Ruiz shown at a portfolio review in 2000, sponsored by the Art Institute of Fort Lauderdale. Every quarter, the Institute invites employers from area design firms to come and view the work of its graduates. A large room at the Fort Lauderdale Convention center is rented so that all design majors can show their work. For graduates, the goal is to find a way to make their work stand out from the rest. Ryan and Julie show us two examples of the best of the concept portfolio.

Julie created an identity system for her portfolio that went far beyond the boards and presentation case. She assembled a concept portfolio that was a study in blue. Julie began by determining the name of her graphic design company: Blue Box Graphics. Then she began to think about an overall strategy for presenting her work. Julie decided to invoke the nostalgia of the 1950s as the overall theme. One of the first items she created was a promotional piece that could be given out at portfolio review. This consisted of a metal lunchbox with her logo on the front. Located inside was a digital portfolio, a "baloney sandwich" CD. A bag of potato chips was relabeled with the blue Box Graphics logo. A small juice container with blue-colored juice was included to complete the fifties look. Julie mounted her resume, based on the same theme, on silver board along with a matching business card. You can see an example of Julie's work in the color insert.

Julie was not afraid to embrace the portfolio interview day experience! She dressed up in a 1950s waitress outfit and gave out lunchboxes containing her work. She got five job offers that day!

Julie's presentation boards were spray-painted with silver glitter and clear coat so that they resembled a sparkly bowling ball from the 1950s. The sketchbook received silver airbrush treatment to match the other colors of the design. A miniature bowling ball attached with a tiny chain was added to connect the sketchbook to the rest of the work. At the portfolio review, Julie completed the concept by dressing as a waitress from the 1950s. Each visitor to her table received a CD that looked like a baloney sandwich. And the tablecloth was selected to extend the retro style.

Here are two examples of Julie's work, showing a tremendous versatility in design. As you can see, Julie not only creates graphic design work, she illustrates beautifully as well.

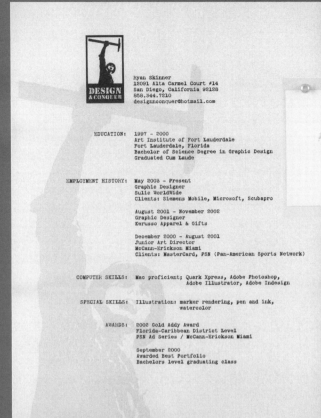

Ryan Skinner
12091 Alta Carmel Court #14
San Diego, California 92128
858.344.7210
designnconquer@hotmail.com

EDUCATION: 1997 - 2000
Art Institute of Fort Lauderdale
Fort Lauderdale, Florida
Bachelor of Science Degree in Graphic Design
Graduated Cum Laude

EMPLOYMENT HISTORY: May 2003 - Present
Graphic Designer
Sulic WorldWide
Clients: Siemens Mobile, Microsoft, Scubapro

August 2001 - November 2002
Graphic Designer
Kerusso Apparel & Gifts

December 2000 - August 2001
Junior Art Director
McCann-Erickson Miami
Clients: MasterCard, PSN (Pan-American Sports Network)

COMPUTER SKILLS: Mac proficient; Quark Xpress, Adobe Photoshop,
Adobe Illustrator, Adobe Indesign

SPECIAL SKILLS: Illustration: marker rendering, pen and ink,
watercolor

AWARDS: 2002 Gold Addy Award
Florida-Caribbean District Level
PSN Ad Series / McCann-Erickson Miami

September 2000
Awarded Best Portfolio
Bachelors level graduating class

above • As you can see, the army theme shows up in Ryan Skinner's self-promotion art book. The paper is a gray-green army-inspired choice.

left • This resume designed by Ryan carries forward his "action hero" theme. He deliberately chose a "rough and tumble" font that "said" army. He carried the theme throughout the entire promotional package.

Julie offered this concept portfolio advice: "Everything must mean something. Each thing you create must represent design in all aspects. Don't just slap a logo on a layout; leave an impression on people. Send a self-promotional piece. Don't be afraid to talk about yourself. Be a creative person all around. Think creatively about everything that goes beyond the norm— it's all about details."

Today, Julie Ruiz is a talented designer who creates promotional pieces for VH1. She's one of the featured designers in Communication Arts Graphic Design Annual 45, for her outstanding design work.

Ryan Skinner is driven by concepts. He began to develop his initial ideas by writing a comic book story about an action hero, a champion of graphic design who would attack and kill problems and create new ideas. Instead of a gun, Ryan's hero would use his weapon of choice: a T-square. Ryan developed different versions and formed new ideas, and kept showing his ideas to his teachers to get fresh feedback. As the concept evolved, Ryan researched the additional support elements, such as paper that would be the right color. "I believe that most conceptual things are right there and are the easiest to understand. Look for the obvious and tailor it to your needs. Talk to everyone about your ideas."

Ryan's extensive research led him to call his company Design & Conquer . "I wanted to design a think-tank company with an army motif. This army would shoot down design problems. Bombs would be the creativity . . . I spent a lot of time online and brainstormed with a friend. Eventually, we came up with the company name. We took every idea and wrote it down."

Ryan's final portfolio used a flipbook system. His self-promotion consisted of a CD case that had the company logo on front and a flip-out printed booklet of his work. Ryan purchased an army helmet, put the logo on it, and placed it on the table. Little green army men were scattered everywhere on the table. On the day of the portfolio review, Ryan wore a business suit. He gave out his fold-out book, resume, and business card.

Here is Ryan's advice: "Don't wait until the last moment. . . . I look back and wish I could have done more. I could have worked a lot harder. . . . Be passionate about your work. See what's going on now in the design world; see what ideas are out there. Live and breathe it. Redesign everything in sight. Professionalism is huge. Know the industry-standard programs. Know what clients want—that they have seen many other designers such as yourself. Don't be arrogant, but do be confident. And don't be afraid to try the newest ways to find jobs. I was hired from the Web site I posted on the internet." An employer saw Ryan's online work and invited him in for an interview.

He arrived at the interview with his portfolio and all of his self-promotional pieces. "The company liked the look, printed the pieces, and showed them around the office. The flip-out book got me the job! Your rough book is very important!"

Today, Ryan Skinner is a creative designer who specializes in collateral material designed to support the overall identity of a company and its advertising campaign (such as pens, mugs, wall and desk calendars, postcards, mailers, or small gift packages). You can see some of his work in the color insert.

Here's a little exercise to help you better organize your thoughts. Write a descriptive introduction for each of the pieces in your portfolio. Then ask yourself:

- What is each piece about?
- How does it represent the client or the assignment?
- Why did you include it? What is it about the piece you are proud of?

A primary objective of your portfolio is to demonstrate to potential employers how much you've invested in your job search. Thus, your career becomes a collection of skills and talents, rather than a series of job titles. As in my experience, an organized and professionally designed portfolio could be just the thing that sets you apart from the other applicants.

abilities. They allow you take your work to the employer in a small easily transported format.

The digital portfolio is another way for you to showcase your best work. It allows you to include all of the items mentioned above, housed in a compact presentation. Digital portfolios are generally created and "burned" (or saved) onto CDs. The CD-based port can be duplicated for a relatively low cost and provide you a way to leave your port for the employer to review at a later date. You'll learn more about digital ports in Chapters 5 and 6, and you can see an example of an effective digital port in the color insert.

Follow-Through

Planning your portfolio means thinking about the end even when you're at the beginning of the process. Ask professionals in your field for specific feedback on your portfolio. Don't know anyone in the field? Ask your artist friends before you assemble the final port. Check for "portfolio days" at area colleges. Frequently, you can attend seminars where industry professionals will be on-hand to offer thoughts about and solutions to problems your work.

Research all prospective employers. Look them up at the library or on the Internet. What type of service or product do they offer? How can you be of benefit to them? If you are to market yourself and your portfolio effectively,

you must know in advance the history and philosophy of the company. The more you know, the better you will be at answering appropriately questions asked of you.

Be prepared to discuss your work. During an interview you will be asked about specific pieces. Your greatest challenge is to prove that you have the skills and experience to do the job. *Never* answer a question with a shrug and an "I don't know," and don't make excuses about the art. The employer will think you have no conceptual skills. Rehearse if you have to, but be ready with answers. And always be positive with your responses. If possible, explain how you can achieve results for the employer.

A Career Development Checklist

This section contains a list of questions and some possible answers to assist you in your career development phase. In business, this process is known as the SWOT technique (for strengths, weaknesses, opportunities, and threats). A SWOT analysis focuses on both the internal and external environments that affect your ability to make a good career decision. A SWOT table generally looks like this:

INTERNAL	STRENGTHS	WEAKNESSES
EXTERNAL	OPPORTUNITIES	THREATS

Using the SWOT Table

Write down answers to the following questions. Don't be modest, but be realistic. Put yourself inside the head of the potential employer as you consider how you will come across during an interview?

Strengths
- What are you skilled at?
- What do you do best?
- Who needs what you have?
- What do other people see as your strengths?

Every time you see an ad for a job, ask yourself, "How do I compare to the competition? Why should this company hire me over everyone else?" When you can answer these questions, you will be well on your way to getting a great job.

Weaknesses

- Which of your job-related skills need improving?
- What are your negative personal characteristics?
- What types of tasks do you find difficult to perform?

A weakness might be that you don't always do enough research before making a decision. Or you may get impatient with yourself or others. Ask yourself if these are characteristics that you see in yourself or that others see in you. Try to be as realistic and honest as you can. Recognize that you can make some changes immediately, whereas others may require some practice and help from others to implement.

Opportunities

- Do you have a clear idea about what you want to do for a living?
- Do you know what size company you want to work for?
- What is the likelihood of job growth in your area?
- Are you aware of any interesting trends in your field?
- Does your knowledge of technology give you a competitive edge? How?
- Would additional education help you to get the job you want?
- Would a change in location enhance your job prospects?

Opportunities help you to define goals. For example, what do you want to be doing in three or five years' time? Are there related career fields for you to explore?

Threats

- What is the likelihood that your field will be downsizing?
- Are you in a dead-end company or field?
- Do you need to change the nature of what you do in order to stay employed?
- Have you been doing the same thing for too long?
- Are there competitors out there with better skills? Who are the competitors and what are their skills?
- What obstacles do you face to improving your knowledge of the field?

This well-thought-out display shows the resourcefulness and vision of the artist. The work is displayed using both traditional (boards and bottles) and state-of-the-art methods (the computer).

- Are the required specifications for your job changing?
- Is changing technology threatening your position?

Decisions, decisions, decisions! Making a career decision is not exactly like choosing where to go for lunch. You have to really involve yourself in the process. By conducting a realistic SWOT analysis, you should be able to see the big picture a little more clearly. If you need more help, ask your family and friends (but be prepared to hear more than you want to know!). Contact a former professor or boss. They may offer some insights to your quest. If your school or college has a career advisory office, make an appointment to consult with someone there.

I always say it's important to know where you are going before you get there. To that end, here is an example of a graphic designer's portfolio checklist. Be aware that for each medium or genre there are very different requirements. Therefore, it is to your advantage to verify what are the required minimums for your discipline. Many of you may already have a checklist from your student days. If not, develop one of you own to help you decide what you need in order to produce a winning portfolio. ∎

Required Pieces	Progress	Date Completed

1. Corporate Identity
- Logo (black and white or color)
- Letterhead (logo, address, phone, fax)
- Envelope (Logo, address)
- Corporate Standard's Manual

2. Folder

3. Annual Report *Must:*
- Meet legal requirements for an annual report
- Be at least 12 pages, plus cover
- Demonstrate continuity of design and concept
- Have a corporate "voice"
- Demonstrate brand image

4. Poster

5. Ad Series

6. Self-promotional:
- Resume plus stationery kit
- One additional promotional piece

7. 3-D Design

8. Web Design *Must include:*
- Overall site plan
- Navigation plan
- Home page
- At least four additional pages

9. Four-Page Editorial Spread
- Cover Page
- Table of Contents

10. Twenty Slides or Print Sheet

11. Digital Portfolio

12. Rough Book

Ten Additional Pieces

You may specialize in a particular area or choose from any of the following:
Advertising
Advertising campaigns, including:
- Print ads
- Broadcast

Required Pieces	Progress	Date Completed

Advertising (con't)

- TV
- Support collateral for your campaigns
  (Post cards, mailers, pens, pencils, fortune cookies with your business card, gift bags filled with small examples of your work—in short, any material that will help the potential employer remember you.)

Graphic Design

- Corporate ID
- Direct mail
- Out of home
- POP (Point of Purchase displays—those neat promotions that you see in the front of the supermarket, such as "back to school or holiday decorations.")
- Package
- Promotional
- Posters
- Multipage documents
- Folder
- Newsletters
- Information graphic

Editorial

- Magazine
- Cover, contents, multiple spreads
- Newspaper
- Books

New Media

- Web sites
- Interactive CDs
- Banners
- Presentations

Illustration/Photography

- Posters
- Ads
- Books
- Editorial

Magazine Layout

●●● LAYOUT AND DESIGN CHECKLIST

Design Elements	Average	Good	Excellent
Is the project visually exciting?	Does it need type?	Does the type support the message? Do the images support the intent of the piece?	Does color enhance the design?
Does it use the principles of designs effectively?	Is there a consistent presentation?	Is there original design?	Do all images and type choice improve the final design?
Does it communicate the intent of the artist?	Is there just too much of everything?	Are the attempts focused and rational?	Does it demonstrate an advanced knowledge of design?
Is it a good design?	It should not be included in the port	It could be improved.	It rocks! Make sure it is seen first!

The Traditional Portfolio
The Resume, Cover Letter, and Business Card

You have created a body of art and now you must determine the best way to showcase it. As explained in Chapter 2, most artists choose either the traditional or digital method, although in recent years many artists are using both. Although digital portfolios have received a lot of attention of late, most employers (and artists) agree that the traditional method is the best overall visual approach, asit allows you to display your work in a structured way. You decide what constitutes your best work. You decide on the display approach.

The focus of this chapter is on the written aspects of the traditional portfolio.

What Goes in Your Portfolio?

As stated previously, your portfolio helps to establish your skills and experience through the quality of your work. It enables the employer to make the connections between your interests and abilities and that of the company. Your portfolio is a collection of projects and achievements that help to define you as a person—your skills, interests, activities, and ability and willingness to commit to the employer. Clearly, then, it should highlight your strengths and areas of expertise.

What you include in your portfolio will, of course, depend on your background and work-related experience. If you are a recent graduate from a college or technical school, your portfolio will primarily be made up of projects completed as a student, and your degree major will determine the appearance of the projects.

Every portfolio should have a unique look and feel to it. In addition to reflecting your special skills and talents as a designer, it should also demonstrate to the potential employer the range of your abilities. All that said, regardless of what you choose to showcase in your port, there are a number of items that you should always include.

- Resume
- Cover letter
- Business card
- Significant samples of your work
- The artist's statement
- Letters of recommendation
- Awards
- Professional memberships
- Portfolio case

Although not considered traditional in nature, the digital version of the portfolio is rapidly gaining in popularity in the design world. We will learn more about the creation of a digital portfolio in an upcoming chapter.

The Resume

Your resume is the document that itemizes for the employer why he or she should hire you. It establishes your knowledge of your profession and gives the employer a good overview of your background. More, the resume sets forth your goals and highlights your accomplishments. Thus, the resume should reflect your experience and establish your credentials. (Note: In Chapter 5, we will take a look at the digital resume.)

Organization is the key to a well-designed resume. So, to design a successful resume, you must first decide on the format. There are two different formats for you to consider: *chronological* and *functional*. There are several factors that determine which format you select, as explained in the following subsections.

The Chronological Resume

Without question, the most widely used format, the chronological resume lists your work experience as history, specifically, in reverse-date form, followed by job titles and responsibilities. Thus, your latest employment is listed first, and continues in reverse order until

When preparing for a job interview, it is important to gather together all of your best work. Your resume, portfolio, and CD all help to establish your credentials.

you have included all your previous relevant positions. The chronological resume makes it easy for the company to see your experience and background in your area of specialization. It is especially effective for accomplished designers with a strong work history.

The problem with chronological resumes is, however, that they tend to focus the reader's attention on what you have done, rather than on what you *can* do. If you are just starting out, you may not have a great deal of industry-related experience, and this format will make that more obvious. So unless you can demonstrate increasing levels of responsibility in a series of jobs, it's probably best to opt for the functional resume, described next.

The Functional Resume

In the functional resume format, you can describe your skills and talents. Instead of listing your experience in chronological order, you can organize your experience according to your areas of specialization. It is particularly useful for college students who have minimal "real-world" experience. Career-changers who wish to enter a different field will also benefit from this format. Likewise, if there are gaps in your work history, say for child-rearing or furthering your education, the functional resume is a good format to consider. Check out the functional resume in the color insert.

The functional resume is not, however, as popular as the chronological resume. One reason is that it is more difficult to write, because it requires a reorganization of information. Another reason is that it makes it more difficult for the employer to determine your contributions to previous employers. That said, a functional resume can be very effective in showing your skills in job-related areas. For example, say you have worked in retail: chances are you were responsible for dealing with customers, organizing merchandise, training or mentoring personnel, and handling purchase problems. These are all skills that an employer will value and want to discuss during an interview.

Parts of the Resume

Name, Address, Phone Numbers

A well-designed resume always begins with basic information about the applicant. Your name and address are important to the employer. (Believe it or not, I've seen beautifully designed resumes on which the designer for-

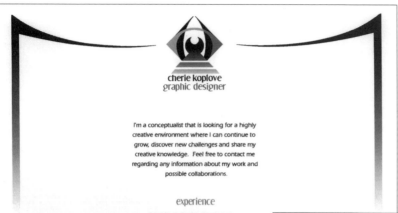

cherie koplove
graphic designer

I'm a conceptualist that is looking for a highly
creative environment where I can continue to
grow, discover new challenges and share my
creative knowledge. Feel free to contact me
regarding any information about my work and
possible collaborations.

experience

Three Years Freelancing Experience
HR Link, LLC - corporate identity, web site development
Kids Can Save Foundation - Theacher's & Student's handboo
P.A.N.D.O.R.A., Inc - corporate identity, advertisements
Lauderdale Yacht Club -poster advertisements, menu desig
Magnivision - brochures, advertisements, point of purchase to
Global Payroll Services - corporate identity
Nation's Health - brochure, advertisement
Stanton - advertisements
Internship at LeftField Advertising

education

Bachelor of Science Degree in Graphic Design – Art Institute of Fort
Attended Northern Essex Community College for a year in their Graphic

design skills

conceptual development, advertisements, package designs, direct m
store and bus signage, displays, brochures, newsletters, catalogs, mag
web animation, web site design and photography.

software skills

Mac and PC platforms
Photoshop, Illustrator, QuarkXPress, Flash, DreamWeaver, Director, F

904 Se 14th St. Apt 2, Fort Lauderdale, FL 33316   978 853 4340   www.what-are-you-look

left • The overall look of your resume conveys
as much about your design sensibilities as the
information you choose to include.

below • A complex resume will benefit from a
"Summary of Qualifications" section. It clearly
highlights the accomplishments of the applicant.

bottom • There should be no doubt in your
mind that this is the resume of a designer! It's
fun, playful, yet conveys all the information necessary to give the background of the artist. It's
a little piece of art in itself.

Debbie Rose Myers
Graphic Designer
1234 East Willow Drive
Anytown, FL 12345
999 • 455 • 1234
dgmyers@webemail.net

Summary of Qualifications

Twenty-four years of diverse college level instruction and curriculum development experience, providing support
to all educational departments.

Over fifteen years of in-depth experience in computers, both PCs and Macs, including installation and maintenance
of over 100 educational computer systems.

Acted as interim coordinator of Graphic Design area at Florida Atlantic University. Hired and trained adjunct faculty
in order to maintain continuity in support of current curriculum. Installed over thirty educational computers in both
educational and support labs.

Created the Art Institute of Fort Lauderdale's desktop publishing and computer graphics curriculum, including both
vector-based and raster-based drawing as well as scanning and image processing. Designed advanced design
courses covering all aspects of modernism and post-modernism.

Organized and implemented the Art Institute's first television production curriculum, including three camera online studio production as well as location shooting. Other topic areas include television graphics incorporating
storyboarding and television camera cards.

A versatile, energetic, and organized educator who has experience originating and implementing curriculum as
well as defining budgetary needs.

Experience

Curriculum Development and Course Evaluation

Responsible for the development of all desktop publishing and computer graphics curriculum. Developed specific
criteria-based objectives in order to design state of the art design curriculum. Originated a new one year evening
division program in electronic publishing while at the Art Institute of Fort Lauderdale. Classes include: Computer
Illustration, Television Graphics, Video Production, Intro to Mass Communications, Color and Composition, and
Graphic Design. Responsible for development of curriculum in Television Production.

- Chairperson: High-Tech Applications in Education Committee
- Chairperson: Advertising Design Computer Curriculum Committee
- Member: SAC's Sub-Committee for Student Support Services
- Member: Employee Recognition Committee
- Member: Advertising Design Portfolio Coordination Committee
- Member: Advertising Design Department Director Search Committee

---

Mario J. Ayerbe
↗ Web .:. Graphic Designer

- Graphic Design ☒
- Web Development
- Corporate Media Kits
- Print Advertising
- Promotional Materials

:Contact

v o i c e	☎	305 . 401 . 6275
f a x	🖨	954 . 322 . 5631
w e b s i t e	🖱	www.mnmdesigns.com
e - m a i l	📫	mayerbe@mnmdesigns.com

Positive and powerful action verbs tell your story effectively. They describe your skills and accomplishments. Used wisely (that is, accurately and with restraint), action verbs make potential employers take notice. Here are several top-quality verbs for you to incorporate in your resume.

Accelerated	Accomplished	Acted	Achieved
Acquired	Adapted	Added	Addressed
Adjusted	Administered	Advanced	Adopted
Advertised	Advised	Advocated	Aided
Aligned	Allocated	Altered	Amended
Analyzed	Answered	Anticipated	Appointed
Appraised	Approached	Approved	Arbitrated
Arranged	Ascertained	Assessed	Assembled
Assigned	Assisted	Attained	Attracted
Audited	Authorized	Automated	Awarded
Balanced	Bargained	Beat	Began
Borrowed	Bought	Briefed	Broadened
Budgeted	Built		
Calculated	Canvassed	Capitalized	Captured
Carried out	Catalogued	Centralized	Challenged
Chaired	Changed	Channeled	Charted
Checked	Chose	Circulated	Clarified
Classified	Cleared	Closed	Coauthored
Coached	Collaborated	Collected	Combined
Commanded	Commissioned	Committed	Communicated
Compared	Compiled	Complied	Completed
Composed	Computed	Conceived	Conceptualized
Concluded	Condensed	Conducted	Conferred
Conserved	Consolidated	Constructed	Consulted
Contracted	Contrasted	Contributed	Contrived
Controlled	Converted	Convinced	Cooperated
Coordinated	Corrected	Correlated	Corresponded
Counseled	Counted	Crafted	Created
Critiqued	Cultivated	Customized	Cut
Dealt	Debated	Debugged	Decided
Decentralized	Decreased	Deferred	Defined
Delegated	Demonstrated	Described	Designated
Designed	Determined	Developed	Devised
Devoted	Diagnosed	Diagrammed	Differentiated
Distinguished	Directed	Disclosed	Discovered
Dispatched	Displayed	Dissembled	Distinguished
Distributed	Diversified	Divested	Documented
Doubled	Drafted	Drew	
Earned	Eased	Educated	Edited
Effected	Eliminated	Employed	Enabled
Encouraged	Endorsed	Enforced	Engaged
Engineered	Enhanced	Equipped	Enriched
Established	Evaluated	Examined	Exceeded
Executed	Expanded	Expedited	Explained
Extended	Extracted	Extrapolated	
Fabricated	Facilitated	Familiarized	Fashioned
Fielded	Figured	Filed	Financed
Fixed	Focused	Followed up	Forecasted
Formalized	Formed	Formulated	Fortified
Fostered	Found	Founded	Framed
Fulfilled	Functioned	Furnished	Furthered

got to include his or her name.) You want the employer to be able to be able to reach you, so don't forget to include your home telephone number and a cell number if you have one; and if you have an email address or perhaps even a Web site, include those as well. The point is, make sure the company has a definitive way to reach you. As soon as you can, buy an answering machine and check it on a regular basis. Check your email frequently. I have a friend who lost a job because he didn't get respond to a telephone message fast enough. The company was in a hurry to reach him and, in the two days it took him to respond, the company hired another applicant. In short, time is of the essence.

Where should your name appear on the resume? It depends on the design style of the resume, but generally your name and address should appearing at the center top of the page, although some prefer to place this all-important information to the right or left, for a slightly different look. This style of design usually works best with resumes that feature a lot of information.

Of course, resumes can be much more creative in their design approach. A well-designed innovative layout helps to balance a resume that is light on content. Take a look at the examples in the surrounding pages. These cleverly designed resumes feature a variety of artistic themes. Notice that there are all sorts of unique compositions; design motifs, such as logos, lines, bullets, and watermarks, give additional appeal. All of these innovative ideas help the potential employer to remember you as a serious designer. The image at the bottom of the previous page shows a clever way to create interest in the simple act of contacting the applicant. It's engaging and visually skillful in its approach.

It is important to think about color (both of the paper and the ink) when you are designing your resume. Color is an eye-catcher and can set you apart from the competition, but it can cause problems as well. Suppose you are asked to fax your resume. Will the color paper you use come out illegible at the other end? Check before you decide.

How long should your resume be? Experts hold many different opinions on this particular subject. When I was a college graduate, the popular length for a resume was one page. The theory was that any resume longer than one page was immediately thrown into the proverbial circular file. The average length of most resumes today is about two pages, but it all depends on your background and level of expertise. My resume is

designer >   **daniel pagan's resumé** | 561 753 8574 | danielpaganone@cs.com ← email me

MY AIM   To work in an environment where the people are as important as the work; practicing design and the creative process keeping in mind the responsibilities I have to society and clients.

EMPLOYMENT

01/01 - 12/01, **AIFL,** Student Financial Services, Fort Lauderdale, FL
Administrative Assistant
Advised students, filed, and organized student files.

08/99 - 08/00, **Walt Disney World Resort,** Epcot Center, Orlando, FL
Guest Services
Provided quality guest service using three different languages, translations, and guest guidance through the park.

01/98 - 07/99, **B/Barquet Architects,** Mexico City, Mexico
Director Assistant
Corporate ID for company, Powerpoint presentations, Word processor documents, data/ spread sheets, revised architects' planes.

above • **Clearly define your goals when writing the objectives section of your resume.**

below • **This applicant's employment history gives a clear picture of the increasing level of work-related responsibilities.**

now four pages long, but I have many years of experience in my area of specialization. If your resume is longer than two pages, it is important to highlight your key attributes for the job. This is usually accomplished by creating a list of career credentials. There are many ways to name this part of the resume. On mine, I use the title "Summary of Qualifications."Alternatives are "Highlights of Qualifications" or "Objectives." In the color insert you'll see an example of a resume that would work equally well for a graphic designer and an interior designer.

If you are just graduating or perhaps are going through a career change, you may not have a great deal to include on the resume. In this case, highlight your important qualifications, achievements, and background. Suggest reasons why you will make a terrific employee. And don't forget, a resume that is interesting or beautiful (especially in the different design professions) counts for a lot! A good rule of thumb for establishing the length of the resume is to balance economy with appropriate depth and detail.

The Objective or Summary Section

You want to grab the attention of the employer. One way to accomplish this is with a philosophy statement or a career mission statement that sets the tone for what is to come. Bullet your accomplishments. Highlight your objectives. Tell the employer what you can do or what you are looking for in a job. This gives the company an understanding of how you can best fit into the structure of the company.

● ● ● **Take Action con't**

Gained	Gathered	Gauged	Gave
Generated	Governed	Graded	Granted
Graphed	Greeted	Grouped	Guided
Handled	Harmonized	Hastened	Headed
Heightened	Held	Helped	Highlighted
Hired	Housed	Hosted	
Installed	Identified	Illuminated	Illustrated
Imagined	Immersed	Implemented	Improved
Improvised	Inaugurated	Indoctrinated	Included
Increased	Incurred	Induced	Influenced
Informed	Initiated	Innovated	Inquired
Inspected	Inspired	Installed	Instigated
Instilled	Instituted	Instructed	Insured
Integrated	Interfaced	Interpreted	Intervened
Interviewed	Introduced	Invented	Inventoried
Investigated	Invited	Involved	Illustrated
Incorporated	Initiated	Instituted	Integrated
Introduced	Invented	Inspected	
Joined	Judged		
Labored	Launched	Learned	Lectured
Led	Leveled	Lightened	Liquidated
Lobbied	Localized	Located	Logged
Lowered			
Maintained	Managed	Mapped	Marketed
Mastered	Matched	Maximized	Measured
Mediated	Merchandised	Merged	Met
Minimized	Mixed	Mobilized	Modeled
Moderated	Modernized	Modified	Monitored
Motivated	Moved	Multiplied	
Named	Navigated	Narrated	Negotiated
Netted	Neutralized	Noticed	Notified
Nurtured			
Observed	Obtained	Offered	Offset
Opened	Operated	Operationalized	Orchestrated
Ordered	Organized	Oriented	Originated
Overhauled	Oversaw		
Paid	Painted	Participated	Passed
Patterned	Perceived	Perfected	Performed
Permitted	Persuaded	Photographed	Pinpointed
Pioneered	Placed	Planned	Played
Pointed	Positioned	Practiced	Prepared
Presented	Preserved	Presided	Prevented
Priced	Printed	Prioritized	Probed
Processed	Procured	Produced	Proofed
Proofread	Programmed	Projected	Promoted
Prompted	Proposed	Proved	Provided
Publicized	Published	Purchased	Pursued
Pushed			
Qualified	Quantified	Quoted	
Raised	Ranked	Rated	Reacted
Read	Realized	Rearranged	Reasoned
Reassembled	Recalled	Received	Recognized
Recommended	Recorded	Recruited	Rectified
Reduced	Referred	Regulated	Rehabilitated
Reinforced	Related	Remodeled	Rendered
Renegotiated	Renovated	Reorganized	Repaired

● ● ● Take Action con't

Replaced	Replenished	Represented	Researched
Reserved	Reshaped	Resolved	Responded
Restated	Restored	Restructured	Returned
Revealed	Reversed	Reviewed	Revitalized
Revised	Revived	Rewrote	Routed
Safeguarded	Salvaged	Saved	Scheduled
Scouted	Screened	Searched	Secured
Segmented	Selected	Sent	Separated
Served	Serviced	Settled	Set up
Shaped	Sharpened	Shipped	Shortened
Showed	Shrank	Simplified	Sketched
Smoothed	Sold	Solved	Sought
Spearheaded	Specced	Specialized	Specified
Speculated	Spoke	Spread	Stabilized
Staffed	Staged	Standardized	Started
Steered	Stimulated	Straightened	Strategized
Streamlined	Strengthened	Stressed	Stopped
Stored	Structured	Studied	Submitted
Substantiated	Substituted	Succeeded	Suggested
Summarized	Superseded	Supervised	Supplied
Supported	Surpassed	Surveyed	Switched
Synchronized	Synthesized	Systematized	
Tabulated	Tackled	Talked	Tailored
Targeted	Taught	Tended	Terminated
Tested	Testified	Tightened	Timed
Took	Took over	Traced	Traded
Trained	Transacted	Transcribed	Transferred
Transformed	Translated	Transported	Traveled
Treated	Trimmed	Tripled	Troubleshot
Uncovered	Undertook	Unearthed	Unified
United	Updated	Upgraded	Used
Utilized			
Validated	Valued	Verified	Viewed
Visited	Vitalized	Volunteered	
Weighed	Welcomed	Widened	Witnessed
Won	Worked	Wrote	

FREELANCE:
- Auto Enhancements 03/03
  Logo design, Corporate Id, Web site
- Ft. Lauderdale International Film Festival 09/02
  Invitation cover design and Photography
- Venice Animal Clinic 01/02
  Logo Design and Corporate Id
- Prudential Financial 07/01
  News Letter
- Triad Housing Partners 03/01
  Logo Design
- Roxy Satellite & Wireless 6/00 - 5/01
  Magazine Layout

James Dunckley | 954-649-8269 | jdunckley@earthlink.net

A good resume lets the employer know what you have already accomplished as a designer. Here is a great example.

reverse chronological order, as already noted. Most companies prefer to see dates of employment.

Your employment history should be more than a listing of job titles and descriptions. It should emphasize your skills and experience. It answers the question: Why will you be valuable to the company? Use this section to highlight how you have made a positive impact on your past employers. To achieve this, you must use action and skills verbs. Incorporate as many of these "can-do" verbs as possible, but don't go overboard! In the sidebar, you'll find a number of such verbs to get you started. But you can find many more in a good thesaurus; and there are many different resources on the Internet. Here are some examples of how to use action verbs to effectively describe your skills and experience:

- Established educational workshops.
- Developed budget requirements.
- Participated in all department meetings.
- Facilitated new tracking system.
- Organized and maintained client files.

What kinds of jobs should you list? There are two schools of thought on this question. Some people believe that you should only list those jobs most relevant to the position you are seeking. Others say it is important to show that you have held down a position for a period of time even if it is out of field. I believe that it is best to play to your strengths. If you have worked in your field, that experience should always be included. If you are a recent graduate with little job-related experience, it is still important to show a steady employment record. Perhaps you have completed some freelance work for a client, friends, or family. These jobs are important and demonstrate your abilities, so be sure to include them.

If you are developing a longer resume, the objective or summary section is important. Without it, you force the employer to read the entire resume to figure out if you are suitable for the company (assuming he or she will read the whole thing!). When a prospective employer finishes reading your key accomplishments, you want him or her to run for the phone to invite you in to interview!

Employment History

Your employment history usually comes after the summary section (unless you believe that your education is your most qualifying feature for the job). This section of the resume traditionally lists your past employment in

Accomplishments

Received honorable mention in the 2002 *Adobe InDesign* competition

Dean's list Summer 2000 and Spring 2002 Honors list Fall 2001 and Winter 2002

above • Have you won any awards? Don't forget to list every accomplishment you have achieved as a designer.

below • It is essential to list all of your accomplishments. Making the Dean's List in college is a notable one!

Education

In this section of the resume, you will list all of your education, in reverse chronological order as you do for your job history. And if you have any certificates or advanced training, list them in this section as well, but be selective with this information. Include only data that will impress the company. If you are in college or a recent college graduate, you do not need to list your high school degree.

If you are still in school but near graduation, include the degree and, in parentheses, the expected date of completion, for example, B.A. (expected 200X). If you are a recent graduate, it is not necessary to include your grade point average unless it is high—3.4 or better. List selected coursework if you think doing so might help you secure the job.

A consistent arrangement is very important in this section. Set the degrees apart so they are easily seen. Use boldface type for emphasis. Make it as easy as possible for the employer to focus on your qualifications. Here is an example:

University of Miami, Coral Gables, FL, 1995–1997
Degree: M.F.A.; Major: Graphic Arts
Nova University, Fort Lauderdale, FL 1992–1994
Ed.S. Computer Applications, Emerging Technologies.
Florida State University, Tallahassee, FL, 1986–1987
Degree: M.S. Mass Communication; Major: Video Production/Advertising.

University of Florida, Tallahassee, FL, 1982–1986
Degree: B.Ed.; Major: Art; Minor: Mass Communication

If you didn't finish your college degree, don't try to hide this fact. Instead, begin with a phrase describing your major, then the name of school and the dates attended. List any continuing education courses you have completed that relate to the job you are applying for. This points to your expertise in the subject. If you have taken continuing education courses after a degree is completed, list those as well.

Honors, Awards and Certifications

What special skills set you apart from everyone else? Always highlight anything that demonstrates a unique set of talents. Perhaps you were invited to participate in an honor's program for designers. If you received any special design awards such as Best in Show, be sure to include this information. And include any academic awards, such as making the Dean's List. If you do not think the resume reader will understand the nature of the award, be sure to include a brief explanation of its meaning and significance.

Professional Affiliations

Are you a member of any professional organizations? Professional groups such as the Advertising Federation, the American Institute of Graphic Arts, or the American Association of Interior Designers usually have student chapters available in your local area. Memberships in career-related clubs or honor societies indicate you are an involved designer, someone who takes an interest above and beyond his or her work. Be sure to list any affiliations that demonstrate leadership skills.

Additional Personal Information

One item frequently left out of the resume is personal information such as your hobbies and interests. Many employers like to see that you have a life outside of work. Outside interests demonstrate that you are a well-rounded person with a natural curiosity about or passion for things other than work.

References or Letters of Recommendation

The popular thinking today is to include a line at the end of the resume that states "References furnished

● ● ● Do's and Don'ts of Resume Design

Do

- Use a direct, active writing style. Begin sentences or phrases with action verbs.
- Pick a resume format and be consistent.
- Make the resume visually appealing. You don't want your resume to look like everyone else's. (For an example of visually appealing stationary, see the color insert.)
- Write with short phrases rather than complete sentences. If you can say it in five words, don't use 20.
- Watch for errors in spelling and punctuation. Ask a qualified friend or colleague to read your resume. I promise you, they will find the mistakes you missed!
- Highlight your accomplishments with positive action words.
- Utilize capital letters, underlining, bullets, or color to emphasize certain items. Use these symbols consistently.
- Tell the truth. Do not skip dates or titles on your resume in an attempt to hide your background or lack of experience. If the employer finds out the real story, you might be fired.
- List sports you were involved in if you are (or were) a college student. Some employers actually seek out athletes because of their teamwork ability and leadership skills.
- Keep the company in mind. Ask yourself, "If I were the employer, would I interview this person?" If you can't answer yes, you're not finished writing your resume.

Don't

- Use personal pronouns (I, my, me) in your resume.
- Give any personal data regarding age, ethnicity, or race; height or weight; marital status, number of children, or health. It is against the law.
- Lay out your resume in such a way that critical information breaks awkwardly at the bottom of a page.
- Include interests or affiliations that might be considered controversial.
- Don't cite your high school degree unless you have no additional schooling.
- Use abbreviations or acronyms.
- Include a snapshot of yourself.
- Use too many big words or the wrong words.
- Mention any salary or vacation requirements.
- Give any negative information about yourself, for example, if you were ever in trouble with the law.

upon request." If you include such a line, be sure you have them handy to supply to the employer who asks for them. Choose your references carefully. Pick people who know your work as an employee, student, or on a personal level (such as a religious contact). Include the name, title, address, and telephone number for each of your references. If needed, add a line or two establishing your relationship with this person.

If you can avoid it, do not use personal friends or family members as references. Simply, they do not carry the same weight as a professional in your area of design. Former clients, former managers, or professors will offer the most credibility in your job quest. Seek their help, but make sure they will be comfortable recommending you and your qualifications. Give each reference a copy of your resume so that he or she is knowledgeable about your history. Explain to all your references that they might be contacted and that you will expect them to respond in a timely manner. I once offered to act as a reference for a fellow professor. Unfortunately, I was unable to respond to the call for several days due to a conference schedule conflict. In that short time, the employer turned to another person for the position.

The Cover Letter

Your friend's birthday is tomorrow and you decide that a book would be the perfect gift. You walk into your favorite bookstore, looking for an appropriate book, only to discover that every volume in the store is devoid of information. Each book has nothing but a plain white cover with the name of the book and the author on it. You see no synopsis, no review, no pictures, no information to help you make a decision.

To the employer, sorting through resumes is a little like this scenario. After placing an ad for a designer in the paper or posting it online, the resumes start pouring in, and there are just too many similar applications to sort through. Obviously, it is important that your application get read, so how are you to differentiate yourself from everyone else applying for the job? One tried-and-true way to achieve this is with a cover letter. Your cover letter is, essentially, your sales pitch. In it, you have the opportunity to highlight your accomplishments and

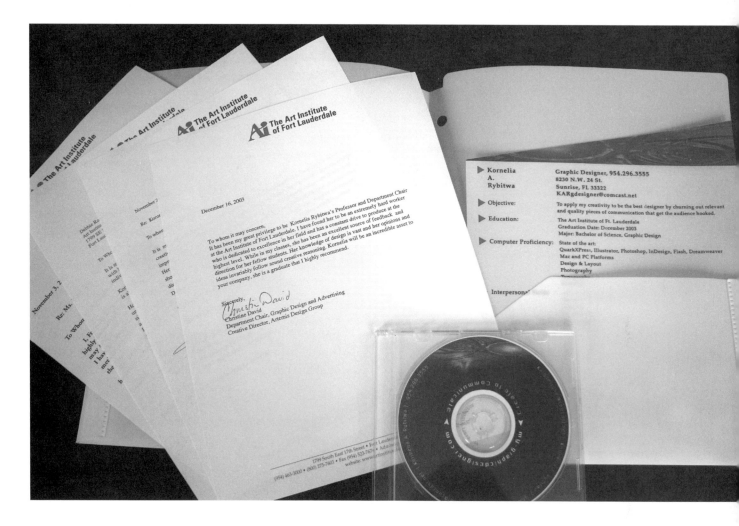

stress to the employers the primary reasons to hire you. A cover letter alone can't get you the job, of course, but it can open doors for the interview process. I assure you, if two people apply for the same job, and only you include a cover letter, you will be called first.

The goal of your cover letter is to, first, introduce yourself to the potential employer and, two, point out why you're the most qualified for the job. A cover letter is most effective when written for a specific employer or a specific job opening; that means you don't use a "boilerplate" letter to apply for every job. It also means you will have to do some research to learn as much as you can about the company. From this research, you can tailor the contents of the cover letter for the job opening. The extra time this takes will pay off in the long run. That research will demonstrate your interest in the job and the company.

Personal letters of recommendation are an effective way to emphasize your talents as a designer, so be sure to include them in your package.

The cover letter generally has three sections:

- Introduction
- Body of the letter
- Closing of the letter

We'll go through them one at a time.

Introduction

In this first section of the cover letter, you introduce yourself and state the purpose of the letter. You indicate

designer > **daniel pagan's letterhead** | 561 753 8574 | danielpaganone@cs.com ← email me

Salutations; Thank you for taking the time to join us at AiFL's June 2003 Portfolio Review.

In the past four years, I have worked towards and attained a Bachelor of Science in Graphic Design. I am eager to continue my education and grow in the field by joining a creative firm. I am interested in developing my skills as a graphic artist and creative developer by filling the position of a designer.

My strengths lie in my personality, design is a product of who I am and what I trust in. I am an ethical, loyal individual and I work towards what I believe is right. I am able to evaluate and adjust my work habits under any given circumstance in order to maximize my level of efficiency. I am confident and trust my judgment. I am always open to constructive criticism, providing that criticism is followed by strong, instructive, and logical reason. Ideally, I would like to work in a well-organized and productive environment.

I would like to practice design and the creative process keeping in mind society and clients. Designing with greater intention is my goal. I am interested in a position that will allow me to grow and enhance my creative and technical skills.

Sincerely,

Daniel S Pagan
Daniel S. Pagan

news > I have since applied overseas to further my education in visual communication. If all goes well, I will depart in October 2003 to attend Huddersfield University, England. In a year I will have completed an MA degree in Creative Imaging. I plan to return to the USA in search of steady work.

practice > problem solving through visual communication

This well-written letter expresses the artist's interest in the employer and points out reason why he would make a terrific addition to the company.

the position you are interested in and how you heard about the opening. If you learned about the job from another person, you might need to indicate who referred you. Use this first paragraph as a lead-in to why you are the best qualified candidate for the position.

If possible, address your cover letter to a person; do not use a generic opening such as "To whom is may concern. Be sure you have the spelling of the person's name correct (call the company to confirm this). Here is an example of an opening paragraph:

Dear Mr. Ross,

I am currently seeking a position as a _____ at _____. I am a hands-on, results-oriented person with a comprehensive background in training, design, and development. My enclosed resume details the specifics of my experience and accomplishments.

Body

In this section, you tell the employer why you should get the job. Detail to the employer understand why your experience and background fit the needs of the company and the requirements of the job. Don't make this part of the letter too long—two or three paragraphs are probably enough. Summarize your experience and give examples. If you have a "Summary of Qualifications" section in your resume, you may use excerpts from it. But do not repeat what is on your resume, except to expand on areas you think the employer might want to, or should, know. Here is an example of the body of the cover letter for a graphic designer:

I have more than five years of in-depth experience in graphic design, on both PCs and Macs, including installation and maintenance of state-of-the-art computer programs. I acted as the interim art director of the graphic design area at _____, where I hired and trained new employees in order to maintain continuity in support of current clients. I also installed additional computers to support growing company needs.

I created the company's first desktop publishing and computer graphics workflow process, from initiation of client contact to fulfillment of final project. I originated advanced procedures to cover all aspects of production. In addition, I organized and implemented the company's first television production facility, including three camera online studio production, as well as location shooting. I designed television graphics, incorporating storyboarding and television camera cards for new clients.

I am a versatile, energetic, and organized designer who has experience originating and implementing production-sensitive layouts, as well as defining budgetary needs for a project.

Closing

In your final paragraph, sum up your experience and express why your qualifications make you the best person for the job. Be very positive about yourself. Close your letter by clearly identifying what you will do next. Write an active statement, such as an offer to contact the employer within a specific period of time. Then do so. Your call shows serious interest, enthusiasm, and willingness to work, exactly what employers want to see. Here is an example of a closing paragraph:

Based upon my job experience and educational qualifications, I am confident that I can contribute to the quality design work provided by _____. I would appreciate the opportunity to further discuss my credentials with you in a personal interview. I will contact you in several days to discuss my credentials with you further.

Yours very truly,

_____

Don't forget, all of the caveats described in the resume section of this chapter apply here. Grammar counts. Spelling counts as much. Always have someone you trust proofread your cover letter. Allow them to criticize your words. This will help you make the cover letter as clear and effective as possible. All employers value your ability to communicate at a professional level. Use this first opportunity to write a cover letter that demonstrates how your background, education, and work experiences can fit the needs of the employer.

The Business Card

The business card may be one of the most overlooked aspects of the designer's portfolio. Most designers spend countless hours creating the work that will be showcased in their port, yet they create their business card almost as an afterthought. This is a big mistake. Think of your business card as a miniature resume. Contained within this small document is much of the information necessary to learn about you, locate you, and get you a job. Ideally, your business card should

Offering a business card is a sign of respect. When you first meet a potential employer, have you business card where you can readily reach it. Don't fumble around looking for it. Then offer the card to the individual with your name side up, so that it can be easily read.

An elegant letterhead design with decorative type conveys an air of sophistication.

convey a sense of who you are and what you do as a designer.

Your business card should have a unique look to it (the color insert has a terrific example of several very unique cards). Once again, the idea is to distinguish yourself from the other applicants. Think about the person who will look at the card, and ask yourself, "Would I hire this person based on his or her card?" Begin by selecting either a horizontal or vertical layout. The standard size business card is generally 2 inches by 3.5 inches. This allows the card to be easily inserted in a wallet or revolving card file.

Check your cards from time to time. Make sure that they are clean, neat and accurate.

Here are some of the items that might be imprinted on your business card:

- Your name
- Your address
- Your phone, fax, and/or cell phone number
- Your email address
- Your job title, if applicable

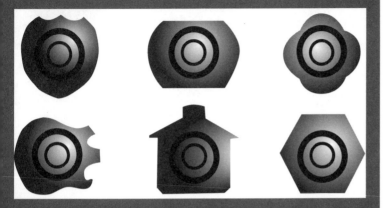

The newest (and possibly) most high-tech way to promote yourself is with a CD-ROM business card. All of your most important information—your name, address, telephone, email, and fax numbers—can all be stored in digital form. But wait, there's more: You can store your entire digital portfolio on a CD. Pictures, animated 3-D graphics, and interactive forms that will link the potential employer directly to your Web site can all happen directly from a tiny CD. The mini-CD can hold between 30 and 50 megabytes of data—more than enough for most digital portfolios. This equals about five minutes of video or hundreds of images or thousands of pages of text.

The mini-CD-ROM works exactly the same as a full-size one. It can be used in almost all CD drives, and carries the same data formats as regular circular CDs. In fact, you can create your own mini CDs. All you need is a computer and a CD burner. If you have an older computer without a burner, local office supply stores in your area can create as many CDs as you require. This is a very cost-effective way to provide examples of your art in a unique format.

What are the benefits of creating a mini-CD-ROM?

- Easier and less expensive to mail
- Compact and convenient to carry

above right • **Don't waste space! Here is a business card that effectively uses both sides. The card is playful and conveys key contact information.**

below right • **This card has a cohesive feeling. The small squares emphasize the design established in the main logo.**

opposite • **All the pieces in this wonderful promotional package are given away in a custom-embroidered pouch highlighted with a catch line about creativity. The student was fortunate to have a relative in the embroidery business, so the cost was minimal.**

- Your Web page, if you have one
- Your logo, if applicable
- Graphic elements

And don't forget to design the back of your business card. while the front of a business card features a person's name and logo, the back can highlight some of their design services or specialities.

The business card is part of your complete business package. In graphic design, this is known as a *visual identity system*. What does that mean? It means that your

business card should have the same look and feel as your cover letter and resume. For example, if you have a logo or graphic on your resume, include it on your business card as well. Take a moment to look at the ideas presented in the color insert to see how you can achieve your own results.

Likewise, use the same fonts from one piece to another. Use a large enough type size so that it is easy to read. (One of my students recently showed me a beautiful business card, but the type on it was so small that I needed a magnifying glass to read it!) Use paper color and texture, logos, and other decorative motifs consistently. And while we are on the subject of paper, don't be pennywise and pound-foolish. Buy the nicest card stock you can afford.

Expanding Your Reach with Business Cards

The world is a much smaller place these days, and we all have opportunities to interact with people from many different cultures. There are a number of books and articles on the subject of international business etiquette. If you are considering an international position, it is essential that you review the etiquette of that country. In Japan, for example, it is considered a faux pas not to both offer and receive a business card.

But wherever you go, never leave home without a stack of business cards! You can hand out this powerful small document and market yourself to a possible employer anywhere. You never know when the job opportunity will arise. A great business card will help a potential employer remember you long after an initial meeting or interview is finished. ∎

As you can see, showing confidence when you present your art makes you stand out from the crowd!

ACCOMPLISHMENTS: Your achievements. The job duties or responsibilities that set you apart from everyone else. Always highlight your accomplishments in your cover letter and resume.

ACTION VERBS: Descriptive verbs used to express talents, experience, or accomplishments. Choose action verbs when you are trying to describe your outstanding skills.

CAREER CHANGE: Progressing from one area of specialization to another. The act of gathering information in order to synthesize, gain competencies, make decisions, set goals, and take action. Most experts agree that the average person will change careers three to five times during his or her lifetime, for a variety of reasons: boredom, downsizing, location change, and others.

CHRONOLOGICAL RESUME: See Resume.

COVER LETTER: An introductory document in which you briefly tell the employer about your interest in the job, and highlight important reasons why you would be the most qualified person. A cover letter should always accompany your resume.

ELECTRONIC OR DIGITAL RESUME: A resume that is created on a computer with the intent of transmitting it electronically. It is traditional in format but is generally sent to the employer via email, or is posted at a Web site.

EMPLOYMENT GAPS: Periods of time when you can show no employment. Whatever the reason—illness, pregnancy, or other circumstances—it is important to be able to account for these gaps in you work history. The interviewer will notice and call attention to the situation.

FREELANCE (INDEPENDENT CONTRACTOR OR CONSULTANT): A person who is self-employed, who pursues his or her profession (frequently in the arts) under no long-term contractual commitments to any one employer or company. Many people enjoy the freedom, flexibility, and satisfaction of working for themselves. Although they do not receive company benefits, freelancers are able to negotiate their own terms and compensation their work.

FUNCTIONAL RESUME: See Resume.

JOB APPLICATION: A form used to document an applicant's qualifications for a job. Although many of the questions on a typical application may seem to duplicate what appears on your resume, the form is a requirement of most company human resources departments.

JOB INTERVIEWING: The process of presenting an applicant's credentials and qualifications to a particular position. The idea is to make the best possible match between the employer and the employee. There are many different styles of interviews, but they all give you a chance to present yourself and your work for consideration.

JOB SKILLS: Your capabilities, knowledge, and talents that add up to your ability to do the job.

KEY ACCOMPLISHMENTS: A summary list on your resume of your key activities and achievements. This is an important section of your resume, as it highlights the work you have done for past employers.

LETTER OF AGREEMENT: A document provided by the employer offering you a job. It details the dates, conditions, and salary structure of the offer.

MENTOR: A person who offers counsel within your profession or organization. Some companies have formal mentoring systems, but most mentoring relationships are informal.

OCCUPATIONAL OUTLOOK HANDBOOK: This guide was created to provide assistance to individuals making decisions about their careers. It provides job descriptions and lists the training and education needed, earnings, and expected job prospects in a wide range of occupations. This document is published by the U.S. Department of Labor, Bureau of Labor Statistics, and can be accessed at the following Web address: http://www.bls.gov/oco/.

PORTFOLIO: A collection of materials that provides a way to visually show your qualifications. It includes your resume, artwork, certifications, and any additional materials that document your expertise.

REFERENCES: A select group of people who have agreed to praise your character and work habits to potential employers. They may be friends, coworkers, or former employers, and are usually selected because they will improve your chances of winning a job. This list of names should be given only when requested.

RESIGNATION: A formal letter declaring that you will be leaving the present job within a specified period of time (usually two weeks). It's very important to leave any job under the best of terms. You never know when you might need that contact.

RESUME: A written summary of an individual's academic history, work experience, and accomplishments, usually for the purposes of finding a job.

glossary

● ● ● ● 4

The Traditional Portfolio
Design and Art Projects

hapter 3 was devoted to an in-depth discussion of the resume, cover letter, and business card. It's time now to turn our attention to the visual components of your portfolio: the art and design projects. These will help to focus the potential employer on your strengths as a creative designer, so it's important to choose thoughtfully and carefully. Each piece should affirm your conceptual skills and problem-solving abilities. In addition, the pieces you include must demonstrate not only your talent, but also your potential for growth.

Most employers agree that the design portfolio should be made of about 10 to 20 pieces of recent, original work. These pieces should demonstrate your strength and experience in design, as well as highlight skill areas of particular interest to you. In sum, you must use your portfolio to create a coherent, comprehensive message about yourself as a designer.

Before we go much further here, though, I want to stress that there really are no right or wrong pieces to include in your port. That said, you should also be aware that the first piece viewed by the employer is the most critical; it sets the tone for what is to come. So a good rule of thumb is to select your finest piece of art as the first. It should be visually provoking and conceptually clear. And it must be perfect: no mistakes of any kind. Remember, you are setting the stage for what is to come. Even a typo in some copy will give a negative impression.

Of course, the job for which you are applying will also influence the pieces you include in the portfolio. Although in general it is best to show a broad base of abilities and styles, resist the temptation to include pieces because you think you have to. If, for example, you are not an illustrator, don't include weak drawings just to prove you've done some illustration. A sad fact of life is that you will always be judged by the weakest piece in the port. If, on the other hand, you have a well-defined art style, you may wish to showcase that talent. Being selective in this manner, however, also has a risk: you may be excluded from certain jobs because you will not be perceived as a generalist.

A tendency among young designers is to include too many pieces in the port. Doing so may make you appear disorganized or unsure of yourself. Remember the old saying: "Too much of a good thing." Most firms will know whether you are qualified for their position after viewing just a few pieces, so don't waste their time. I learned this lesson the hard way, when once I was asked during an interview to stop my presentation, which had gone on for too long. It was very embarrassing!

above • A smile belies any nervousness you might have during a job interview. Relax! This is supposed to be fun!

below • Always dress appropriately for an interview. When you dress up, you show respect to the potential employer.

Organizing Your Portfolio

How you organize your portfolio is almost as important as the work you choose to include in it. Similar to the resume, you can arrange your art chronologically or categorically. Using the chronological system, you arrange your projects with the most recent work at the front of the port and continue in reverse order by date. This is a logical way to order your work, but only use it if you're confident the first piece in your port is a strong one. Also note that this style of arrangement works best if all of the pieces are of one category. If you have a wide variety of work, then the categorical system may be a better choice. This system allows you to divide your portfolio into well-defined sections. A graphic designer, for example, might arrange his or her work into sections such as logo design, collateral pieces, or editorial spreads. A fashion designer might instead divide the port into formal wear, casual wear, and beach attire. The categorical system also allows you to prioritize the pieces that are the most relevant to the job you are applying for.

Professional Portfolio Presentation

In Chapter 2, I introduced the various portfolio case options available to the designer. Here I want to begin by saying it doesn't really matter which style of portfolio you choose as long as it thematically supports your work and presents a professional appearance. The following are some factors to consider regarding which port case is right for you:

Most cases are about 1 to 1-1/2 inches in depth, but if you have a lot of work or some bulkier pieces, you might need a wider case.

Buy the best binder or case you can afford. To check out different portfolio options, visit the art (or craft) supply store in your area. You will see a full spectrum of sizes and formats. Or visit a few of the many art stores on the Internet as well.

● ● ● STYLE	SIZE
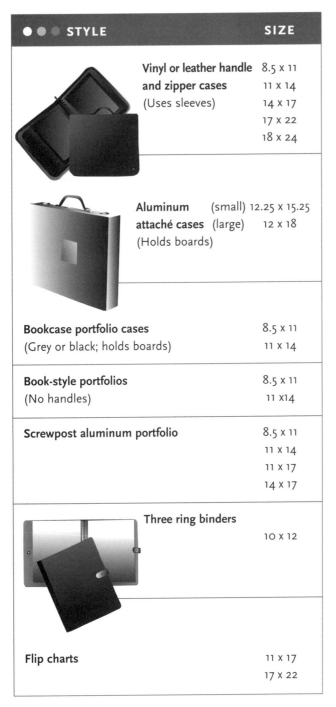**Vinyl or leather handle and zipper cases** (Uses sleeves)	8.5 x 11 11 x 14 14 x 17 17 x 22 18 x 24
Aluminum (small) **attaché cases** (large) (Holds boards)	12.25 x 15.25 12 x 18
Bookcase portfolio cases (Grey or black; holds boards)	8.5 x 11 11 x 14
Book-style portfolios (No handles)	8.5 x 11 11 x14
Screwpost aluminum portfolio	8.5 x 11 11 x 14 11 x 17 14 x 17
Three ring binders	10 x 12
Flip charts	11 x 17 17 x 22

Should you show your portfolio work on boards or books? The answer is simple. Use whichever method is easiest and most convenient for you. Both styles of display allow you to replace the art, to keep your selections up to date. Boards, though they tend to be heavy, allow the viewer to pick up the work and examine it closely. Furthermore, boards make it very easy to rearrange your pieces based on the job at hand. In contrast, the portfolio book is much lighter and easier to carry, but it is difficult to find one whose pages don't "catch" when they are repeatedly turned. So before you choose one of these, insert your artwork in the book and turn the pages. Do they move easily without crimping the binder? Also consider whether the book or the case is awkward to handle; if so, you will feel clumsy during an interview. One final word of caution: Whether you select a book or a case, make sure that it holds the art securely in place.

There is nothing more exciting (or nerve-wracking) than the moment when the prospective employer opens your portfolio case for the first time! Help to calm yourself at the same time you make it easy on the interviewer by choosing the portfolio that best addresses all of the above criteria.

To give you a jump-start on shopping for a portfolio, the chart on the left details a number of the different sizes and styles of portfolio cases:

Pay Attention to Detail

A major factor in developing a professional presentation is choosing a unifying theme or style to link what's in your portfolio to the style of the case. You can do this graphically by using a consistent page color, border design; or logo. But whatever you do, don't draw attention away from your work. Stay away from wild patterns or loud color schemes that take the viewer's eye away from the focal point of the port—your art. Most portfolio cases come supplied with black or gray paper inserts. You can usually change these, but always opt for neutral colors.

Prepare Your Work for Viewing

You have your portfolio case, so now let's talk about how you're going to prepare the actual artwork. If you are a graphic, interior, or fashion designer, many of the pieces you have created are probably on disk. (We'll talk more about fine art in a moment.) The pieces must be printed,

If your work is unusual, perhaps consider a more avant-garde style, such as one made with steel exteriors; or a fashioned wooden case, designed to look like it came from the Old West. If you're very handy, you might even consider constructing your own case.

● ● ● How Much Will It Cost to Create a Portfolio?

Typically, an artist may expect to spend anywhere from $150 to $500 for printing the art, making the slides, buying the portfolio case, compiling a stationary package, burning CD-ROM disks, and producing other materials (such as self promotional pieces). But that cost may be much lower, depending on how much you can accomplish at home versus how much you have to outsource at print shops such as Copyright or Kinko's. Print shops charge an hourly rate based on how much time you spend sitting at their computers. And should you require additional services, such a scanning your art, expect to pay about $10 per scan (although you can generally negotiate an hourly rate if you are doing the scans yourself using the shop's equipment).

If you do need to use a print shop's computer, arrive prepared and organized. As I just said, you are going to be charged by the hour, so you don't want to waste any time. Each scan takes about one to two minutes, so costs can add up pretty quickly. Another word of advice: Don't waste time color-correcting or resizing your images at the shop if you have a computer at home. Save your work and leave as soon as you are finished scanning. Those extra minutes will really add up!

If you are creating a digital portfolio, expect the pay for materials such the CDs themselves, the jewel cases to put them in, and duplication and printing costs (should you decide to label the CD with your name and logo). These costs can vary, but generally run about $.35 for the do-it-yourselfers to about $3.50 each with a minimum order of 500 through a CD specialty company. Color-printing a multicolor logo, for example, will increase the cost by about $.20 per color.

The good news is that once you have completed the portfolio, you have incurred the greatest cost. Maintaining a portfolio is never as expensive as the initial creation cost. As you create news pieces, you simply have them printed and add them to your port.

The CD case is another way for you to showcase your design talents. Here is a great example where the art on the cover is in harmony with the CD and the business card.

but which method is best? Should you use a home printer or a commercial printer?

Using a Home Printer

There are many fine color printers available for the home market today. Epson, Hewlett-Packard, Brother, Minolta, Lexmark, Canon, and Olympus all make high-quality inkjet printers. Though they can be a bit slow, the price can't be beat, and the results are spectacular. All sorts of papers are available for these machines, from photo glossy to holiday card stock, from T-shirt transfer paper to large-format papers, there is a printer and a paper for you.

Take some time to research which printer will best suit your designs. If you will be doing a lot of large-scale printing (for example, 11 x 17 inch), you will probably want a printer that is capable of handling oversize paper. Then you will be able to print full size, and trim down to the correct size. That way your pieces will look like they have a "full bleed" to the edges. This makes a very professional presentation. And speaking of professional, that is the name of the game! It doesn't really matter which printer you use, as long as your final outputs look great.

Once you have selected a printer, you will have to decide what kind of paper you want to use. You can

● ● ● Inkjet Tips

If you have an inkjet printer, don't set up the paper in a stack to feed through the printer. Why not? Because the ink is still wet on the paper when it comes out of the printer. If you run the paper through automatically, one page after another, the ink is going to smear and you'll be wasting time, money, and supplies. Print each page one at a time and give it time to dry; and by all means keep all wet pages separated—ideally in a room without humidity. Give the prints a day or so to dry thoroughly before you mount them in your portfolio.

Two more tips: Be aware that inkjet papers will fade in time. To maintain the quality of your prints, store your work in a dark area, free of direct sunlight. And keep your unused paper as dry as possible.

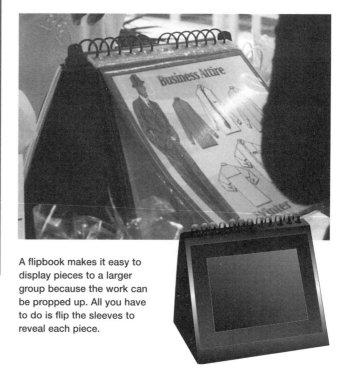

A flipbook makes it easy to display pieces to a larger group because the work can be propped up. All you have to do is flip the sleeves to reveal each piece.

achieve striking results with both glossy and matte paper stocks, but which one should you chose? A good printer alone can't guarantee fabulous color prints, but a little knowledge about paper, along with some printing hints, will net you great results.

Inkjet paper comes in a range of different weights, textures, and colors, so before you buy, again take the time to research out what each one offers. Go to your local computer or office supply store a look at the samples provided by the manufacturer. If you can't see samples of the printing results, don't buy the printer. If possible, ask the store personnel print something for you, preferably one of your designs.

Paper, as I just noted, is available both in glossy and matte stocks. Glossy paper was invented to produce prints that mimic the typical photograph. It generally produces a deeper, more intense color. Semigloss paper can also be purchased should you wish to produce work with a more understated shine. Matte papers feature a low degree of gloss. They are good when your intent is to produce softer, subtler shades of color in your design. Matte papers typically are available in light weights, good for printing, say, a brochure that will be folded. Glossy papers, because of their heavier weights, are difficult to fold cleanly.

Using a Commercial Printer

What if you can't afford a printer? No problem! There are many small print shops, such as the aforementioned Kinko's or Copyright. They have color printers and bindery equipment available for your use. You bring in the file on disk or CD, sit down at one of their computers, and output your work. You are charged only from the time you log on. And you can work whenever it suits you, as most of these shops are open 24 hours a day.

Mounting Your Work

Now that you have printed your design work, how do you mount it? There are two different ways to display your art: *flush mounting* and matting. In the past, artists always used the matting system. An opening just slightly larger than the artwork would be carefully cut in the matte material. The art would then be slipped into place in between the matte and a board placed just under the piece. It was a little like making a sandwich. Though the presentation was highly professional looking, the two boards made each piece of art heavy and bulky to handle. Therefore, these days, mattes are used primarily for displaying fine art in homes and offices.

Flush mounting is a much more practical solution for those who wish to display their work on boards (as opposed to on paper sleeves in a port case). The work is carefully centered on the board. A fine mist of spray mount (a type of glue) is spritzed lightly on the back of the art. The art is then pressed to the board.

This magnificent sculpture by Steven Bleicher is entitled *Ancestor Fetish and Vessel.* It is constructed of wood and raku (a pottery-firing technique). But it is 12 inches high, and so requires special consideration for a portfolio. As you can see, the image clearly shows the details of this handsome piece.

● ● ● **How to Display Artwork for Interviews?**

The answer to this question requires a bit of thought. Let's begin with the size and weight of your case. Remember, you'll have to lug it from interview to interview, so, as cautioned earlier, keep size in mind when you go shopping for a case. Color is also an important consideration. You want the case to show off the work, not overwhelm it. Select a neutral color. (Most artists prefer black.) Some portfolio cases come with stands or easels, enabling you to prop the work up. These are quite effective, but they can be a little awkward to work with until you get accustomed to the setup. Most people prefer the old-fashioned way: standing and looking over the work as it is presented page by page.

What if you have a lot of awkward pieces that need to be pulled out and examined, such as cards, product samples, or booklets? In this case, you must strive to create a portfolio that it is professional, yet manageable and practical. Portfolio sleeves require that you reach inside to pull out the piece. Instead, paste the piece down, rather than build a clear pocket holder for the piece to nest in until you are ready to remove it.

Displaying Three-Dimensional or Folded Pieces

Three-dimensional art pieces and folded materials cause unique display problems. Art pieces such as sculpture, folders and brochures, and package design must be exhibited as effectively as possible to accommodate their dimensionality.

Let's examine sculpture first. Most pieces of sculpture are fully articulated, that is to say "in the round." This presents a unique challenge. How do you convey the full sense of the art in a two-dimensional environment? There are two answers:

- *You could photograph the piece from all sides.* Then you would generate a series of slides or prints. In this way, the viewer would be able to see the piece from all angles. A series of mounted prints would allow you to represent the art from many different angles.
- *You could videotape the piece.* This method, too, gives you a way to show the piece from all sides, but using it you run the risk of not being able to play the tape during the interview (the employer might not have the proper equipment). Therefore, a videotape should only be used to supplement the printed work (or converted to a digital Quicktime movie).

What about folded pieces? One way is to use folder pockets and corners. They provide a practical way to display folders and brochures until you are ready to bring them out for further examination. These pockets are useful for both brochures and folders. Corners are

turfs up dude.

Truly Nolen has been keeping
lawns a sea of green since 1938.

Black Widow

TRULY NOLEN PEST CONTROL

These wonderful ads for Truly Nolen were created by Christine David's agency, Artemis Design Group.

also sensible for pieces that may require a lot of handling. The sleeve or corner keeps the work from sliding around in the portfolio.

Once you have decided which of the display methods to use, carefully measure the board or paper insert so that once the system is in place, it will present properly.

Protecting Your Work

A photography portfolio generally consists of prints, color slides, and tearsheets. Most photographers go to great lengths to protect their work. Frequently, prints are window-mounted between white or black boards, then slipped into acid-free sleeves, to ensure that the art is not harmed. Some artists prefer to laminate their photos between two sheets of clear plastic. This fully protects the art, and any smudges can be easily wiped off. Black card masks are excellent for color transparencies. They come in an assortment of sizes and allow the viewer to see many different pieces (both horizontal and vertical) on one page.

Here is a section from a promotional piece designed by the award-winning graphic designer Paul Kane. His design skills are clearly apparent, hence this piece would make an excellent way to showcase his portfolio.

If you are a professional photographer, you may have a selection of tearsheets. Tearsheets are provided to the photographer by the publication once a piece has been selected to appear in print. They can include anything that has been published from a magazine editorial to a print ad. Tearsheets are usually placed in plastic sleeves inside a good-quality display book. Because most tearsheets are produced in a standard size, the 14 x 17 inch display book is a good option. It is just large enough to hold the work and offers a nice black border around the art.

As discussed earlier, for most designers, the design case with a zipper on three sides and a ring-binder mechanism on the spine is the most popular format for carrying work. But for the photographer this may not be a practical solution. Because photos need to be seen up close, they have to be removed. For this reason, professional photographers prefer briefcase style portfolio cases with a hinged lid and open interior. These are more flexible for displaying different-size pieces.

● ● ● Portfolio Summary Tips

- Include *only* your best work.
- Include only recent work—from the past two or three years.
- Create a diverse and broad range of work—that is, demonstrate your experience.
- Consider writing short explanations about your work.
- Resist the urge to use fancy or strange typefaces! Make sure your words are readable.
- Check and recheck for spelling errors.
- Don't crowd large images, for example, a three-ad series on one page.
- Use neutral color pages in your presentation case.
- Always include your rough book or concept journal (described in the next section).
- Never let the pages you select to hold your designs detract from the art. Use smooth or matte papers
- Do not use distracting borders around your designs.
- Put your best work first in the portfolio; likewise, put some of your best work last.
- Keep everything in proportion—nothing too large or too small.
- Make sure that all images are aligned with the edge of the page; do not make your interviewers swivel their heads.
- Make sure your portfolio is always neat and clean.
- Purchase a portfolio case large enough to house your art comfortably.
- Keep your portfolio and your art in a dry place.
- Strive to be different—explore beyond the obvious.
- Let your personality, perspective, and passion show—these are the things that make for distinctive portfolios!

Additional Display Guidelines

You might use the list of guidelines here as checklist as you begin to compile your portfolio. Not all will apply to you or to every piece of your art, but they are good reminders of the professional viewpoint:

- *As much as possible include only original work in your portfolio.* Stay away from photocopies, as they are inferior to inkjet outputs. Once a printer piece has been copied, it tends to lose its sharpness—the

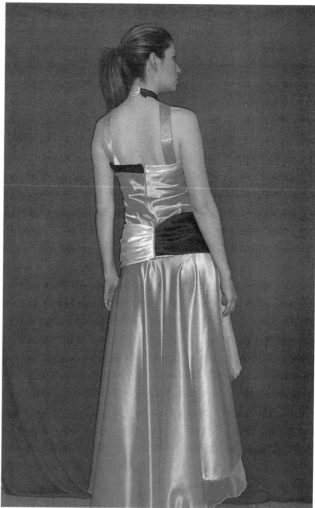

Carrie Cochran's designs, shown here, are fresh and modern. Her work has been featured on Sharon Osborne's talk show. It is difficult to display, as it must be photographed from various angles to convey all the features.

color washes out. It is far better to take a photograph of the piece. Then your work will always be crisp, and you can alter the photo size to match the portfolio.

- *Consider using cover sheets.* The cover sheet is usually a small piece of paper that offers the viewer an explanation of the nearby art or to comment on the scope of the project. Architects frequently add explanations of a design project using this method. Perhaps you have been involved in a graphic design project, for example, a promotional package; you helped create a piece, but had only limited involvement. A cover sheet accompanying the work would enable you to give a short explanation of the role you played in the production of the piece. Cover sheets aren't always necessary, but

they can be an effective tool in portfolio design.

- *Display pieces that demonstrate knowledge of your industry.* Even if your portfolio comprises mostly student work, that does not mean it should look amateurish. As an example, a graphic designer must always be concerned with the "production process" of art. Don't, then, design a building interior that only the top 5 percent of America could afford to buy. It might look interesting or exciting, but potential employers will wonder whether you can make practical decisions on behalf of their clients.
- *Keep it clean!* This may seem like stating the obvious,

but when I tell you some of the things I have found in portfolio cases I have evaluated, you'll understand why I include it here—dog hair, coins, the smell of cigarettes. . . . Double-check your portfolio. Erase smudge marks from projects. If the pages are scratched and torn, the port will look unprofessional. I once had a student tell me that he was going for the "messy art look" as his port style. He ripped, tore, and burned his boards. They looked horrible. It might have seemed like a good idea to him, but the final product looked dreadful, which brings me to my next point . . .

- *Always purchase additional sleeves for your portfolio.* As you use the port, some of the plastic will get scratched or tear. Periodically, replace worn sleeves with new fresh ones. You always want the port to look great.
- *Look your portfolio with fresh eyes.* Turn a critical eye to your port. I know it's your baby and you love everything in it, but consider the point of view of the potential employer. Remove any material that could be offensive under certain circumstances. Bright shiny sports cars with beautiful models might be great if you want to design for a car magazine, but you won't score any points with an in-house graphic design firm whose major clients are banks or hospitals. And stay away from controversial topics unless you can show both sides objectively. I'm not saying you can't show editorial work, but you must be sensitive to the opinions of others. Don't lose a great job over something that could have easily been avoided. Always have others evaluate your portfolio. If several people question the same piece, you really should pull it.

Portfolios for Different Design Disciplines

Each of the design disciplines uses the traditional portfolio in a slightly different way. This is due in part to the specific projects that each discipline generates. For example, a fine artist might generate large multipaneled paintings, whereas a graphic designer will design both small ads to fit magazine formats and large billboards. Likewise, an architect's drawing will vary in size based on the scope of the design. And the fashion designer will be creating clothing both in two-dimensional (on

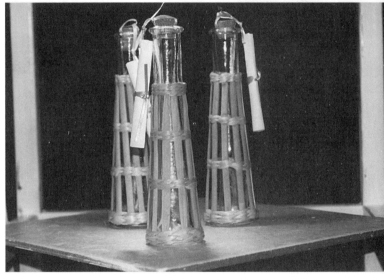

This is an effective display for a great self-promotional piece design by Raquel Passley.

paper) and in three-dimensional (on a model) forms. As the needs of the artist changes, the display method utilized must change as well.

Consider for a moment the portfolio of the fine artist. The painter, the printmaker, the photographer, and the sculptor each produces art of various sizes. Many of these pieces will be too large to fit into a portfolio. (And it sure is hard to carry a 3 by 5 foot painting around with you!) Large-scale work requires special attention. The artist has several options. As you already know, he or she can take a series of slides that show both the size and detail of the piece. These slides can be mounted in special photo sleeves that serve to showcase the work, which are then inserted in the portfolio case. There are other options available to you as well. Some fine artists feel it is important to project the art in slide form at the interview, and so will bring a special portable light table to show the artwork. An artist may also print a piece as large as he or she feels is necessary to properly show the scope of the work. As long as the prints fit easily into the portfolio case, the work will be properly displayed.

Graphic designers will also need to give some consideration to challenging display problems. A beautifully designed three-dimensional package had to be displayed to show all sides of the project. This would require the artist to display the piece as a flat two-dimensional piece and in a finished form. The artist could take a picture of the final package as it would appear on a shelf to show the application.

This innovative little package display is difficult to capture in pictures. Nevertheless, it is important to try to feature the piece in its best possible light, by taking a series of photos from different angles so that the viewer can see it from all sides.

Architects and interior designers frequently prepare boards for clients that are 24 by 36 or even 30 by 40. Although it is possible that the work may be kept in a large format, frequently, the work is reduced to accommodate the interview process. Design models will be photographed from a variety of vantage points and mounted on boards to show the various angles of the design. Drawings of the design in process are included to show the project from concept to completion.

The Sketchbook

You know you are a remarkable talented, creative, and incredibly insightful art and designer, but now you have to prove it in the professional arena. To help you do that, in addition to your portfolio, it's a good idea to provide a sketchbook. Your sketchbook (sometimes known as the *rough book* or concept journal) is a compilation of doodles, quick ideas, drawings, sketches on the backs of napkins, musings, visual references, and anything else that shows how you conceptualize design. Think of it as your brainstorming process in action. Employers know that great ideas are typically slow to evolve, from careful thought coupled with research of the needs of the customers. They like to see this thought process.

What? You don't have one? Start developing one now! Employers will not hire you based on a pretty portfolio alone. They also want to know how you arrive at your designs. And unlike the portfolio, you don't have to worry about the look of your sketchbook. It may very well be messy and that's perfectly acceptable. The idea is to show the development of your ideas.

In your sketchbook, it's a good idea to show alternate solutions to each problem. It is unlikely your first idea was the final one, so be prepared to show how you went from point A to point D, or F, or even Z. And try to keep the sketchbook somewhat organized, to more clearly demonstrate your process.

The Artist's Statement

As part of the portfolio process, most art students are asked to develop an *artist's statement* before they are permitted to graduate. The artist's statement is an essay that describes the philosophy of the artist. Usually the

statement discusses the meaning of processes, or techniques involved in art making.

In preparation for writing this statement, take a moment to think about what you want to achieve with your art, as well as what kind of message you are trying to communicate as your portfolio is viewed. Your objective is to promote yourself in a way that sets you apart from other artists. Thus, your artist's statement should give the reader compelling insights about you.

The statement usually includes the college history of the artist from freshman year until just before graduation, and frequently discusses the influences of other artists. The point is, you want anyone who reads it to gain valuable insights into you and your work. The following subsections will help guide you in the creation of your artist's statement.

The Introduction

The first paragraph of the artist's statement sets the stage for all of the information to come. It should be informative, but brief, giving some insight into your art and your philosophy of art making. Invite the reader to learn more about your goals and ambitions. You want to pique his or her interest. The first paragraph should only be three to five sentences long.

Here is a beautiful architectural rendering by Frank Balzano. But because it is so large, it will have to be either photographed or scanned in segments.

The Body

The purpose of this section is to discuss several of your pieces and provide the reader with some insight into your art-making process. The pieces you choose to talk abou, will be the focal points of your statement. Therefore, for each piece provide critical information, such as the title and dimensions of the work, the medium utilized, and an explanation of why you included the piece. Explain each piece. Explain your ideas and describe your artistic vision. Communicate your inspirations and influences and how they intertwined to produce the final piece.

As you describe the art, provide some analysis for the reader. Use artist's terminology that helps to characterize the piece, such as "color," "negative space," "texture," "movement," and "emphasis." Interpret the piece for the viewer. Clarify the message that is being communicated. Mention well-known artists who have influenced you and your work. Be passionate about what you have to say. Help the reader to understand

above • These two pieces are by Howard T. Katz. On the above left is a sketch for the painting entitled *Code of Honor: Valor.* The drawing shows the value of keeping a sketchbook to work though ideas. The piece on the above right is the finished painting that was produced as a result of the sketch. The final painting is part of a series designed to explore the traditional code of chivalry, and asks the question, "Does chivalry still have a place in today's society?"

left • Karan Sanok's computer drawings feature fantastical landscapes. They are completely designed and rendered on the computer, and take hundreds of hours to create.

why you believe the piece to a successful work of art. This may be an uncomfortable thing for most you to do, but you must learn to promote yourself.

Final Thoughts

As you close your artist's statement, draw some conclusions. Be honest and direct in expressing your final thoughts. The statement should not be so erudite or difficult to comprehend that you lose the reader's interest. And never make excuses for your art.

Before you distribute your statement, ask some professionals in the field to read it. Accept and consider their thoughts and criticisms. Fine-tune your statement as necessary. Your artist's statement may just be one of the most effective promotional tools you have. ∎

ARTIST STATEMENT: A short essay written to help potential employers understand what you believe to be the most important aspects of your art. It may also discuss techniques and artistic influences.

BINDING: The methods used to hold various amounts of paper together. These include:

- Saddle-stitch binding—One or more staples are inserted in the center of a page.
- Side-stitch binding—One or more staples are placed on the side of the page. Not as professional looking as saddle stitching.
- Perfect binding—All pages are pressed together on one side. Once the pages are flat, glue is applied on the outside edge.
- Case binding—All pages are glued to a gauze strip, then glued again to end paper. The end papers are attached to a hard cover. Books are produced using this technique.
- Plastic comb binding—Plastic teeth are inserted into a series of tiny holes (square or round) that make up a stack of paper. The spines can be removed easily as needed. Very inexpensive, but not as professional as perfect binding.
- Three-ring binders—The standard binder that comes with three metal rings. Used mostly for reports and found in most stores.

BINDERY EQUIPMENT: A machine used to fasten paper together. There are many different types of bindery machines on the market. They vary by price and features.

CD-ROM: Abbreviation for compact disk read-only memory. An optical digital storage device, capable of holding about 650 megabytes of information.

COVER SHEET: A short piece of paper used to add comments on the scope of a project. The cover sheet is generally a brief explanation about the purpose or artistic style of the work.

FLUSH MOUNTING: A method of placing art on a page by gluing it directly on the page with no extra protection (such as a matte). The drawback is that the art is not fully protected (unless it is placed inside a sleeve as well).

MATTING (OR MATT BOARDS): A mounting process whereby an image is slipped between two thin boards. A "window" is cut in the top board so that the art may be viewed. The art is well protected. This is the traditional way to present portfolio work if you don't want to use page sleeves in a binder.

GLOSSY PAPER: Paper that has a shiny coating, as that typically used to print photographs. It is excellent for high-resolution digital images.

JEWEL CASES: Small, hinged plastic cases used to store CDs. They come in a variety of colors and sizes.

MATTE PAPER: Paper that has a soft lusterless surface, used to print images with a more subdued feeling.

PORTFOLIO CASE: The binder, case, or folder used to hold images and other pieces of information.

PRINT SHOPS: Also known as pre-press houses (such as Copyright or Kinko's), these are stores that offer a variety of printing services. Prints shops also often provide computer rental and design services.

SKETCHBOOK: A collection of doodles, quick ideas, and drawings that show how an artist thinks and processes concepts and ideas. Also known as rough book or concept journal.

SPRAY MOUNT: A type of glue that comes in a spray bottle or can. Light amounts can be applied to paper to help adhere it to another surface. It is generally used for flush mounting.

TEARSHEET: A page torn from a publication. Used as proof by the publisher or the advertising agency that an ad or article appeared in a specific issue; used by the artist to display printed work.

glossary

● ● ● ● ● **5**

The Digital Portfolio
CD-ROMs and Web Sites

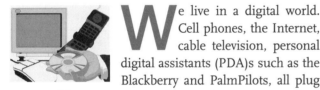

We live in a digital world. Cell phones, the Internet, cable television, personal digital assistants (PDA)s such as the Blackberry and PalmPilots, all plug us in and keep us connected. It won't surprise you then to hear that having a digital portfolio will give you a leg up on the competition. What employer could possibly resist a state-of-the-art presentation with sound and animation? A print portfolio is a great marketing tool, but a digital portfolio is an experience

Armed with just a small CD-ROM containing your designs, you can easily apply for jobs anywhere. Want to relocate to another state? Simply send your CD for evaluation to remote locations. Or post it on the Web or attach it to an email.

Ah, sounds great, you say, but how to begin? I won't deceive you, an electronic portfolio can be challenging to create from scratch. There are many details you must consider—which computer program to use, which graphic format; file sizes, presentation styles, and copyright issues. These are just some of the things you will have to think about. Fortunately, once armed with some basic information, you will be able to create a terrific tool with which you can promote yourself. And that's the purpose of this chapter, to examine the process of creating

both CD and Web-based portfolios. In it, I evaluate both the strengths and weaknesses of each format so that you'll be able to determine the best program for the job. I'll also introduce you to some of the support software available for multimedia authoring.

CD-ROM or Web-Based Portfolio?

Any discussion of electronic design begins with the question, which format should I use to create my portfolio? Should I create a Web site? Or produce a CD-ROM? The answer is, it depends. In fact, there is not much difference between the two formats. Both follow a very similar set of rules. The difference is one of speed. On the Web files take longer to download, so they must be smaller in size. CD-ROMs do not have the same speed restrictions, hence files can be much larger. That said, with a little planning, you can create a project that works effectively in both formats.

The most important point to remember is that all interactive media-based projects are fundamentally the same. You create a user interface that allows the viewer to navigate through your resume and art projects. The final product may be different, but the interface principles remain the same. We'll take a closer look at some of

Who will win the 2004 World Cup?

The Internet makes it possible for your work to be viewed 24/7 from virtually anywhere in the world.

the problems associated with the various forms of multimedia is bit later. For now, let's take a look at some of the software necessary to create an interactive portfolio.

The best way to create a successful electronic presentation is to produce a portfolio that is not reliant on any other program. With a stand-alone presentation, the original software need not be present in order to view the work. There are several programs available to help you build an interactive portfolio. Some are easy to master, while others require a bit more effort. All will help you achieve your goal: to create an interactive portfolio. Before we explore some of the more popular programs, let's evaluate the strengths and weaknesses of the two formats.

The CD-ROM-Based Portfolio

For all intents and purposes, a CD-ROM (remember, this acronym stands for compact disc read-only memory) can be considered, simply, a storage device for your designs and resume. Whatever your specialty—fine art, photography, architectural rendering, or fashion design—a CD can be used to display your work. As a simple art storage device, a CD lists all of the files that contain the various elements of your portfolio. The user double-clicks on any of those files, which opens the creation program to display the contents of the file.

The primary disadvantage of this method is that the viewer must have the software you used to create the art, or he or she will be unable to open the file. Fortunately, there are now several different ways to make your files "play" without dependent software. We will talk more about these solutions later.

One major advantage of creating a CD-ROM-based portfolio is that you can reproduce it as often as necessary. As soon as a hot job prospect comes your way, you "burn" a CD containing your work and send it quickly on its way to the potential employer. Most new computers today come with CD burners that enable you to reproduce your work in a matter of minutes. If you have an older computer, you can buy an external CD burner for under $100. Or you can have your digital portfolio reproduced at most local print shops.

The CDs themselves are inexpensive. One costs about 49 cents. And if you buy in bulk, the price reduces to about 25 cents per disk. Furthermore, CDs are lightweight, so it doesn't cost much to send one through the mail, a real cost savings if you plan to do a bulk mailing. And for a professional touch, you might want to consider buying a software package that will enable you to create special CD labels with your contact information. Some of these programs will also allow you to add graphic images. Then you can include the logo you use on your business card. Very professional!

CD-ROMs can hold a lot of data, about 650 megabytes. That a lot, but it is not unlimited. A Photoshop file sized to 11 by 17 (a typical two-page spread) and created at 300 dots per inch (dpi) is typically about 24 megs (see the Glossary at the end of the chapter for definitions of these computer terms). This means that you will be able to store about 26 images on your disk. If you plan on displaying larger images or want to run an authoring program, you will have to dedicate more space.

The single biggest problem associated with a CD is the time required to load large images. Fortunately, this problem is not insurmountable. It just requires a little knowledge and creativity.

CD-ROM discs hold huge amounts of artwork, and the cost to you is minimal and the rewards are potentially vast!

How to Burn a CD

Here are the basic steps to burning a CD:

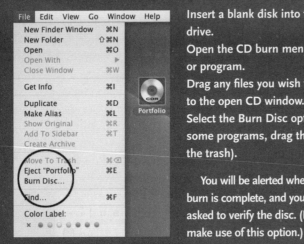

Insert a blank disk into the CD drive.

Open the CD burn menu option or program.

Drag any files you wish to burn to the open CD window.

Select the Burn Disc option (in some programs, drag the disc to the trash).

You will be alerted when the burn is complete, and you may be asked to verify the disc. (I always make use of this option.)

Note that, unless you own a rewriteable CD burner and discs (CD-RW), you will only be able to burn data on the disk once. You will be able to read files from it, but you will no longer be able to write anything to the disc or modify the contents of the disc.

The Web-Based Portfolio

Using a Web-based portfolio is probably the fastest possible way to promote your abilities as a designer to potential employers. Anyone interested in your work can log on and visit your Web site in a matter of seconds, from anywhere in the world.

A well-designed Web-based portfolio generally consists of a main, or home, page that contains links to other areas of the site. In many ways similar to the CD, a Web site offers the viewer a variety of ways to navigate and interact. Like the CD, a Web site is created in a nonlinear fashion.

Designing for the Web does, however, have its own set of unique problems—first and foremost speed. Art created for the Web must take dial-up user limitations into account. Any file that takes too long to download risks losing the patience of the visitor. Clearly, you don't want the viewer to click away from your site out of frustration.

Other Web portfolio issues you'll have to address include:

- *Color.* Color shifts occur between print and Web-based output. There are color differences between displays on PCs and Macs.

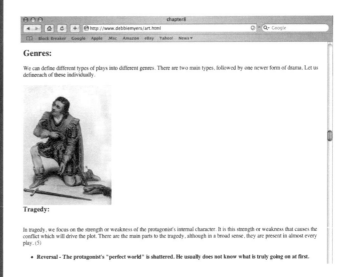

This Web site offers lots of information is a pleasing format that invites the viewer to stay and learn about the theater.

- *Copyright.* You have to protect yourself as much as possible from theft. A few tricks will help keep your files safe.
- *Ease of navigation.* If the viewer can't figure out how to navigate your site quickly and easily, he or she will leave quickly. (We will deal with technical problems in detail in Chapter 6.)

Size and Speed: Primary Criteria

As I've already stated, working with media files can be challenging for the simple reason that they are big. Really big! This is especially true of large-scale images, sound, and video files. For example, a 24-megabyte Photoshop file prepared for print will never be acceptable as a digital file. Why not? Let's say you have a project that you plan to publish both on the Web and on a CD. (Remember, file size makes a big difference in this situation because the Web is much slower than a CD player.) Now assume that your final project size is 1 megabyte. To download that file would, depending on the method of transfer take:

Method of Transfer	Transfer Time
28.8 modem	1 minute, 44 seconds
64k ISDN	50 seconds
T1	10 seconds

Now add to those numbers the amount of people on the Web at any one moment. At certain times of the day, there may be only a few million online, but at other times there may be many, many more. Think about rush hour on the expressway. It takes a long time to get home when everyone else is trying to do the same thing. The Web is like that. A file that streams nicely across the country late at night may take twice as long in the middle of the day. And most folks are pretty impatient these day. They will only wait so long before jumping to another site. So expecting someone to wait 50 seconds to download your project is probably expecting too much.

Now let's consider that same 1-meg file on a CD. The ability to access information on a CD depends on several factors, including drive speed of the player, buffer size (memory), and how fast that disk can get up to full spin speed. To clarify, let's say that drive speed is represented by an X factor where each X indicates an access speed of 150 kilobytes per second. As an example, a 40X CD-ROM drive can access information at a rate of up to 6 megabytes per second. That same 1-megabyte file can be accessed in a fraction of second! At least that's the way it is supposed to work. The problem is that the CD has to get "up to speed" (known as *spin speed*) in order to access the file. This works well for single files, but if you want to take multiple files (such as your entire Web site), with its multiple file links, and burn it on a CD, the CD will have to "ramp up" every time your Web page accesses a different link.

As you can see, you have to give a lot of thought to how you approach your initial files. You have to always keep in mind the viewer, and how long he or she will be willing to wait to see your project.

Deciding Which Multimedia Authoring Program to Use

There are a number of terrific multimedia programs on the market today, offering an impressive range of features. The newest multimedia software features floating palettes with "drag and drop" capacity. You decide on the look of the project and the software helps you to create the interface. Let's peek inside a couple these packages and find the one to suit our needs.

Linear versus Nonlinear: Choosing a Presentation Program

News Update:
On April 18, 2005 Adobe Systems announced a $3.4 billion deal to acquire Macromedia. This giant merger of campanies will help create a new range of multimedia and desktop publishing programs.

PowerPoint: Viewing from Point A to Point B
One of the most popular presentation programs on the market today is Microsoft PowerPoint. PowerPoint is a relatively uncomplicated program used to create portfolio slide shows. Images as well as type can imported to preexisting templates (or to those you create from scratch). The newly created "show" can then be controlled via buttons or by creating a timed presentation. You can also demonstrate the process of creating a piece from sketch to completed project with a transition build. This allows you to sequentially add art images one picture at a time on a single slide. This is a nice effect if you want to show the evolution from concept to finished piece. Neat transitions such as "wipes" and "dissolves" can take you from image to image; and you can add music to enhance the experience. Simple animations are also possible if you want to add a little something extra. You can see an example of the PowerPoint interface in the color insert.

PowerPoint is easy to learn. Most important, for many, PowerPoint will be all they need to create a quick electronic portfolio. One of the most useful features of the program is the "Package for CD" (PC) or "Make Movie" (Mac) function. This feature allows you to take your finished electronic portfolio and export it as a standalone environment. Once you select "Package for CD" (PC) or "Make Movie" (Mac), PowerPoint embeds the PowerPoint Viewer as part of your presentation. Potential employers viewing your portfolio will not need PowerPoint in order to look at your work. They need only double-click the starting icon and the slide show begins.

The main drawback to PowerPoint is that it is a linear program. That means a slide show can be run only forward and backward, one slide at a time. If the viewer wishes to revisit an earlier image, he or she will have to sequence through each of the in-between slides to get there. This can frustrate the viewer, who may be unwilling to backtrack in this fashion. Still, PowerPoint is a

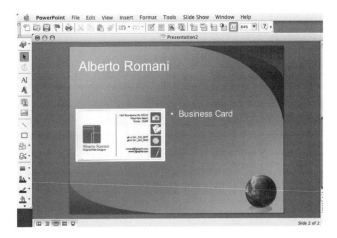

This PowerPoint slide show features a template that works well to support the artist's business card design.

great little program if you need a quick and easy presentation for your work.

The Flexibility of a Nonlinear Presentation

If you want to make it easier for your viewers to navigate your portfolio, you'll need to prepare a nonlinear presentation, one that allows them to "bounce around" your portfolio. First the viewer might look at your resume, then pay a visit to your "gallery." Once in your gallery, he or she may veer off into mini-galleries, where more of your designs are on display. At any time, the viewer can, simply by clicking, move directly to another area of your port without having to back out of the section he or she is currently viewing.

Nonlinear authoring programs offer additional flexibility. They give you the ability to import many different file types, so no matter what your area of design, chances are that you will be able to transfer your projects into a format that these programs will understand. With these and many more features, such multimedia programs can really showcase your work. You can design almost unlimited interface styles. You can make the project as friendly and approachable as you wish. In sum, nonlinear programs are very attractive to potential employers. They offer a sophisticated way for you to display your work, and they point to your level of design expertise in the process.

Several programs are available to create nonlinear portfolios and two popular programs are Macromedia Director and Macromedia Flash, now owned by Adobe.

For many years, Macromedia Director has been the program of choice for multimedia authoring. Director serves many different purposes and professions; it not only enables you to build your digital portfolio, but it can also help you to create simulations, tests, and even games. What gives Director the edge over other authoring programs is its capability to handle a wide a range of media. Director can import all sorts of graphic formats, music, even long-format video and 3-D.

Consider, for example, how effective it would be to take one of your sculptures or architectural drawings and model it in a 3-D space (programs such as 3D Studio Max, Form Z, and Maya can be used to create the model). You could then import the project to Director where the viewer could look at your model from all sides.

A word of caution is in order here, however. Director has a higher learning curve than many other authoring programs. But once you master it, you'll find it to be very flexible and capable of producing very sophisticated interface design. Director uses a computer language called Lingo to create what are called "markers." These markers represent the various sections of your interface. (Note: You can create a digital portfolio without the use of Lingo, but all the best features of the program can be achieved only with its usage.) Check out two examples of Director in action in the color insert.

For those who prefer to create multimedia with as little programming as possible, Macromedia Flash is the program of choice. Flash utilizes a highly graphic interface that allows you to create an interface in a relatively short amount of time. Floating palettes abound, to make your design work easier. And the programming code, ActionScript, used in Flash helps you control major sections of your project. Although ActionScripting can be difficult to learn, Macromedia makes it easy on those of us nonprogrammer types. All sorts of scripts come prebuilt to help you on your way. These snippets of code, called Behaviors, allow you to control parts of your project without actually having to write in the ActionScript language—meaning you don't need a lot of programming knowledge to build your portfolio. Templates are also included, to help you with the creation of slide shows and video presentations. You can see a typical Flash screen in the color insert.

One of the most important reasons for using Flash is speed. Flash uses vector-based technology to create interfaces. (A vector image is up of many individual points arranged by the underlying math of the graphics program.

Because they are math-based objects, vector graphics can be output at any size without sacrificing quality.) This enables you to produce dazzling animations, yet keep file sizes down to just a few kilobytes. What does that mean? Little or no wait time at your Web site or on your CD.

But what really sets Flash apart from other multimedia authoring programs is its flexibility. Are you an architect? Flash can import files from AutoCad. Do you have files created in graphic programs such as Photoshop or Illustrator? No problem: Flash can import files from those programs as well. Moreover, a wide range of features make it easy for you to use the program to suit your individual needs. Animators make it possible to create cartoons for the Web. In fact, Flash can help you create projects that go way beyond portfolio design. Corporations can extol their fine consumer products with Flash-based demonstrations; weather and stock information can be sent graphically to cell phones or PDAs; and kids are encouraged to learn facts about the world with clever Flash-based games. Flash has become so popular of late that you'll hear people refer to their projects as "Flashed."

Which Program Is Right for You?

So which program should you choose? Linear or nonlinear: Answer: It depends. Each program has strengths and weaknesses, advantages and disadvantages. If the thought of doing even the least amount of programming leaves you weak in the knees, then PowerPoint may be the clear choice for you. If, however, you can double-click to generate a few lines of code, you might be surprised at how easy Flash is to learn. And, of course, the more time you spend working with a program, the more sophisticated the interface will become as a result. It is easy to create a quick little interface, but the really great ones take time (lots of time). So if time is of the essence, choose the quickest route possible to your final project.

Master of the Web: Choosing a HyperText Markup Language (HTML) Program Editor

Just as there are a number of multimedia authoring programs that can help you to design an interactive CD, there are numerous programs to help you design Web pages for your projects. Though it is possible to design Web pages

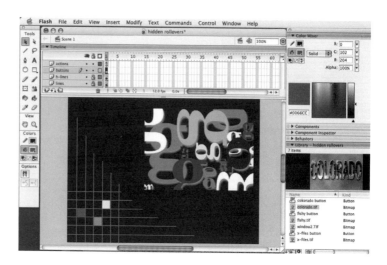

This Flash interface features a "rollover" effect. The viewer rolls over one of the buttons located at the lower left and artwork pops up on the screen.

using nothing more than a simple text editor, most experts agree that using what's called a *drag-and-drop* program will simplify the process considerably. The code generated by these text editors isn't always perfectly clean, nevertheless, they do offer powerful design and programming tools.

In some ways, creating a Web site is similar to producing a CD-ROM. Images, text, and sound are combined to create a series of "clickable" pages. Many designers use both multimedia authoring programs and HTML editors to create a total viewing experience.

Shopping for an HTML Editor

Let's take a quick look at some of the more popular HTML editors, to give you an idea what's available.

Adobe GoLive

The sometimes tedious work of building Web pages is easy with Adobe GoLive. GoLive features a great set of floating palettes that make the Web design process much more enjoyable, as well as *rollovers,* those buttons that change color when you roll over them with your mouse pointer.

But Adobe GoLive is much more than just an HTML editor; it is a complete site management tool. This means that if you want to work on a site with several other designers, everyone can create pages and bring them together easily. GoLive includes plug-in support for each of the major media packages such as Flash

above • Images can be imported and placed in layouts that work to inform and engage.

below • What makes Dreamweaver so unique is that it gives you the ability to create layouts that don't look like ordinary Web designs. This gives you free rein to be an artist without worrying so much about how the layout will look once it is uploaded.

(for Web animation), QuickTime and RealPlayer (these are video players for movies and animations), and Scalable Vector Graphics (SVG; a new format for Web graphics that uses math to represent designs similar to vector-based drawing.). The learning curve on this capability can be a little steep for the beginning Web designer, but the rewards are many for those who persevere. You can see what is possible with GoLive by checking out the example shown in the color insert.

Dreamweaver

The Macromedia entry into the HTML editor market is Dreamweaver. Like Adobe GoLive, Dreamweaver is a drag-and-drop style HTML editor, with extensive layout tools, and its features and results are quite similar to GoLive. Macromedia products are well integrated, meaning that Dreamweaver works well with Flash (not surprisingly, since Macromedia produces both products).

Dreamweaver is notable for the clean HTML code it creates. Using the program, you can work directly in code view, in a page layout mode, or in a split view where you can see both your code and the preview, as shown in the color insert. In addition, should you ever decide to become a more advanced HTML designer, Dreamweaver provides excellent support for scripting languages such as Active Server Pages (ASP; special embedded scripts that can be written for web page development), Java Server Pages (JSP; a scripting language for creating interactive Web pages), and ColdFusion Markup Language (CFML; one of the main languages used to design Web databases).

Adobe Acrobat

Adobe Acrobat is especially useful for graphic designers who are comfortable with page layout software. Using Acrobat, you can create files that rework layout-style pages (such as QuarkXPress and InDesign) into Web links. The program converts those files into a special format called Portable Document Format (PDF; a cross-platform file format that accurately displays font and graphical elements displayed in a publication). The program can also embed multimedia content such as sounds and movies. And because fonts cause one of the biggest problems facing multimedia designers (standard TrueType fonts on PCs do not always work on Macs), Acrobat embeds font information directly in the document.

Moreover, using Acrobat, pages can be created that contain index links, enabling visitors to click on any link and be immediately taken to its corresponding page. Acrobat also has the capability to reduce file sizes (which means they take less time to download), and is great at creating electronic magazines. Once a document has been designed in Adobe InDesign or QuarkXPress, it can be easily converted into an Acrobat document. The new page can move seamlessly to the Web, where it becomes available for viewing.

Making a Choice

Which program should you buy? The choice of course depends on what you want to do and how much you are willing or are able to pay. Graphic designers would do well to learn GoLive or Acrobat, as both programs do a good job of creating Web pages that follow layout rules

Here is an example of Acrobat Reader output. Once a file has been created in Acrobat, you can open it and examine it in Reader. Notice that all of the pages are available as previews on the right of the layout.

they are familiar with. These two programs are also efficient at designing a small- to medium-sized sites that feature a fair amount of static content. If, however, you are a budding techie who intends to move into programming environments, then Dreamweaver is your best bet. It has the capability to work with the most modern computer languages, allowing you create sites that feature electronic shopping carts.

Putting It All Together: Additional Software Options

You have created a print portfolio. It may consist of printed pieces, along with 3-D pieces such as sculpture or package design, drawings, slides, and/or photographs. Now you must convert that print portfolio into a digital format. Where do you begin? How long will it take? How do the different programs work together? To answer those questions and more, in this section we'll examine some of the programs that can help you to convert your work to the digital format.

As you have learned, the building blocks for any multimedia project center around the final environment you are targeting (Web or CD) and the authoring software you have selected. To finish the final project, you will need additional support software, and choosing the correct program and file format is important to produce a successful project.

The software necessary to complete the transformation from print to digital generally falls into three categories: raster-based programs, vector-based programs and page layout programs. Here is a quick rundown of the features of these types of programs.

Raster-Based Programs

Raster-based images (sometimes called bitmapped graphics) are created pixel by pixel within a grid of pixels, or points of light. These images have a fixed resolution, which is defined as the dpi, which stands for dots per inch, determined when an image is first created. A typical screen resolution is 72 dpi. Any image you create or modify at a set dpi should never be resized because each of the individual pixels are *fixed*, or absolute, in size. Any attempts at resizing will make the image appear "soft." Raster-based images are great for continuous-tone images such as photographs, as they allow for smooth gradients and subtle detail. A comparison of a raster-based and vector-based image is shown in the color insert.

Adobe Photoshop
In this category, Adobe Photoshop is without a doubt the leading image-editing program on the market today. Photoshop comes with powerful tools to create and manipulate images. Its list of features is impressive. There are tools for color correction and auto removal of dust and scratches. One particularly interesting tool is the Healing Brush. It erases wrinkles, minor skin defects, and other small flaws from images of the human face. And Photoshop's selection of special effects provide endless possibilities for image manipulation. Other features such as improved masking and a spellcheck really smooth your workflow.

Photoshop works in conjunction with many of the

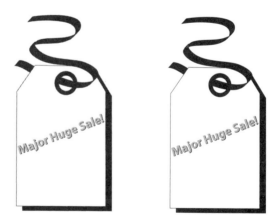

As you can see with these two images, a bitmapped image (such as Photoshop) always make images look pixelated. However, images created with vector-based programs allow images to be resized as much or as little as needed. The image will always look crisp.

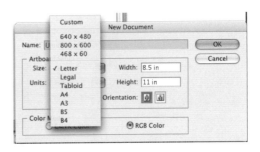

Here is a typical setup page in Photoshop. Notice that you are offered a wide range of options for the initial page setup.

above • **Adobe is the industry standard when it comes to image manipulation, and it's easy to see why. Its full set of sophisticated features make it easy to create complex images.**

below • **This astonishing illustration by Valen Evers shows what a great artist can do with Painter. Complex "natural art brushes" make it possible to simulate a real-world art environment. Whether you want to create watercolor or Conte crayon images, Painter has the tools to you.**

popular scanners, allowing you to transport your images directly into the program—a real time-saver. Moreover, several formats for saving are provided; and there are numerous options for importing your images to the authoring programs.

Photoshop also comes bundled with another image editing program called Image Ready. Image Ready helps you to prepare your files for display on the Internet. You can customize each picture by specifying the level of compression. The program also gives you constant feedback on the time to download an image—very useful for Web designers!

Corel Painter

But perhaps you're looking for a program that is geared more toward fine art than graphic art. In this case, Corel Painter might be a good choice for you. Corel Painter is what's known as a *natural media painting program*. As such, it offers a large assortment of media to work with, including oils, acrylics, colored pencils, felt pens, chalk, charcoals, crayons, and airbrushes, to create realistic artwork. You can also select the "paper" type (such as watercolor or charcoal) for your project. You then apply the medium to the paper where it acts as it would in the natural world. The painting brushes are pressure-sensitive; that is to say, they work with drawing tablets to control the amount of paint or the thickness of the lines you apply to the drawing. The program also comes with lots of filters so that you can include additional effects to your designs. Painter also features a Publish to Internet command, which enables you to preview the effects of various compression settings on your images.

Vector-Based Programs

Vector-based drawing programs are very different from raster-based programs. They use math to describe the points or shapes that make up an image. (Fortunately, you won't have to know these mathematical equations!) The advantage of using math to describe a shape is that it doesn't have a set resolution. Furthermore, file sizes are very small, and the images may be resized as much or little as necessary. All that said, vector-based programs have one major disadvantage: They are terrible for converting continuous-tone images such as photographs.

Vector-based programs include Adobe Illustrator, Macromedia FreeHand, and Corel Draw.

Adobe Illustrator

For many years, Adobe Illustrator has set the standard for vector-based drawing programs in print production. This professional graphics program enables image creation with clean PostScript output (very important in the print industry) and tight integration with Adobe Photoshop. The program lets you create new pages with either the Web or a CD in mind.

Illustrator also offers superior drawing tools, such as the Warp Effect tool, which allows you to customize text in unique ways. Another highly useful tools is the Magic Wand, which allows you to select objects in your document with a set of attributes that you like and reproduce those attributes directly onto another shape. The Magic Wand also makes it possible to specify which attributes to look for, including fill color, stroke color, stroke weight, opacity, and blending mode. If you are a professional designer or artist looking for a stable, powerful drawing program, look no further than Adobe Illustrator.

Macromedia FreeHand

If you are looking for tight integration with Flash, the leading authoring program for Web animation, Macromedia FreeHand is probably a better choice. FreeHand is a great program for creating illustrations and layouts for print and, especially, the Web. Macromedia's package includes multipage support and the ability to create and manage up to 32,000 master pages in a single document.

FreeHand provides a number of great tools. My favorite is the Contour Gradients tool. It blends colors based on the outline of an object—an excellent feature for adding realistic shading. It's also possible to automatically trace an imported raster-based photograph, turning it into a resizable vector-based facsimile of the original. (With Illustrator, you have to buy a separate package—Streamline or Silhouette).

Much like Dreamweaver and Flash, FreeHand now incorporates a similar type of menu layout. And FreeHand excels in its interaction with Flash. It has the capability to edit files and import back and forth. You can launch and edit Flash MX files with FreeHand; and FreeHand files can be launched and edited with Flash MX. This one feature alone makes the program a real asset for designers moving to the Web.

CorelDraw

CorelDraw continues to be a cost-effective way to "set up shop" with everything you need for drawing and Web animation. CorelDraw is easy to master, and it ships with a superior interface and features set. Working with

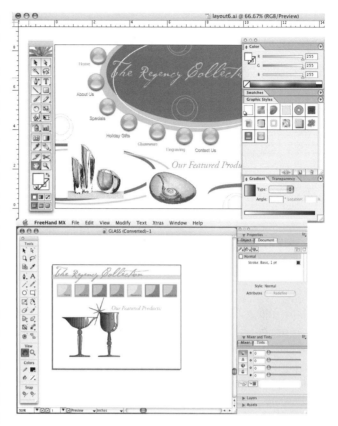

above • When it comes to vector-based illustration, there is no doubt that Adobe Illustrator leads the way. The interface is straightforward, and the options are boundless.

below • Macromedia FreeHand is a great choice if you intend to move your designs to Flash. The two programs integrate tightly to give you more drawing options than you would have with Flash alone.

vector-based images can be difficult, so one of the most useful features of the program is its capability to quickly join multiple paths into a single object. It also features pressure-sensitive Smudge and Roughen tools and excellent filters, which can add bulge and ripple effects to an object. Text is easy to control, and unlike other vector-based programs, text boxes can be linked, so that text can "flow."

Using CorelDraw, you can also embed graphics within a paragraph of text. CorelDraw also does a good job of creating and optimizing Web images, and can generate rollovers for Web design. In sum, the product offers a number of great features, including enhanced drawing tools, text tools, fills, textures, patterns, and interactive tools.

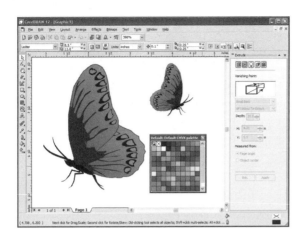

CorelDraw has a sophisticated set of palettes that allow you to produce complex drawings. The program also offers color systems for print and Web output.

Macromedia Fireworks

Macromedia Fireworks is a bit of a hybrid program. It utilizes both raster-based and vector-based capabilities to create pictures. It is also a full-scale image creation and manipulation program, similar to Adobe Photoshop. Live Effects is the Fireworks answer to manipulating text to create some pretty cool effects—all in real time. In Fireworks, every aspect of a graphic, including text, objects, and image maps, is fully editable and can have effects applied at any time. For Web-based design, Fireworks offers a good assortment of tools, including image slicing (which cuts an image into separate segments to prepare it for HTML) and JavaScript rollovers. The ability to optimize Graphic Interchange Format (GIF) images with browser-safe colors, as well as the capability to import files from Photoshop, FreeHand, Illustrator, and CorelDraw make Fireworks an excellent program choice.

Page Layout Programs

QuarkXPress

QuarkXPress is the cream of the crop when it comes to layout programs. Most newspapers, magazines, pamphlets, and posters today are created with this program, and with good reason. QuarkXPress features a clear, easy-to-understand interface, and it comes with a complete set of type tools and the capability to work with complex pages. Of late, Quark, Inc., the makers of QuarkXPress have turned their attention to the Web

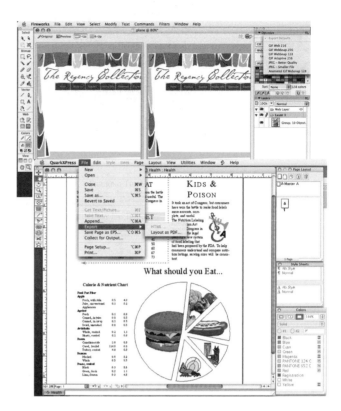

above • Fireworks simplifies the work of preparing images for Web design. The program allows you to "slice up" your images into small pieces that can then be dropped into Web layouts.

below • When it comes to page layout, QuarkXPress has long been considered at the head of the pack. The latest version allows you to create Web pages directly from your page layouts.

design market. Included with the program now are features that allow you to produce Web pages that contain hyperlinks, image maps, and rollovers. You can also choose compression settings for your images on an individual basis, to gain more control over your pictures. Exporting HTML on QuarkXPress is straightforward, but you will have more control over the look of your final Web pages with an HTML editor. Still, for designers comfortable with the program, this is a good starting point.

InDesign

InDesign is another excellent page layout program. Much like QuarkXPress, InDesign offers a full set of page layout features. It makes excellent use of the familiar Illustrator/Photoshop-style interface and offers several of Illustrator's vector-based tools. Images can be dragged directly in from either program, bypassing the usual import step in other programs. InDesign is especially strong at previewing images in a layout. You can view images in high-resolution mode or in the quicker Typical Display mode. InDesign also makes it possible to perform multiple undo's—a very useful capability! InDesign writes relatively clean code, although as with QuarkXPress you are still better off using an HTML editor. InDesign can also convert your Tagged Image File Format (TIFF) images to Graphic Interchange Format (GIF) or Joint Photographic Experts Group (JPEG) files on the fly when you export them.

Program Review

At this point, you've been introduced to a number of programs, all designed to, in one way or another, help you produce your digital portfolio. To help you sort through all the information, the table starting on page 63 gives you a form on which you can make notes for each of the products we've discussed.

Once you have completed this form, which will give you a basic understanding of the software available for multimedia authoring, you will be ready to make a buying decision. I suggest that you include at least one vector-based and one raster-based program, along with an authoring package, based on your final output. At one point or another I have used all of the programs discussed above, and they all feature outstanding options for the designer. That said, here are my personal recommendations:

For raster-based image creation: Adobe Photoshop
For vector-based image creation: Adobe Illustrator
For page layout: QuarkXPress or InDesign
For CD-ROM authoring: Flash
For Web design: Dreamweaver

Here are some additional points to ponder when you are evaluating software:

• How software-friendly is it? If you have only a couple of weeks to design the interface, you probably won't have time to learn a complex program. Look for programs that offer tutorials and help screens. Ask yourself, "Can I figure out enough of this program to design an effective interface in the time I have?" And consider purchasing a book that offers lots of visual instructions.

Adobe InDesign is a relative newcomer to the page layout market, but it has already won legions of followers thanks to its clean interface, which is so much like its sister program Illustrator.

• Does the program feature good text and graphic options and an easy way to manipulate text? Does it let you choose from numerous fonts, colors, sizes, and styles? Can be type be "broken apart" into vector-based shapes that no longer require the font?
• What graphics features does the program have? Can you produce special effects, such as "warped" or 3-D?
• Does the program come with any prebuilt options, such as animations?
• Can images be readily imported and manipulated from other programs?
• Does the program accept sound?
• Which sound formats are available within the program?
• Can you import sounds and music from other sources?
• Can you modify the sound once inside the program?
• What level of interactivity does the program offer?
• Is the program a linear or nonlinear authoring program? Will linear design be enough to satisfy you, or will you require a more advanced authoring environment?
• What is the cost of the software?
• Can you purchase the software with a student discount?
• Are free trial versions available?
• Will "light" versions of the program be enough to get the job completed? How much do updates cost?
• Can you edit images within the program?

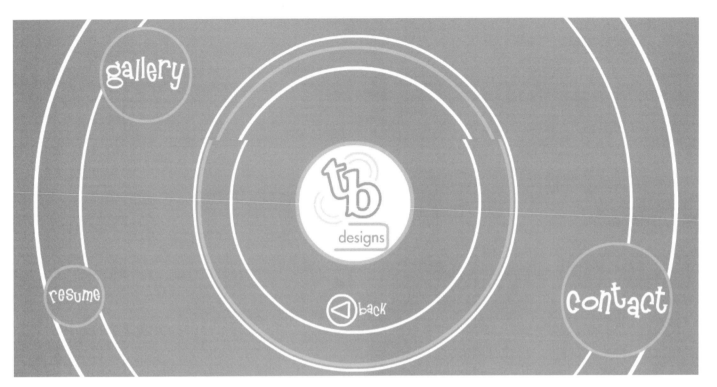

This enjoyable interface is reminiscent of design from the 1950s, with its colors of aqua, yellow, and blue. It is clear to the user which options are available.

- Does the software come with a spell-checker and thesaurus?
- Will the program self-check for programming errors?

Now that you know a bit more about authoring programs, you are almost ready to design your digital interface, and in the next chapter, you will begin the process of building your digital portfolio. But first let's turn our attention to a more complete discussion of Web design.

Planning Your Web Design Project

Though, as I've said, designing an interface for the Web and a CD are similar, there are a few special considerations. When it comes to proper planning, the key is to ensure that your Web site design goes as smoothly as possible.

And to help you to focus your thoughts and design ideas, I want you to complete the following exercise: visit at least five portfolio Web sites, and complete the ques-

tionnaire that follows for each site. The purpose here is simple: How can you design a site if you don't know what you want or like? You need to take time to check out sites by other artists such as yourself and identify what you like and don't like about each site. Pay particular attention to the overall design, graphics, speed, and ease of navigation. (Note: Don't worry if you can't answer all the questions here. You will be able to after you read the next couple of chapters.)

Now, don't just sit there: Start brainstorming! Grab a sketchbook, start drawing, and don't stop until you like what you have created. Ask yourself, "What is the mood I am trying to create?" Simple, outrageous, or elegant—it doesn't really matter. But one thing's for sure: you can't begin to create the interface until you know what the site will look like. Good design equals good navigation (see the color insert). Put yourself in the shoes of the employer. What will really grab the attention of the visitor? An effective opening? Examples of your work? A clean navigational system? The success of your site is based primarily on the logic you apply to the introduction and first page. The next chapter is devoted to design techniques, so stay turned for more on this shortly. But for now, consider these questions:

- Do you have a site map and does it make sense?
- Do you have the skills necessary to create the interface you have designed?
- Are you getting your message across?
    Does your choice of colors, graphics, and fonts support your design theme?
    Do you include a logo on the site?
    Can your designs be grouped into logical categories?
    Should you include image descriptions and photos?
    Do you need music or video?

- Do you have the following items?
    An updated resume that uses good actions verbs and good typography?
    A gallery of your designs? There should be at least 10 to 15 outstanding pieces available for viewing.
    Did you include a description of each piece?

- Do you have a contact page?
    How do you want prospective employers to contact you? E-mail? Telephone?
    Did you provide a place on the site for this information?

- Is it fast?
    If it takes more than 10 seconds for the first page to load, you'll lose your viewer. Do not use Web designs that larger than 50 to 80 kilobytes. In the case of Web interface design, smaller equals faster.

If you are serious about designing a Web site, and you follow all of the steps outlined in this book, you will create a winning portfolio Web site. ■

glossary

ActionScripting: An object-oriented programming language developed by Macromedia for use in its Flash animation grogram. The language is designed to work most effectively with vector-based graphics, but it can also work with raster-based files.

Address: In this context, the series of series of letters and numbers by which the Internet identifies you or the location where information is stored. Examples include your E-mail and Web addresses.

Adobe Type 1 Fonts: Developed by Adobe in the early 1980s, Type 1 technology uses the PostScript page description language to render fonts on the screen and in print. Type 1 fonts have two parts: the screen font and the printer font. Both must be present on the computer in order for a file to render (print) properly.

Application: A program or software that tells the computer to do what you want it to do. Examples include Safari, Netscape Navigator, Microsoft Internet Explorer, HTML editors, Flash, GoLive, and QuickTime.

Bandwidth: The amount of data that can be sent from one computer to another through a particular connection in a certain amount of time. The higher the bandwidth, the faster your page will load.

Bookmark: In this context, a method of saving a Web site location to an electronic "address book." Creating bookmarks allows you to return to previously visited Web addresses.

Browser: A program that allows users to visit and access information on the World Wide Web. Popular browsers include Netscape Navigator, Safari, and Internet Explorer.

Buffer size: The access time or the speed by which data is made available to your computer for processing from a CD.

Bug: A programming code error that causes a program or computer system to perform unpredictably and in some extreme cases, crash.

Copyright: The rights to an original creative work held by an individual or corporation. Additional rights may be gained in such areas as film, broadcasting, computer programs, logo, and many other items. Unauthorized use of these items is punishable by law, and can include fines and jail time.

CD-ROM Read/Write Speed: The maximum rate at which a CD drive records data to a disc. The read (or transfer rate) is how fast the drive reads data off a disc. The speed of the drive is historically compared to music CDs (where 1x or 1-speed gives a data transfer rate of 150 kilobytes per second).

DIAL-UP CONNECTION: The capability to connect to the Internet through a land-based telephone line. It is the most common form of Internet connection.

DOCUMENT SOURCE: The HTML code created to generate a Web page. Many Web sites allow you to "view the source code" of the pages, although sometimes the code is hidden to protect the designer's copyright.

DOTS PER INCH (DPI): A measure of resolution for printers, scanners, and displays. Magazines are typically printed at 300 dots per inch. Large-scale commercial typesetters (e.g., for fancy catalogs) can print at about 1200 dpi.

DOWNLOAD: The transfer of files from one computer to another, or from the Web to your own computer.

DRAG AND DROP: A common method for manipulating files that involves clicking on a a file to highlight it, and then dragging it via the mouse, from one location to another, where it is released. A typical example would be to drag and drop a file attachment into an email.

EMAIL ADDRESS: An electronic postal address. An email address consists of a series of characters, such as gail@yahoo.net, that uniquely identifies the mailbox of a person who can send and receive electronic mail.

EXTENSIBLE MARKUP LANGUAGE (XML): A variation of HTML that is suitable for use on the World Wide Web.

HYPERTEXT MARKUP LANGUAGE (HTML): A set of tags and rules used to develop hypertext document design for the World Wide Web.

INTERFACE (OR USER INTERFACE): An interface based on graphics instead of text. A typical interface relies on a series of icons and pictures and uses a keyboard and mouse as an input device.

INTERNET: A vast collection of interconnected computers linked together through a series of networks throughout the world.

LINK (ALSO KNOWN AS A HYPERTEXT LINK): An association that is established between two Web pages. The connection is usually devised by creating a graphical icon that indicates a connection is available. A way to navigate digital interfaces.

LINGO: An object-oriented animation scripting language developed by Macromedia for use in its Director authoring animation gromgram. Lingo is designed to work most effectively with vector-based graphics, but it can also work with raster-based files.

MARKERS: A prompt created to act as a position holder for moving within an authoring program. Markers are created to assist in programming.

MEGABYTE: A unit of measure equal to 1 million (1,048,576) bytes. Generally refers to the amount of memory a computer or a hard drive has available.

MULTIMEDIA AUTHORING PROGRAM: A software program that has been designed to help in the creation of digital interactive files. Director, Flash, and GoLive are examples of multimedia authoring programs.

RASTER-BASED GRAPHICS: Also known as bitmapped graphics, raster-based graphics are images created pixel by pixel within a grid of pixels or points of light. Raster images have a fixed resolution that is defined as the dpi.

STAND-ALONE PRESENTATION: An interface that is created to be device-independent. A stand-alone presentation does not require the original program in order to run.

TEXT EDITOR: A utility program to help create and modify text files. It can refer to an HTML editor or a word processing program.

TRUETYPE FONTS: Fonts that use a single font file for each. It is fully scalable and generates bitmaps (screen versions) as the user creates text in a layout or drawing program. Type 1 fonts were introduced by Microsoft in 1982.

VECTOR-BASED GRAPHICS: A system of design that use math to describe the points or shapes that make up an image.

WORLD WIDE WEB CONSORTIUM (W3C): A group of people and companies that work together to define the commerce, communication, and language standards for the Internet.

● ● ● WEB SITE EVALUATION FORM

1. Name of Web Site	URL (www._____.com)	Does the URL make sense?

2. Was there an opening?	Was it appropriate for the site?	If not, why not?
Did you like it?	☐ Yes	
	☐ No	

3. Does the site open quickly?	☐ Yes	
	☐ No	

4. Do a thumbnail sketch of the site.
   Compare it to the other sites you visit.

5. Does the homepage reflect the	☐ Yes	
overall message of the site?	☐ No	If not, why not?

6. Does the homepage require a lot of scrolling?	☐ Yes	
	☐ No	If not, why not?

List the design elements.	1.
Do they work to support	2.
the theme of the site?	3.
	4.
	5.

Do the links make
effective use of color?

7. Do the links make sense?	☐ Yes	
	☐ No	If not, why not?

8. Do the links work?	☐ Yes	
	☐ No	If not, why not?

9. Is the text easy to read?	☐ Yes	
	☐ No	If not, why not?

10. Are there frames? Do they work?	☐ Yes	
	☐ No	If not, why not?

11. Is there good content?	☐ Yes	
	☐ No	If not, why not?

12. Is there a background color	☐ Yes	
or graphic? Does it work?	☐ No	If not, why not?

13. Is there animation? Is it effective?	☐ Yes	
	☐ No	If not, why not?

14. Is there sound? Does it support	☐ Yes	
the theme of the site?	☐ No	If not, why not?

15. Were links included to other	☐ Yes	
sites, such as colleges?	☐ No	If not, why not?

16. Was there a contact page?	☐ Yes	
Does the email work?	☐ No	If not, why not?

17. Did you have any technical difficulties? List them.	1.
	2.
	3.
	4.
	5.

18. What is your overall	1 = Needs a major overhaul
rating of this site?	10 = Outstanding!

Program Name	Primary Purpose of the Software	Technical Features	Learning Curve
Microsoft PowerPoint		1. 2. 3. 4. 5.	
Macromedia Director		1. 2. 3. 4. 5.	
Macromedia Flash		1. 2. 3. 4. 5.	
Adobe GoLive		1. 2. 3. 4. 5.	
Macromedia Dreamweaver		1. 2. 3. 4. 5.	
QuarkXPress		1. 2. 3. 4. 5.	
Adobe Acrobat		1. 2. 3. 4. 5.	

● ● ● SOFTWARE EVALUATION FORM

Program Name	Primary Purpose of the Software	Technical Features	Learning Curve
Adobe Photoshop		1. 2. 3. 4. 5.	
Corel Painter		1. 2. 3. 4. 5.	
Adobe Illustrator		1. 2. 3. 4. 5.	
Macromedia FreeHand		1. 2. 3. 4. 5.	
CorelDraw		1. 2. 3. 4. 5.	
Macromedia Fireworks		1. 2. 3. 4. 5.	

The Digital Portfolio
Technical Elements

Now that we have spent some time looking at the various multimedia authoring and support programs available to help you design your electronic portfolio, you may be wondering how these programs work together. It is as this point that the graphics file format comes into play, and in this chapter, you will learn how to analyze some of the multimedia industry's graphic formats. Fortunately, no matter what type of images you plan to add to your portfolio, the format selection process is pretty much the same.

But before we get started, recall from Chapter 5 that computer graphics fall into three main groups: raster-based programs, vector-based programs, and page layout programs. But it is also possible to have what are called metafiles, a type of hybrid file containing both vector and raster images (Flash, the multimedia authoring program, falls into this category).

Preparing Work for Digital Presentation

Working with Raster-Based Images

We'll begin with the use of raster-based images. Raster images, as you will recall, are produced by such pro-

grams as Adobe Photoshop and Corel Painter, as well as scanners and digital cameras. There are many different file formats to choose from, but the most common raster-based formats are:

Tagged Image File Format (TIFF)
Joint Photographic Experts Group (JPEG)
Graphics Interchange Format (GIF)

The format you select will depend on a couple of factors: the image itself (such as a photo requiring a lot of detail, or a logo) and how the image is to be used (e.g., CD-ROM or Web). Remember, images created for print can be large, whereas images for the Web must be well compressed to enable efficient download. You also need to be aware that not every program is capable of importing every file format. In general, you are better off using the three formats listed above. It is important to use standard formats, otherwise, though your files may import correctly to an authoring program, they may not work well with once the files are available for viewing.

Working with Vector-Based Images

Vector-based images, remember, use math to describe the points or shapes that make up an image. Common vector

Your computer is your most valuable tool in creating a digital portfolio. Having a friend alongside to assist you is just as valuable.

images include 2- and 3-D architectural drawings, illustrations, flowcharts, logos, and fonts. The advantage of using math to describe a shape is that it doesn't have a set resolution, so the file size tends to be much smaller; hence, vector-based images can be more easily transformed or resized than raster images. Vector images are typically created and displayed within drawing and animation programs. The shapes generally consist of lines, curves, and other shapes, which can be assigned colors and given outlines or other special effects such as drop shadows.

Common vector-based formats include:

Scalable Vector Graphics (SVG)
ShockWave Flash (SWF)
Encapsulated PostScript (EPS)

Working with Page Layout Files

A word of warning: Page layout file types present a problem. Neither InDesign (INDD) nor QuarkXPress (QXD) provide file extensions that are fully compatible with most multimedia programs. As a general rule, you will have to export the page layout file into another program as an intermediate step. The file can then be saved in a more universal format that the authoring programs will understand. For example, a file created in QuarkXPress

can be exported as an EPS file to Photoshop. Once in Photoshop, the file can be saved as a JPEG. Now the file is ready for digital usage. InDesign can export your file as a PDF, but that format is still not completely accepted in the multimedia world (although the format is quickly making inroads). PDF files can be downloaded and burned to CD (PDF is not the best choice for Web design). Page layout formats include:

Encapsulated PostScript (EPS)
Portable Document Format (PDF)

Working with Metafiles

A graphics metafile is a computer file that contains a set of data records describing a graphical image. These files may contain either bitmapped or vector graphics data. They are also used to describe information about layout, fonts, and graphics to a printer or display device. Metafiles transport graphical information between different types of computers and computer applications. There are different type of metafiles, including Page Description Language (PDL), Computer Graphics Metafile (CGM), Encapsulated PostScript (EPS), and PDF. Vector formats like Flash or SVG can also function as metafiles, because they are capable of including raster information.

Coordinating Graphic Formats

By now you're probably feeling as though you're swimming in alphabet soup—EPS, TIFF, PDF, CGM, and so on—but fortunately, all this comes together fairly easily.

It all begins with the final output. Once you have determined how your portfolio will be viewed, you can select the authoring program you plan to use that will

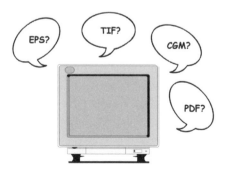

best serve your needs. The authoring program you select has import requirements and restrictions. Knowing these in advance allows you to work backward as you prepare your images electronically for the digital portfolio. In a moment, we will take a file from the beginning to its final destination in an authoring program, but first let's examine some of the import requirements for each of the multimedia packages. (Note: This is not the complete list, but will serve to highlight some of the possible formats you may encounter in your travels through multimedia design. An asterisk indicates a popular format choice.)

Microsoft PowerPoint
Joint Photographic Experts Group (JPEG)*
Tagged Image File Format (TIFF)
Macintosh (PICT)
Windows Bitmap (BMP)
Encapsulated PostScript (EPS)*
Graphics Interchange Format (GIF)*
Windows Metafile (WMF)

Macromedia Flash
Joint Photographic Experts Group (JPEG)*
Tagged Image File Format (TIFF)*
Photoshop Proprietary Format (PSD)
Graphics Interchange Format (GIF)*
Macintosh (PICT)
Windows Metafile (WMF)
Encapsulated PostScript (EPS)*
Windows Bitmap (BMP)
(WAV)* (Waveform Audio; cross compatible with
    Mac and Windows)
QuickTime movie (MOV)*
Flash Player (SWF [ShockWave Flash])*
AutoCAD 10 (DXF [Drawing Interchange Format])*
FreeHand Proprietary Format (FH10)
Silicon Graphics Image (SGI)*

Macromedia Director
Joint Photographic Experts Group (JPEG)*
Tagged Image File Format (TIFF)*
Photoshop Proprietary Format (PSD)
Graphics Interchange Format (GIF)*
Macintosh (PICT)
Windows Bitmap (BMP)
QuickTime movie (MOV)*

Rich Text Format (RTF)
PowerPoint (PPT)
(WAV)* (Cross compatible with Mac and Windows)

Adobe GoLive
Graphics Interchange Format (GIF)*
Joint Photographic Experts Group (JPEG)*
Flash Proprietary Format (SWF)*
Portable Document Format (PDF)*
Cascading Style Sheets (CSS)
QuickTime movie (MOV)*
(WAV)* (Cross compatible with Mac and Windows)
Director Shockwave Proprietary Format (DCR
    [Director Shockwave Proprietary Format])*
Microsoft Excel Proprietary Format (XLS [Microsoft
    Excel Proprietary Format])

Dreamweaver
Graphics Interchange Format (GIF)*
Joint Photographic Experts Group (JPEG)*
Flash Proprietary Format (SWF)*
Portable Document Format (PDF) *
Cascading Style Sheets (CSS)
QuickTime movie (MOV)*
(WAV)* (Cross compatible with Mac and Windows)
eXtensible Markup Language (XML)
Director Shockwave Proprietary Format (DCR)*
HyperText Markup Language (HTML)
Microsoft Excel Proprietary Format (XLS)

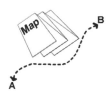

Inserting, Resizing, and Moving Graphics

Creating and working with images designed for multimedia is quite different from working with images for other media. You already know that file size plays a big part, but there are other technical considerations. One of the most important decisions you must now make is screen size, because this will determine all later choices you make when you resize each of your projects. My first word of advice here is to resist the temptation to use the default size of the multimedia authoring program. The reasons is that you mist make a selection based on the final application, that is, whether Web or CD. Why? Because each of these environments uses a different page layout configuration. Let's examine the differences.

The page layout you initially select for Web and CD-ROM design will be based on two factors: one, the size of the monitor and, two, the screen resolution. Your electronic portfolio will be displayed under a variety of different conditions. For example, it may be viewed by potential employers whose monitors are set to 640 horizontal × 480 vertical pixels. Other companies may have their monitors set much higher, to, say, 1024 × 768 and beyond. Some companies will have screens as large as 21 inches, whereas others may look at your work on screens that are only 15 inches. As a multimedia designer, you need to be sure your project will display no matter what the circumstance.

And never assume that the people viewing your portfolio will have updated equipment, or use the same programs you have on your computer. Take my friends Bob and Robert. Bob is into technology big time. He owns three desktop computers, plus one laptop. He also has the latest digital camera and printer, and everything is networked. When you design for someone like Bob, you need not be concerned about whether your project will display to its best advantage. But my other friend Robert is just the opposite. He hasn't bought a new computer in almost five years, and his monitor is only 15 inches and displays at 640 × 480, which is seriously out of date. Plus, his eyes are weaker so he needs larger type. But as long as Robert can surf the Net, he's happy. My point is, you may well encounter both Bob and Robert types when you submit your electronic resume, so it's a good idea to keep this diversity in mind. On August 14, 2004, according to Upsdell.com (a weekly newsletter for Web site designers: http://www.upsdell.com/BrowserNews/stat.htm) and StatMarket.com (a Web site optimization service:http://www.statmarket.com/), the percentage of people using the most popular screen resolutions break down as follows:

640 × 480	2 percent
800 × 600	28 percent
1024 × 768 and higher	70 percent

You might be wondering why this is so important. When you create pages that are larger than the monitor size on which they will be viewed—that is, pages that exceed the viewable area—artwork may be cut off or in some cases disappear. So keep these recommendations in mind to ensure that all of your artwork displays properly, even under less-than-ideal conditions.

So which size should you select? For CD-ROM design, the answer is pretty clear. A project created at 800 × 600 has the best chance of being seen in all its glory. For Web design, you must factor in the browser window title bar at the top and the scrollbars on the sides. These additional elements take away some of your design "real estate." Thus, to design a Web page for a monitor set to 800 × 600, choose 760 × 410. When the project is loaded into a Web page browser, it will fit perfectly.

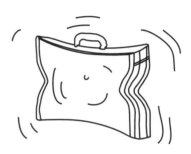

Compressing Files to Reduce Size

Most completed design projects do not conform to either Web or CD size requirements. Sculpture, paintings, clothing designs, and interior renderings are created for a client, not multimedia. They have to be converted to digital information. And although many graphic design projects are already in digital form, they are usually not in a size that conforms to specific multimedia format. And, as I've mentioned numerous times, typically, the files are huge. Here's why.

As I explained previously, raster-based images are created pixel by pixel within a grid of pixels, or points of light. Each pixel contains information that helps define the color. As such, they tend to be quite large. For example, a typical file created to be printed would utilize a 24-bit red, green, and blue (RGB) image. Each image uses 8 bits of data for each channel of color, for a total of 256 possible values for each color and 16.7 million colors. To print, graphic files must be converted from RGB to CMYK (cyan, magenta, yellow and black). The CMYK file now has four channels of color information, so these files are even larger. Even a 24-bit image created with the digital portfolio in mind would be 800 × 600

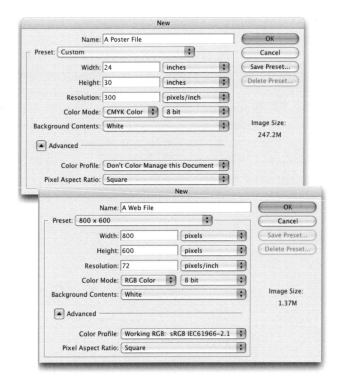

As you can see, the file size difference between the poster design and the Web design is significant. Any files created at such a large size will have to be reduced to fit the limitations of the Web.

pixels as a page size, and would result in a file of around 1.37 megabytes. That's way too large for your purposes. For example, a poster designed for, say, an upcoming festival might be designed to be 24 × 30 at 300 dpi, in CMYK format, for a file size of 247.2 megs!

Screen resolution (again, that's dots per inch, or DPI) also plays a role in a raster image's file size. Most graphic design image files are created at 300 dpi. Files created for the Web are always 72 dpi. Obviously a 300-dpi file will be substantially larger than a 72-dpi file. Always keeping in mind that time is a factor in your multimedia presentation, there are several different techniques you can use to reduce the download time for your viewers. The first is to apply a compression system to the image. With a little work, the image size can be dramatically reduced.

Image compression systems can be either *lossless* or *lossy*. Lossless compression has been around for some time. The system is generally applied to files types such as TIFF, LZW and PKZip. It compresses files through algorithms that reduce file size. A lossless compression

can reduce an image to approximately 50 to 75 percent of its original file size. When extracted from the compressed condition, the file is completely restored to its original state, with all of its original information intact. The lossless system, however, while great for archiving files, is not useful for multimedia work, because the files will still be too big and the format is not generally accepted by Web browsers.

In contrast, lossy compression can dramatically reduce the size of your files. Depending on how much compression you apply, the image can be reduced to as little as 1 percent of its original size. This is achieved by removing small to large amounts of pixel information contained within the file. However, the end result is the loss of both information and quality. The higher the compression, the more visible the degradation of the image. If you open a JPEG, alter it, and resave it, there will be about a 10 percent loss of information. Open and close that file a couple of times and you will end up with graphics garbage! To maintain file quality, always save your multimedia files in their original format (TIFF, EPS, etc.) and compress them under a different name at the last minute. File formats that utilize lossy compressions (JPEG) should be used primarily for display on the Web and CD.

In general, JPEG compression is very useful, but there are certain conditions under which you do not want to apply it. Some programs will attempt to apply a compression for you when you first output the file, and you never want to apply compression on top of a compression. Your image quality will really begin to degrade. We will talk about this potential problem, along with some solutions, in more detail a bit later.

Using Color Spaces for Multimedia Design

A *color space* is simply the range of colors that a viewer has available. The color space for a graphic designer is CMYK (again, that stands for the colors cyan, magenta, yellow, and black). CMYK projects are typically used for work that is intended for printing, as ink on paper. For a multimedia designer, the color space is usually RGB (red, green, and blue). The RGB color space is applied in files that are created for use on-screen. Here is the reason why. When the Internet was first being developed, most monitors were limited to a palette of 256 colors

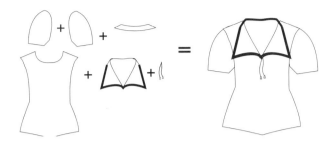

Armed with a few pieces of simple art, you can create a fabulous garment. Here you see the process of piecing together a blouse with a set of basic elements.

(known as "Web-safe" colors). Any additional colors were automatically eliminated. Today's monitors can display millions of colors, but Web designers still use the original the Web-safe palette. (For an example of this, refere to the color insert.) In fact, many Web designers use Index colors, derivatives of RGB color, but with an even more limited palette. Using Index colors makes it possible for the multimedia designer to produce a project that will be seen in its proper colors under the most diverse possible conditions. It also assures the fastest possible download.

Which color space should you select? Use RGB for all multimedia projects, including CD-ROM and Web design. Use Index colors for Web design once you gain some technical proficiency.

Transferring Artwork into the Computer

The key to successfully transmitting art into the computer is to know which programs work together in the most efficient way. Sometimes this is quite easy, requiring just a couple of mouse clicks. Other times the process requires a bit more knowledge about the programs and how they work together. To clarify this concept, we'll step through a couple of projects.

Two-Page Editorial Spread for a CD

Most graphic designers have completed a couple of magazine design projects. Typically, the programs utilized to complete such projects are Adobe Photoshop, Adobe Illustrator, or QuarkXPress. A project such as this may exist on board, but for the purpose of this discussion, we'll assume it is archived on a zip disk or CD. We'll also assume that the project is in digital QXD (QuarkXPress's native file format) format, which is not compatible with any of the multimedia programs, so the file will need to be converted.

The first step is to export the file using the Save Page As EPS command. Then the file will be exported as an

EPS. Once the file has been converted, it can be opened in a raster-based program, such as Adobe Photoshop (this works pretty the same in all versions of the program). Before this EPS file can be used in a multimedia authoring program, however, it will need to have the following five changes applied to it:

1. *It will have to be resized to fit an 800 × 600 screen.* And if the final resolution is 800 × 600, the file will actually have to be sized slightly smaller to allow for the placement of other items on the page, such as navigational buttons.
2. *It will need to be converted to RGB format.* Although Photoshop gives you the option of opening the file as either CMYK or RGB, it is better to first open the file as a CMYK and then

● ● ● Naming Your Files

File naming is a tricky issue when it comes to interface design, so here are a couple of guidelines:

Do no include spaces in filenames.

Keep the names short.

Do not use characters such as the asterisk (*), the slash (/), or a hyphen (-). These are special reserved symbols. You may, however, use the underscore character (_); for example, my_name@yahoo.net.

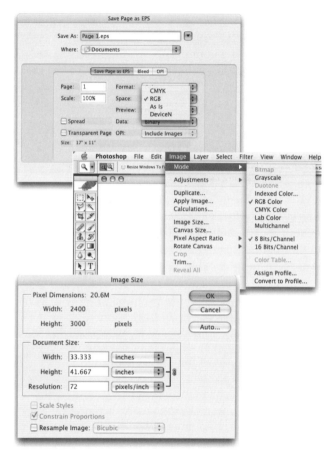

From above • The Export option of QuarkXPress allows you specify which color space will be used once the page has arrived at its final destination.

As you can see, there a lot of different choices when it comes to color and design. T-shirt designers prefer the Indexed option, whereas graphic designers usually choose the CMYK option, and multimedia artists use the RGB option. The one you select will depend on your final output.

The Image Size dialog box is where you to "resample" (reset) the dpi of your layouts. All images created for either CD or the Web must be saved as 72 dpi files.

convert it, because the colors will remain truer to your original layout.

3. *The file must be resized to 72 dpi.* You have the option of selecting 72 dpi when you first convert the file, but I recommend completing each step separately. This gives you the opportunity to try out different settings.

4. *Save the file as a TIFF or a JPEG.* I usually select TIFF for Macromedia Flash. Why? Flash can apply a JPEG conversion for me when I publish the file and I can instruct Flash as to how much compression I want the file to have.

5. *Import the TIFF file into Flash.* The final destination for the editorial spread is the Library, Flash's holding area, where it will be when you are ready to insert it in the final project.

A 3-D Sculpture for a Web Page with a Digital Camera

For our second example, we'll assume you want to display a series of images that show one of your recent sculptures from all viewpoints. For this type of art we have to start at a different point than we did for the editorial spread.

First the project has to be photographed, and for this step we're going to assume it will be done using a digital camera. This will simplify things considerably, because it eliminates. the hassle of running to the store to have the film developed, then scanning the image. All you have to do is transfer the photo from your camera to your computer. Let's get started.

1. *Take the photographs.* I recommend you take several photos from different points of view. Your sculpture is three-dimensional, so you will want to showcase it from several vantage points. Don't rush. Take time to consider the best way to show your work. You will need to determine the dpi your camera uses to "capture" (see step 2). It has different quality settings for different types of photographs. Consult your manual for dpi equivalents. Remember, you are trying to achieve 72 dpi. Some cameras also allow you to control how the image is saved. If possible, save it in an uncompressed format. This might be TIFF or as an unprocessed image (RAW; a native format of many digital cameras).

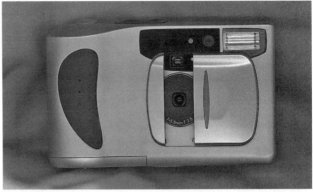

above • **Photoshop's File Browser feature allows you to see small thumbnails of your images before you load them. This is a valuable time-saver.**

right • **It doesn't really matter what type of digital camera you use to photograph your art. Because the final destination is a CD or the Web, the image doesn't have to be super high quality. As long as the picture looks good on your screen, it will look good on just about any screen.**

2. *Capture the photographs.* A digital photograph is downloaded to your computer via a Flash memory card. Once on your computer, the file can be opened by a raster-based image program, such as Adobe Photoshop. Photoshop 7, and later versions, has a nice feature that allows you to "browse thumbnail images" of your photographs.

3. *Rotate the photographs if necessary.* If you had to turn the camera sideways to photograph the entire image, you may need to rotate the photo to its upright position.

4. *Use the RGB format, and make sure the file is 72 dpi.* Most digital cameras use RGB as their default when capturing pictures, but it's best to check and make sure. If you captured at a higher setting than 72 dpi, be sure to change the file.

5. *Resize the photos to fit a 760 × 420 screen.* And, as I explained earlier, if the final destination is 760 × 410, the file will have to be sized slightly smaller to allow for the browser window and the placement of other items on the page. Some artists like to display the image as a thumbnail first. Then,

when the visitor clicks on the thumbnail, a larger version of the picture opens on the screen. This feature is quite easy to implement. Create the image in the large size you want, then size it down to a thumbnail and save it a second time under a similar, but different, name.

6. *Save the file as a JPEG.* JPEG compression is always best for the Web when photographs are involved. But you'll have to decide how much compression to apply to the image. Use the lowest possible setting that won't detract from the quality of the image, always keeping in mind that the smaller the file, the faster the download. Most Web designers try to keep their image size under 50 kilobytes. You can, however, create a file as large as 80 kilobytes only if you have no other choice.

7. *Import the JPEG file into Dreamweaver.* This is the final destination for your photographs. Import the small and large JPEG images and bring them onto your newly designed Web page.

above • **Linda Weeks** created this marvelous display showcasing her design talents. Not only did she create the package designs, but she produced the visual display for the packaging as well.

right • A closer view of Linda's product reveals the elaborate stand designed to hold the cosmetics.

Package Design

The Lowdown on Downloads

You've been there; we all have. You've gone to a Web site that sounds interesting to you, and now you sit staring at the your monitor waiting...waiting...waiting. Finally, an image appears. But it's blurry. You click one of the icons to head to the next page. When you get there, the text is small, and white reversed on a black background, so you can barely read it. On the next page is an animated image. But it never stops spinning and the colors are blinding. On the last page is a large button, which is obviously a link. You click on it, but nothing happens. Finally, you leave the site in frustration, vowing never to return.

Don't let this happen to visitors to your Web site. Images are an important part of interface design, but you must be careful not to let them frustrate your visitor. You want their experience to be aesthetically pleasing, but don't make them wait forever for the experience to begin!

Rules for Using Images for Your CD or Web site

Of course you'll want to include buttons, pictures, image maps, thumbnails, logos, and other images to your design interface, but you must use caution in this regard. Simply put, don't get carried away. A picture may be worth a thousand words, but not if the viewer has to

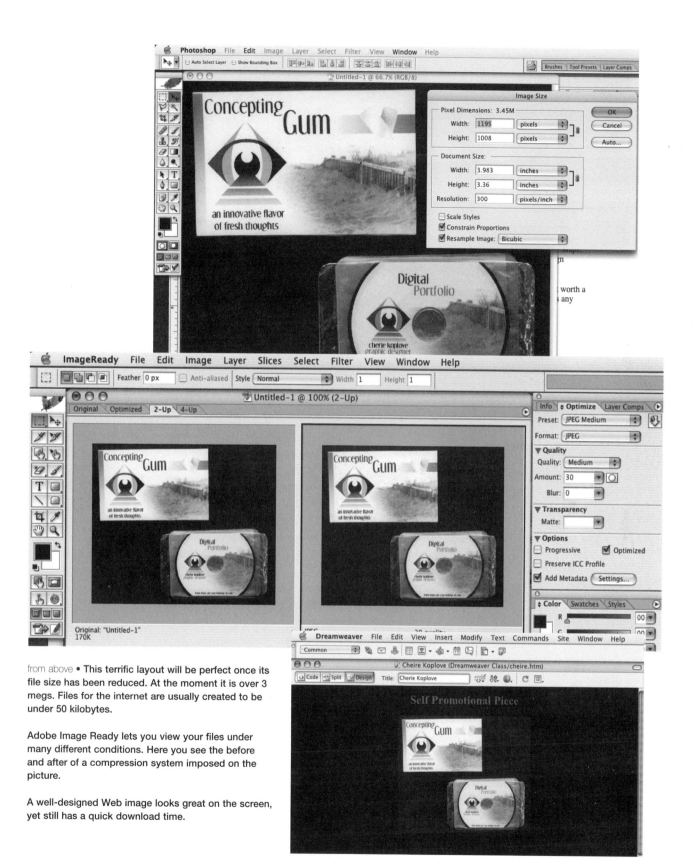

from above • This terrific layout will be perfect once its file size has been reduced. At the moment it is over 3 megs. Files for the internet are usually created to be under 50 kilobytes.

Adobe Image Ready lets you view your files under many different conditions. Here you see the before and after of a compression system imposed on the picture.

A well-designed Web image looks great on the screen, yet still has a quick download time.

The Importance of a Master File

As you begin to develop all of the support material for your project, remember to always keep the original, or master, files. I cannot tell you how many times I completed a freelance job for clients only to have them change their mind at the last moment. CD burners and low-cost zip disks make backing up your files a no-brainer.

A Bit about Bit Depth

Bit depth is the number of bits used to store information about each pixel. The higher the depth, the more colors are stored in an image and the larger the file. Most images are scanned at 24 bits to retain the maximum color definition for the image.

Lowering bit depth is a great way to reduce file size while still maintaining quality.

wait a thousand seconds to see it. I've said it before, and I'll say it again because it's so important: Smaller images equal faster downloads. Look at the file size of this "Concepting Gum" image created in Photoshop. Notice the dimensions as well. At 3.45 megs, this file is huge. The figure at left shows what the image will look like after it has been optimized in Image Ready a Web optimization program that comes with Adobe Photoshop. Notice that Image Ready tells you that the file is now 8K and will take about two seconds to load. Not bad! The figure at right shows what the images will look like on a web page.

Not only does the image look good, but the file size is conveniently small. Here are some tips to help you keep you interface downloads lean and mean.

Resize Your Images and Icons

When you are creating graphics for an interface, do not to use images that are any larger than the actual size of the final design interface. For example, if the final page size of your interface is 800 × 600, any graphic you use should size well under that amount. If you have a photograph that's 4 × 5, at 300 dpi, you will need to resize it to under 800 × 600; and make sure to change the pixels to 72 dpi. Image Ready is a great program for this, as it presents a live preview as you work with the image.

Test the image in the interface. Make sure it looks as clear as possible. The object is to make the file small while retaining clarity. Yes, it's a lot of extra steps, but it must be done.

Optimize Your Images

As you have already learned, the two most commonly used image formats are GIF (Graphics Interchange Format) and JPEG (Joint Photographic Experts Group). GIFs are best for graphics that have only a few colors; JPEG is best for photographs. These formats can be optimized in other ways to decrease download times. For example, if you have a picture with a white border, remove (or crop) the image to remove that space. By doing so, you will reduce the file size.

JPEG files will look better at reduced sizes if you blur the image slightly before the compression is applied. If you have a scanned image, chances are it has

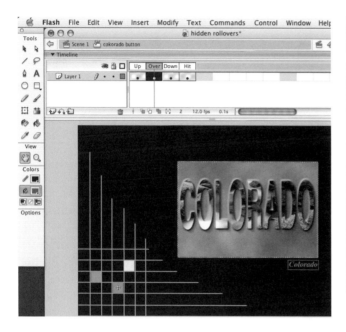

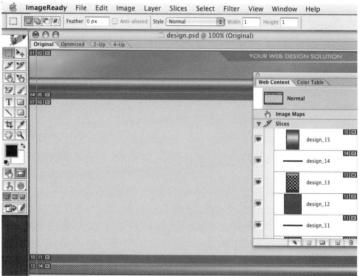

above • **This rollover effect was created in Flash. When the user's mouse rolls over the little square, an image pops on the screen. The square could also be a small icon of the large image.**

right • **This is an example of "image slicing." Notice the lines that slice or cut the image up into smaller images. Each of these sections will be saved under a separate filename and loaded into a table layout in a Web design program.**

a high *bit depth* applied to it. Reducing the bit depth will decrease the file size. (See the sidebar on bit depth.)

Use the Same Icons Again and Again

Using the same graphic or icon repeatedly on different pages within your interface decreases download time. The reason is that there's less new information for the system to load, so naturally it will be faster. And if you are clever about the repeated use of graphics, no one will notice.

Use Thumbnails

I mentioned this briefly earlier, Thumbnails are miniature versions of larger images. When the user clicks on one, a full-sized version of the image appears. The larger image is either reduced in a graphics program and saved under a different file name, or the image is reduced directly in the authoring program. Once the thumbnail is inserted into the digital page, it can be linked to the larger image. Creating a thumbnail saves the user time download time and keeps the overall file size small.

Slice Up Your Images

This little trick also serves to speed download time. And it's easy, too. Take your image into a program such as Adobe Image Ready or Macromedia Fireworks and break it up into small chunks, then save each mini-file. Each image will display as it loads. This gives the user the impression that things are happening a bit faster (and they are!).

Don't Overanimate

Flash and Director files, JavaScripts, GIF animations, and scrolling marquees can be a lot of fun, but they are doomed to failure if no one ever sees them. These files, as you know by now, can become gigantic, and the more you insert on your page, the longer it will take to load. And aside from the lengthy download time, the page will look unprofessional, which is the last thing you want. I recently visited a Web page that had five animations. I didn't know where to look! You want your interface to be the star not the animations.

Scaling the Learning Curve

At this point, you may be asking yourself, "How long is it going to take me to learn how to do all this?" Of course, that depends on your patience and your tenacity. Some authoring programs have a pretty steep learning curve, and you will have to spend as much time as it takes to become proficient using them. You have a lot of pictures to coordinate in the computer. You have to

● ● ● Stay on the Right Path

Take a moment right now to look at your computer desktop. Are files scattered all over the screen? If so, you need to clean things up. When it comes to interface design it is imperative that all your files reside in the same folder. HTML creates "paths" (or trails) for your files to follow. If you create a link for a file that works on your home computer, but doesn't work once it is uploaded, you have probably changed the path without realizing it. Here is an example:

MyHardDrive>Myfolder>MyNewWebsite>MainStuff>picture.jpg. This file is buried deep inside the computer in the area called MainStuff. Nothing wrong with that, but as you start to upload the file to the Web, you realize that you need to remain rename one of the folders to:

MyHardDrive>Myfolder>MyNewWebsite>Images>picture.jpg

This is now an entirely different path as far as your web page is concerned. The web link that was established is looking for the folder "MainStuff," but that folder no longer exists because you renamed it.

If you have created any links on your page that look for the original path to load that picture, nothing will load. Why? Because the HTML code will still be looking for the old path.

What's the solution? Create subfolders within the main site folder for your project and make sure its name is exactly the same as it will be once it is uploaded. If you move images and pages around after the folders have been created, your links will break.

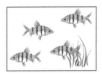

A small GIF animation such as this one is effective. Five such animations on one screen will junk up the screen. Use animations only if they enhance your overall concept.

design an interface. Yes, it is a lot of work, but the reward will be your beautiful electronic portfolio.

What kind of time commitment are we talking about? I have produced complete projects in about as little as 20 hours, but I have also spent as much as 45 hours. But I consider this work a labor of love. If you are enjoying the challenge, you will hardly notice the time you spend.

If you find yourself overwhelmed by all of this information and feel you need training from an expert, don't hesitate to sign up with a tutor or for a class at your local community college. You will find a variety of classes offered, including on many of the software programs mentioned in this book. Or cruise your area bookstores. There are dozens of books available on every conceivable software program on the market. The Internet is another great resource. There you'll find user forums and tutorials for virtually every need. In short, do what you have to in order to get you up to speed in as short a time as possible. ■

24-bit: Describes a scanned file or preview image made up of RGB color information. An 8-bit per pixel card can generate 256 colors; 24 bits per pixel yields 16.8 million colors.

Bit: The smallest unit of computer information. The value of a bit is 1 or 0.

Bitmap: A digital graphic image that consists of a map of dots or squares. Each square has a color value represented by either 1 bit (simple black and white) or up to 32 bits (high-definition color). Bitmaps include GIF, JPEG, and other file formats, which can be read by such programs as Adobe Photoshop and Corel Painter.

Clip art: Royalty-free images that can be brought into art programs and presentation applications. Clip art can be edited or used as-is. Additional images, including some in bitmap format, are available from commercial suppliers and online.

Color space: The range, or gamut, of colors, available to a viewer. The color space for a graphic designer is CMYK (cyan, magenta, yellow, and black).

CMYK: The four process colors used in printing: cyan, magenta, yellow, and black. These four colors when printed appear to the naked eye as full color.

Graphics Interchange Format (GIF): One of two popular file formats for graphics on the Internet (the other is JPEG). GIF files have a limit of 256 colors, and provide sharper black-and-white images than JPEGs. GIF is popular because it reduces image file size without losing any information the process. There are three different GIF types: (1) Animated GIF (89A), which allows storage and playback of a sequence of still images to create the illusion of animation. (2) Transparent GIF, which enables a designer to designate a color (usually the background) of an image to be transparent. Only GIFs can accomplish this. (3) Interlaced GIF enables progressive rendering of images, meaning that the focus slowly sharpens to reveal the entire picture.

Interlacing indicates to the viewer that the image is loading.

Index color: A color system that minimizes the number of colors and file size of a graphic image to 8 bits or less. Used primarily for Web design.

Image file formats: The common graphics file formats. GIF and JPEG are the formats used in Web design. TIFF and EPS are the common file formats used in publishing.

Image map: A graphic that contains several "hot spots," or invisible buttons that link to other pages. For example, an image map of the world might contain links to Europe, Asia, South America, and the United States.

Image optimization: The process of making your images suitable for the Web. The main factors that influence the display of graphics for the Web are the size, physical dimensions, and bit depth of the image.

JavaScript: A programming language for use in Web pages that allows for user interaction. An example is filling out a form to get more information about a product or service.

Joint Photographic Experts Group (JPEG): The standard for storing images in compressed form. JPEGs can contain up to 24 bits of color information (16.7 million colors) making them more desirable (but larger) than GIF files. However, most user monitors are capable of displaying only 8-bit color.

Logos and trademarks: A symbol, usually composed of letter and/or shapes that identifies companies, organizations, products, and so on. Logos are crucial for name recognition and branding.

Master file : An original file. A master file should never be altered in any way.

Optimize: To reduce the size of a file to allow for faster loading. Graphics files are typically optimized through a number of different ways such as reducing physical dimension and dpi and fine-tuning color information.

Path: The direction to a file on a computer. For example: MyHardDrive >MyNewWebsite is the path for MyHardDrive>MyNewWebsite>picture.jpg.

RGB: The primary colors—Red, green, and blue—which are used on most computer monitors to display images.

Screen resolution: The width and height of pixels on a computer's screen. Typical values are 1024 x 768, 800 x 600 or 640 x 480.

Thumbnail: A small version of an image. When the user clicks on one included on a Web page, a full-sized version of the image appears. This saves file space and download time.

glossary

⬤ ⬤ ⬤ ⬤ ⬤ ⬤ ⬤ 7

The Design Phase

What do potential employers regard as the most important element of your digital portfolio? If you answered creativity, you're right! But they're looking for much more. They will examine your portfolio as a reflection of your logic, vision, versatility, artistry, and computer skills.

As I've said many times throughout this book, your electronic portfolio gives the viewer a better understanding of your particular design strengths and knowledge. And the way you choose to arrange the portfolio gives the viewer an understanding of your intellectual and organizational skills, as well as your ambition.

Don't be afraid to let your sense of humor shine through, as Kwesi William does here.

Employers want designers who do what is asked for, and who then is willing to go the extra mile. Therefore, an innovative electronic portfolio will reveal that you will make the effort to continually raise the bar, to produce higher-quality, more innovative work. An accomplished digital portfolio says essentially, " If you ask for two comp designs, I'll come back to you with three."

To help you produce that kind of digital portfolio, this chapter explains the process of planning, with a focus on the theory and use of color.

Organize, Organize, Organize

I've stressed the importance of being organized in earlier discussions. When it comes to developing an effective electronic portfolio, organized planning is the most important effort you'll make, and it begins well before the design process. Simply put, the more time you spend planning your electronic portfolio, the easier it will be to assemble the components.

There are a number of organizational strategies you can employ to make the multimedia part of your life easier. Begin by gathering all of your project materials together. Sift through all that work and select the best for inclusion in your portfolio. Let's call this your artist inventory checklist. (Chapter 4 discussed this process in much more detail.) Always keep in mind that this work must represent the best of what you can do, so be very selective, with a focus on articulating your vision. Remember, your work should not only highlight your skills and abilities, but also reflect your artistic philosophy. If you have other projects you were involved in, such as copywriting or marketing, you may include them as well, even if no actual artwork was involved. There are clever techniques available to showcase those accomplishments in your digital port.

You should have already completed your resume, ready for conversion to a digital format. Don't forget to include other materials such as logos or artwork created on a more personal level in your inventory checklist. The color insert displays examples of these components. Finally, select 15 to 20 pieces for your digital portfolio.

Know Where You're Going

After you have determined which projects to include, you need to determine the best way to arrange them for the multimedia presentation. You are going to have a lot of information to include in your final portfolio—your projects, resume, list of awards and accomplishments, along with your contact info. All of these materials have to be organized into a coherent system. Here is a list of some sections that you might consider including in your port (the color insert shows several screens with a number of these elements displayed):

Summary of qualifications
Objectives
Employment history
Artist statement or design philosophy
"Gallery": A body of work
Sketches, drafts, and works in progress
Education
Honors and awards
Community service
Memberships, certifications, and achievements
Letters of reference
Letters of recognition
Contact links

And it all has to be in some logical sequence. The best way to approach this challenge is to map out the major sections of the portfolio, then create subcategories. Let's call it the "divide and conquer" strategy.

There are many ways to approach the organization of the material for your digital port, but I think the best way to begin is to list *all* of the possible categories. Don't worry at this stage how long the list is or if certain categories overlap. Your goal is to arrive at a complete inventory of everything you might want to include in the digital interface. Then start sorting by subject matter. You might want to sketch out this information; or you might prefer to cut and paste the categories into groups.

Don't stop after one attempt. Try out a couple of different systems. When you think you have one that will work, refine it a little further. Some of the items you list may fit into more than one category, so take some time to determine the best way to combine the material. For a graphic designer, the list above might be arranged to look like this:

Main or Home Page
Resume
    Summery of Qualifications
    Objectives
    Education
    Employment History
Honors and Awards
    Community service
    Memberships, Certifications, and Achievements
    Letters of Reference
    Letters of Recognition
The Gallery
    Sketches, Drafts, and Works in Progress
    Graphic Design
        Editorial Spreads
        Poster Designs
        Annual Report
        Package Designs
        Logos
        Photography
    Personal Art
        Paintings
        Drawings
Contact Links

The next step is to develop a visual schematic to assist in the arrangement of the major sections—a flowchart. A flowchart maps the way that list you just

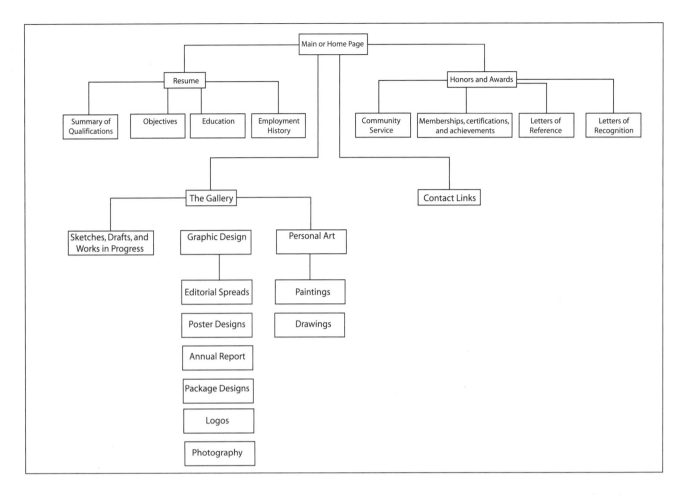

The flowchart of a digital portfolio might look like this.

created will be represented on your portfolio. It helps you to visualize a clear arrangement of material that will make it easy for anyone to navigate your portfolio, while still offering something unusual and unique. In short, think of a flowchart as a way to visually index the contents of your portfolio.

Take a look at a similar flowchart designed for the Web. The interface on the next page was developed by Giselle Lopez. Notice that the interface offers a clear way to navigate to the home page. You can get another view of this design in the color insert.

Next time you're online, visit a couple of Web sites with the express purpose of taking not on how they are arranged. Is the arrangement of the information clear? Do you find it easy to navigate the site? If so, consider sketching a flowchart to describe that site. It will help you to visualize how different sites are compiled. And keep in mind, there is no one right way to develop a flowchart. It's simply a tool to help you once the actual work begins.

Gather Your Art

It's time to get your project off the ground. By now you have your art projects, rough book, sketches, photos, boards, sculpture, and anything else you need to begin the process of multimedia design. You have taken the time to inventory your projects and you have selected the pieces you want to include in the port. You must now convert the art must to a digital format.

If the art is two-dimensional, a scanner is ideal. Most scanners can control the size and dpi of the image as it is converted. This will save you some time. The more functions the scanner can perform, the easier it will be for you to finish the prep work on the file once it is in the raster editing program. Whenever I scan artwork, I take some time to figure out the size of the final file. Then with the art on the scanner, I input appropriate dpi numbers and reduce the file enough so that it fits comfortably within the layout. This shortens the time I have to spend in Photoshop (or any other program) and makes me more productive.

Art that is too big to fit on a scanner presents a special challenge. Package designs, sculptures, large-scale renderings, and clothing designs all require a different approach. Larger pieces will need to be photographed with either a digital or traditional camera. Digital photos can be downloaded directly into the computer. Traditional photos will have to be developed, then scanned. Large flat pieces can be scanned in segments, then merged back together in Photoshop. There's quite a bit of prep work to get all your art ready for the authoring program, but it's important to take your time and get everything just the way you want it.

Remember to keep backups of all digital art. Once the images have been captured and saved, create extra copies! Burn CDs or DVDs or save to an extra hard drive—use whatever method you prefer to archive your work, but do it. Here's why it's so important. Suppose you want to save your work for the Web. The art will be saved as a JPEG. As you will recall, the JPEG format compresses art by eliminating extraneous pixel information. If you keep an original copy of the art before you create the JPEG, you will always be able to alter the original. You will have to do this more often than you might imagine. As your portfolio needs updating, for example, you may find it necessary to change dates, colors, or the size of the art.

Designing a Visual Theme: Making Your Portfolio Unique

All the art is properly scanned, sized, and saved. You have created a flowchart for your interface and selected a multimedia authoring program. The next step is to design a visual theme for the interface, to tie the project together. Through the use of color, buttons, sound, images, and type, you will give a viewer a complete art and multimedia experience. This presentation is every bit as important as the art itself. In the same way that a beautiful painting shown in an inappropriate frame will make distract from its beauty, a poorly designed presentation will detract from the designs you worked so hard to produce.

Clean, crisp, and uncomplicated, this portfolio by Giselle Lopez accomplishes everything necessary for a good design.

There are a countless ways to present information. Which way you go depends on how you want to present yourself. Are you playful or serious? Do you fancy yourself traditional or avant-garde? Do you like lots of color or neutral shades of gray? Your personal style sense is a good place to begin the design process, but there are other factors. The art you will be showcasing also influences the interface look. Pieces that feature a lot of bright colors need to be shown against neutral background colors. Keep in mind that it is always about the art, not the interface.

Take care when you select style and theme choices. Never forget that your portfolio will be viewed not only

This fabulous package display piece was designed by Linda Weeks, a graphic designer in the South Florida area. The best way to present this large display in a portfolio would be with a series of photographs that show all the angles.

directly but indirectly as well. This means that the viewing experience will expose the underlying meaning of who you are and how you perceive yourself as an artist. What you may see as a really innovative idea for an interface others may be patently offended. Consider your audience at all times, and steer clear of themes that might be unfavorably viewed. An interface can be fun and innovative, yet carry a serious message. Remember the retro fifties look you saw earlier in the book? Music, colors, and type of the decade created an amusing presentation. You, too, can create an interface based on novel motifs or unconventional ideas. Think about your hobbies, cultural heritage, places you might like to visit. Do whatever you have to do to get your create juices flowing.

You will need an opening theme, in the same way so many television shows use a theme song. It's their signature. Even a simple animation will dazzle the spectator. We have been talking a lot about the overall look and feel of the main (or home) page of the digital port, but you can also design an opening that will set the tone for everything to come. While it is not mandatory to create an introduction for your port, a clever one hints at your skills as a multilevel designer. A well-designed opening gives your viewer an engaging and interactive experience. It creates

the environment. The opening gives the viewer the "wow experience." So take some time to sketch, storyboard, conceptualize, and sketch some more. Figure out the best approach for your introduction and start creating it.

Once the opening is complete, you will need to design your home page, the pivotal area, or hub, of your site. From the home page, the user navigates through the rest of the site, discovering the many sections you have produced. Therefore, it is the most important of all your pages. Remember first impressions are the most important. The information you insert on this first page should demonstrate a clear understanding of the navigational needs of the user. Home pages generally contain the following design elements (see the color insert for an example of these elements):

Your name
Clear links to other pages
Effective use of color that creates a unified design
Images that serve only to support the design
Common interface design elements

What is the most important part of your home page? Your name! Place your name in a prominent location.

Diana Sanmiguel uses icons as her method of navigation in this modern, yet playful digital portfolio.

Remember, the portfolio is about you; it may be in logo form or created with type, but it must be there. Place any other elements you wish on the home page, but make sure your name is right up there where the viewer can see who created the awesome portfolio.

Navigation: How to Get There from Here

Navigation is all about the user. Buttons, navigational bars, and text provide the visitor with the tools to go every-where on your site from wherever they are at the moment. A well-designed set of graphic links within your portfolio pages will direct users beyond your home page.

Make sure navigation buttons and bars are easy to understand. Do not assume that the user will "hunt" around looking for a hidden link. And make all navigation buttons consistent throughout the site. Never design anything without considering how it will function for the user. You can create several different types of links such as buttons, bars, images, text rollovers, and image maps. Each of these represents a design metaphor. Use any of the methods you wish as long as the method supports the overall design. Buttons should always be small and quick to download. We'll discuss more about them in Chapter 9.

This series of screens created by Frances Ortiz have an interesting retro feel that invokes the 1950s.

In Camillo Montilla's interface, the building blocks are always located in the location throughout. It is important to create a theme that works at all times to support your message.

● ● ● ● All Buttoned Up

You can buy buttons that are ready to use. As I mentioned previously, there are lots of Web design clip art packages on the market. But as I also mentioned, the problem with such packages is that everybody else has access to them. That said, let me tell you about a great Web site, Button Generator (www.buttongenerator.com). At this nifty little site you can customize buttons and menus based on their designs. You can also choose from a nice selection of type and color choices. Here are just a few of the many buttons ready for you to modify.

You can also choose to make a multiple-state button, which offer an up, down, and over effect. This makes it much easier for the user to see when the button is active and will link to somewhere else.

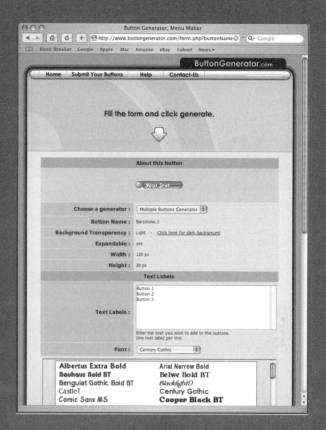

At Button Generator.com, you can create great buttons in the wink of an eye! Everything you need to make a button is just one click away. A variety of fonts and buttons styles are available for you to choose from, and the final results are worth the effort.

A basic button is generally a circle, square, or rectangle that represents a link to another area of the portfolio. Buttons may include informational text and may be three-dimensional or stylized graphic symbols called icons. For example, you might use an icon of a small house to indicate the link back to your home page (see the color insert).

A navigation bar is used to display a collection of buttons. As such, they usually reside at the top or bottom of the page. So-called text buttons are not buttons at all, but rather a text that acts as a link. Text buttons are frequently designed to change colors (known as rollovers) when selected, to indicate their function as a link. Small images can also serve as links. They can be created to change colors or morph into another image when selected. An image map is a picture with several links or "hot spots" embedded into the file. When the user's mouse passes over the hot spot, it changes in some way to suggest a link to another area.

Here are three sites that give you the opportunity to generate custom designs.

Free Alpha Button: free.alphabutton.com/index.php
My Imager: www.myimager.com
Flash Buttons: www.FlashButtons.com

There are also a number of Web sites that offer relatively inexpensive programs to generate your buttons.

Up   Over   Down

above • **These shapes show the change that will occur when the user rolls over them with his or her mouse.**

right • **These are examples of buttons designed in Macromedia Dreamweaver, which gives you the capability to create Flash-animated buttons in a variety of styles and colors. Each button can be customized with the type of your choice.**

Here are a few to check out:

Just Buttons: www.lincolnbeach.com/justbuttons.asp
Crystal Buttons: www.crystalbutton.com
1 Cool Button Tool: www.buttontool.com
Xara Webstyle 4: www.xara.com/products/webstyle
FreeButton.com: www.freebuttons.com/index.php

Of course, you can always make your own buttons! In the color insert are a few I designed with Photoshop. It's not that difficult. Armed with a little knowledge you can design some great buttons just by combining different colors and shapes.

Using Color Effectively

Although every element on the home page contributes to the cohesiveness of the design, color plays the most important part. Color is a major form of communication. Color can symbolize and trigger emotions and associations, both positive and negative. Color adds impact. Color points to what is important for the viewer to see and understand. Color (both in type and as a background) can act as a unifying theme. In short, the ineffective use of color can jeopardize your message.

As an example, think about Valentine's Day. What colors come to mind? Now think about fall in Vermont. Can you see the color of the leaves? Color is important in all aspects of life. So-called green rooms are used in Hollywood to relax an actor. Red is used in restaurants to stimulate appetite. Department stores designers have found that reds, blacks, and blues have a positive impact on impulse shoppers (at least for the store!). However, the interpretation of a color depends on many different factors such as age, gender, cultural background, training, and personal experience. Men react to color differently than women; they tend to prefer blue and orange. Women like red and yellow. In general, the colors red, orange, and yellow are considered to be "exciting" colors; purple, blue, and green are thought to be "calming" colors.

The Psychology of Color

All this is by way of saying that selecting color for your portfolio should be based on how you want to market yourself. Don't use a color simply because you like it. Recognize that the colors you choose will have an effect on each person viewing your portfolio, regardless of his or her background or culture. To help you in this regard, let's examine briefly what's called the *psychology of color.*

Red and Pink

Red suggests excitement, strength, passion, or courage. But it also has implications of violence and aggression, as it may trigger images of blood or war. Studies have demonstrated that red can even raise blood pressure. In China, red symbolizes luck.

In most Western cultures, pink symbolizes of innocence, romance, and femininity. Pink often conjures images of softness and sweetness, like of a baby. It is also thought to be calming and tranquilizing.

These two screens are from the digital portfolio of Jennifer Worley. She likes to use strong contrast as a way to showcase her art.

Orange and Yellow

Orange is a warm and vibrant color, hence invokes warm and cozy feelings or images of an autumn afternoon. But orange has also been shown to stimulate the appetite; and it symbolizes health.

Yellow, as you might imagine, signifies sunshine, warmth, and happiness. Yellow is considered a positive, bright, cheerful, and optimistic color. But it has its "evil twin," as it can also symbolize cowardice or fearfulness.

Green

Green is seen as a refreshing color that symbolizes growth and abundance. It also represents health, freshness, new growth, and tranquility. Green is powerful, too, in that it communicates wealth, and so is frequently used by banking institutions. Green's "bad" image comes from its link to the negative emotions of jealousy or envy, as well to lizards, toads, and other creepy-crawly things.

Blue and Purple

Not surprisingly, the color of the sky and the sea is considered a calming color. It communicates trust, wisdom, generosity, reliability, dignity, and intelligence. Blue is known to be an appetite suppressant, and can also be used to express depression and melancholy. Blue is one of the few colors that is universally accepted by all cultures.

Purple is a soothing yet powerful color, as it is associated with royalty, wealth, and creativity. It is also considered spiritual and mysterious. Lighter shades of purple are thought to represent romance and nostalgia.

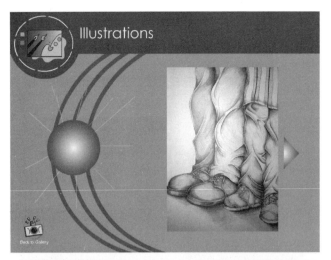

above • **This beautiful interface designed by Sandra Cruz shows her love of illustration both in the main image and with her drawing at the top left.**

below • **Barbara Gaterman clearly illustrates the choices available to the user with a clean, straightforward approach.**

in weddings and christenings. It also connotes spirituality and cleanliness, and is used to express youth and vigor. And in contrast to most Western cultures, it symbolizes mourning in Eastern cultures.

Gray is a conservative color that implies intellect and symbolizes a conservative point of view. It is considered a dignified color that speaks of maturity and dependability. It is also considered to be a futuristic color and so is used frequently for technology-related design concepts. It is currently a very "in" color in Web design. But gray can be depressing and may symbolize sadness, old age, and decay.

Brown

Brown is a natural color that depicts earthiness or the outdoors. It brings to mind the rich image of coffee or chocolate. Brown also may be used to represent the future, as it makes people think of comfort, credibility, and stability. It is a restful color. And in India, brown is the color of mourning (see the example Web site provided in the color insert).

Color and Your Portfolio Interface

After evaluating your approach to the colors you will use for your interface, the next step is determine how and which colors can be used together. Color choice will, of course, always come down to personal preference, but there are some guidelines you should follow to ensure the best response from the widest possible audience.

Limit the Number of Colors: The Three-Color System

Too many colors will give the page a too-busy feel, and the viewer will find it difficult to locate the important information. Too many colors also can make the eyes tired. Conversely, using too few colors can make a page boring or uninteresting. Color should be used to draw in the viewer and encourage them to see more, to see it all.

One good way to limit the use of colors, yet still produce and interesting interface is to use the three-color system. That means you design your interface with a primary color (see the color insert), a secondary color, and a highlight color. The primary color is the main color of your design. It will occupy most of the design space.

Unfortunately, purple can also suggest cruelty and arrogance (see the color insert for a good example of the use of the color purple by Sandra Cruz).

Black, White, and Gray

Black is a very powerful color in that it connotes so many things: power, elegance, and sexuality; death, evil, mystery; fear, unhappiness, and grief. Black is frequently used in packaging design to convey product sophistication; it is also used to invigorate other colors, It is stimulating in small quantities.

White is considered to be a cheerful color that reflects innocence and purity, hence its widespread use

SORAYA SALTIEL
DESIGNING BRIGHT GRAPHIC DESIGNER

244 NE 14th Ave. Suite 22
Ft. Lauderdale, FL 33304
954 763-7996
954 303-0930

OBJECTIVE:
To use my creative knowledge and technical skills in a position as a graphic designer in the advertising field.

PROFILE AND SKILLS:
· Graphic Designer specializing in advertising, print design, layout, corporate ID/collateral design, package design, and campaign advertising design.
· Experience with event planning and design, illustration, fine arts and web design. Great communication and research skills, as well as sales experience and customer service.

LANGUAGES:
English and Spanish.

SOFTWARE:
Adobe Illustrator, Adobe Photoshop, Adobe InDesign, Adobe Acrobat.
QuarkXpress, Macromedia FlashMX
Mac OS X and up Windows 2000 and up.
Microsoft Word, Excel, Power Point and Entourage.

EMPLOYMENT EXPERIENCE:
Cenuco Inc. (Boca Raton, FL) June - December 2003
   Sales Associate for Barrington University
   Graphic Design assistant in online advertising
   Marketing and Advertising Research Assistant

Marquina Publicidad (San Juan, PR), May 2001 - September 2002
   Graphic Designer, Advertising Sales Associate
   Team Manager/Art Director for two full campaigns.
   New Business Department graphic designer

Distribuidora Flamingo Inc (San Juan, PR). May 1996 to August 2000
   Sales Associate, Merchandise input manager.
   Assistant Secretary, Show Room display designer
   and coordinator.

Freelance.
   · AIHE of Puerto Rico
      Annual Gala Invitations for 2001-2003.
   · Distribuidora Flamingo INC.
      Corporate ID, web site design
   · The Opera Theater of Puerto Rico.
      Spreads for program guide for
      "La Flauta Magica", September 2003.

EDUCATION:
The Art Institute of Ft. Lauderdale. (Ft. Lauderdale, FL)
   Bachelor of Science in Graphic Design
   March 2004.

Campbell University. (Buies Creek, NC)
   Graphic Design
   May 2001.

PORTFOLIO AND REFERENCES AVAILABLE UPON REQUEST

left • This beautiful resume is part of a complete self-promotional package that includes business cards and envelopes.

below • Julie Ruiz turned to the 1950s for inspiration. Her self-promotional piece is not only sharp, but fun as well!

above • Ryan Skinner's self promotion book uses a consistant design theme throughout every provided piece of art.

right • Here is a wonderful example of a digital portfolio. Notice that the artist's name is on both the container and the CD-ROM. It is important to incorporate a total design package.

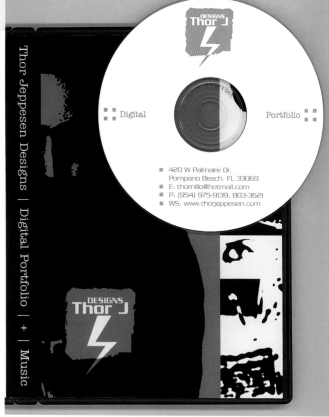

Digital   Portfolio

420 W Palmaire Dr.
Pompano Beach, FL 33069
E: thornillo@hotmail.com
P: (954) 975-9139, 803-3621
WS: www.thorjeppesen.com

Thor Jeppesen Designs | Digital Portfolio | + | Music

below • This resume is an effective example of communication technique, as it offers numerous ways to contact the designer. In addition, the colors selected look great in print, and will also fax well.

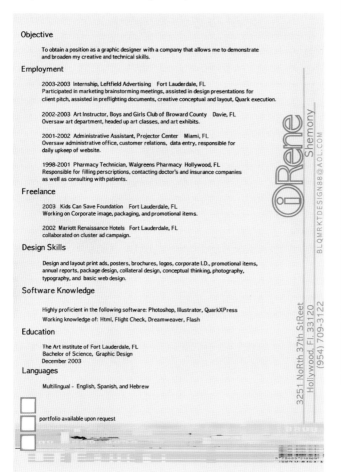

Objective

To obtain a position as a graphic designer with a company that allows me to demonstrate and broaden my creative and technical skills.

Employment

2003-2003 Internship, Leftfield Advertising   Fort Lauderdale, FL
Participated in marketing brainstorming meetings, assisted in design presentations for client pitch, assisted in preflighting documents, creative conceptual and layout, Quark execution.

2002-2003 Art Instructor, Boys and Girls Club of Broward County Davie, FL
Oversaw art department, headed up art classes, and art exhibits.

2001-2002 Administrative Assistant, Projector Center Miami, FL
Oversaw administrative office, customer relations, data entry, responsible for daily upkeep of website.

1998-2001 Pharmacy Technician, Walgreens Pharmacy Hollywood, FL
Responsible for filling perscriptions, contacting doctor's and insurance companies as well as consulting with patients.

Freelance

2003 Kids Can Save Foundation Fort Lauderdale, FL
Working on Corporate image, packaging, and promotional items.

2002 Mariott Renaissance Hotels Fort Lauderdale, FL
collaborated on cluster ad campaign.

Design Skills

Design and layout print ads, posters, brochures, logos, corporate I.D., promotional items, annual reports, package design, collateral design, conceptual thinking, photography, typography, and basic web design.

Software Knowledge

Highly proficient in the following software: Photoshop, Illustrator, QuarkXPress
Working knowledge of: Html, Flight Check, Dreamweaver, Flash

Education

The Art institute of Fort Lauderdale, FL
Bachelor of Science, Graphic Design
December 2003

Languages

Multilingual - English, Spanish, and Hebrew

portfolio available upon request

Rene Shemony
BLQMRKTDESIGN88@AOL.COM
3251 NoRth 37th StReet
Hollywood, Fl. 33120
(954) 709-3122

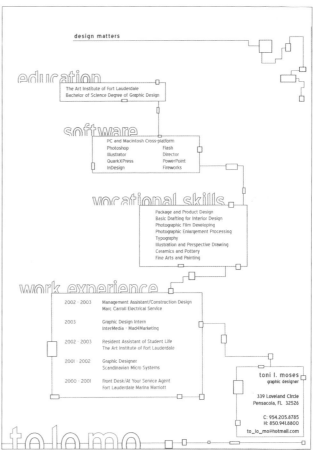

above • This resume would work well for either a graphic designer or an interior designer. The technical look is entertaining and conveys the style of the artist.

design matters

education
The Art Institute of Fort Lauderdale
Bachelor of Science Degree of Graphic Design

software
PC and Macintosh Cross-platform
Photoshop   Flash
Illustrator   Director
QuarkXPress   PowerPoint
InDesign   Fireworks

vocational skills
Package and Product Design
Basic Drafting for Interior Design
Photographic Film Developing
Photographic Enlargement Processing
Typography
Illustration and Perspective Drawing
Ceramics and Pottery
Fine Arts and Painting

work experience

2002 - 2003	Management Assistant/Construction Design Marc Carroll Electrical Service
2003	Graphic Design Intern InterMedia · Mad4Marketing
2002 - 2003	Resident Assistant of Student Life The Art Institute of Fort Lauderdale
2001 - 2002	Graphic Designer Scandinavian Micro Systems
2000 - 2001	Front Desk/At Your Service Agent Fort Lauderdale Marina Marriott

toni l. moses
graphic designer

339 Loveland Circle
Pensacola, FL 32526

C: 954.205.8785
H: 850.941.8800
to_lo_mo@hotmail.com

to lo mo

DOUG VOLKERT
graphic designer

10190 Boca Entrada Blvd #223 Boca Raton, FL 33428
phone: 954.242.1647 email: dvolk55@aol.com

left • This very attractive design features a series of circles and lines that tie in with the logo. It is very clean and elegant.

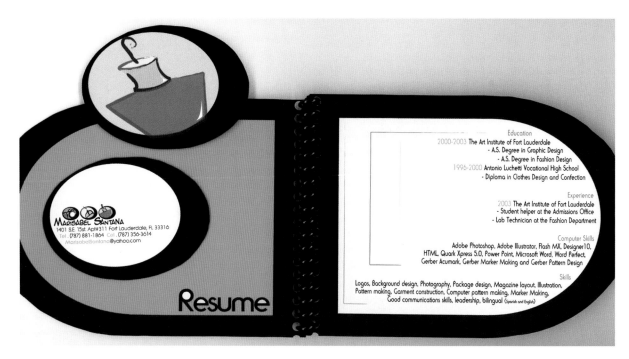

above • Here is another fabulous self-promotional piece, one that has a consistent theme of color and style. Note the use of black as a border for both the business card and the resume.

left • Circles are the running theme of this design, as you can see. Individual pieces of art have been arranged to fit on the circle that slips into the circular holder. The color is spring green, a very cool and calming color system.

right and below • As you can see, each of these visual identity packages has particular elements that carry over from cover letter to resume to business card.

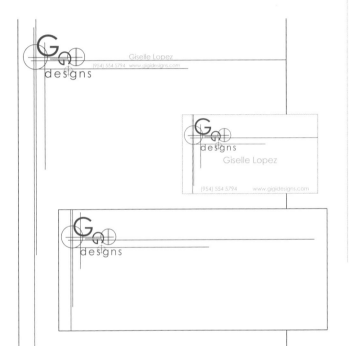

Experience
Internship at *The Sports Authority*, Visual Department
Concept development and copy editing
March - June 2003

Ad design for The *Renaissance*, The *Marina Marriott*
and The *Harbor Beach* Hotels,
Fort Lauderdale, Florida
June 2002

Logo design for Dream Musicians
Fort Lauderdale, Florida
December 2002

Design Skills
Logo Design, Ad Design, Corporate Identity, Package Design,
Collateral Design, Photography, Posters, Layout, Digital Imaging,
Editorials, Web Design

Software Skills
Macintosh and PC Platforms
Illustrator, Photoshop, QuarkXPress,
InDesign, HTML, Flash

Language Skills
Bilingual: Spanish / English

Accomplishments
Received honorable mention in the
2002 *Adobe InDesign* competition

Deans list Summer 2000 and Spring 2002
Honors list Fall 2001 and Winter 2002

Education
The Art Institute of Fort Lauderdale, Florida
Bachelor of Science in Graphic Design
September 2003

Universidad de Los Andes
One year of Industrial Design

Graphic Designer

Diana Sanmiguel

401 Golden Isles Dr. Suite 712,
Hallandale, FL 33009
• 954 - 2618335 ▪

Diana Sanmiguel
Graphic Designer a

401 Golden Isles Dr. Suite 712, Hallandale, FL 33334 • 954 - 261 8335 • dia_s45@hotmail.com ▪

right • PowerPoint has a user-friendly interface. It's easy to learn and comes with lots of premade templates, such as the one you see here. This example was made with a background and images placement slide that comes standard with the program.

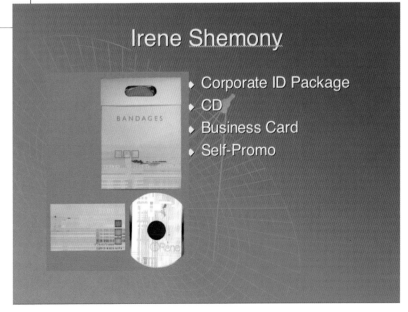

right • This Director project is for a children's "game show." The program makes it easy to create an interface that is both inviting and engaging.

middle • Director has the capability to let you design nonlinear interfaces. This means you can create a design that allows for maximum flexibility. During the quiz, the viewer can navigate forward to more questions or return to the home page to begin another game.

below • When it comes to animation for the Web, Flash can't be beat. The vector-based art is simple to create and the file sizes are conveniently small.

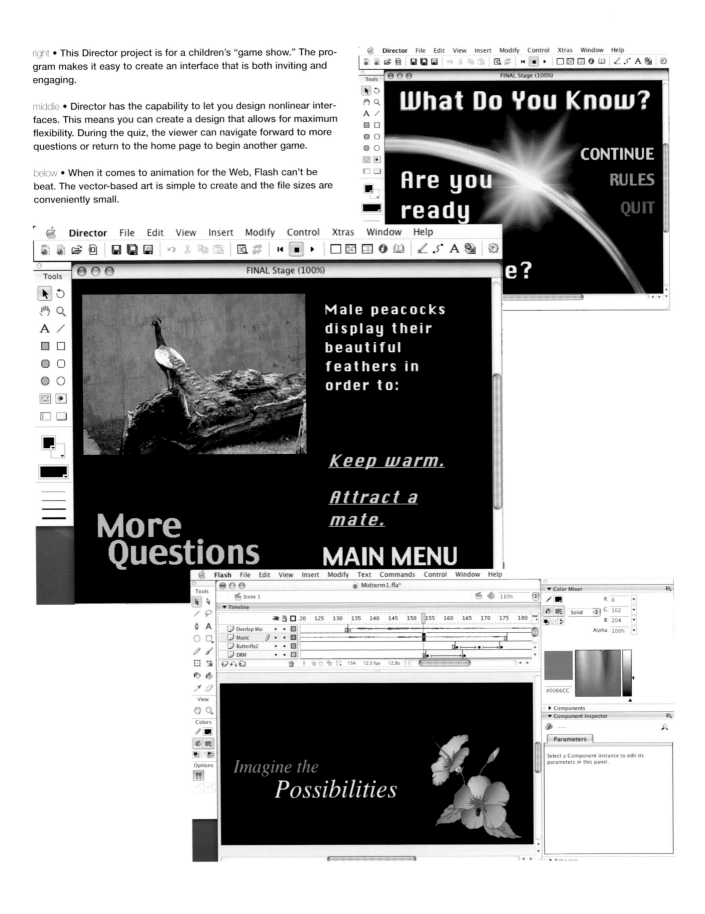

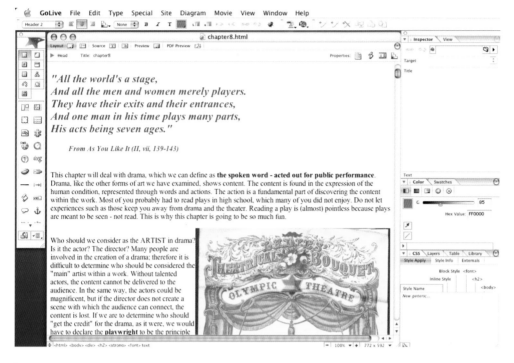

left • Adobe GoLive makes it effortless to create complicated Web designs that conform to current online standards.

below • Macromedia Dreamweaver allows you to view your work in both design view and code view. Notice the HTML code that is generated for this interface.

above • As you can see by these two images, the raster-based file on the right always shows the pixels when enlarged. Raster-based files are fixed-size images. This means that they will always looks jagged up close. Vector-based images, such the one on the left, will always look clean, even up close, because the shapes are drawn based on mathematical algorithms.

below • You can clearly see the navigation system in place for this digital portfolio. You have the option of viewing art, visiting other areas, or returning to the home page.

right • Here is a great display. A metal mesh letter stand doubles as a display rack for resumes. Business cards and mini CDs prop up nicely against the holder.

below • A well-designed layout, such as this one created by Kwesi Williams shows a logical navigational system.

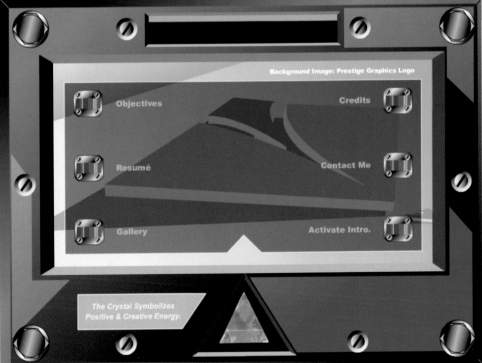

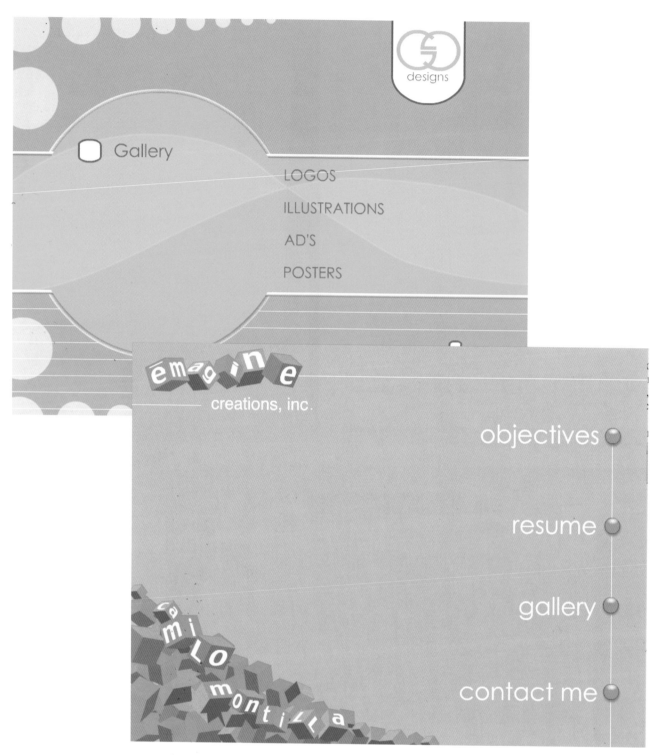

Gallery

LOGOS

ILLUSTRATIONS

AD'S

POSTERS

émagine

creations, inc.

objectives

resume

gallery

contact me

above • The consistent look and feel of this layout makes it easy to know where you are in the interface at all times.

below • This clever interface featuring building blocks was designed by Camillo Montilla. Note how he spells out his name in blocks. It's not traditional, but much more fun.

left • Photoshop is a great resource for button design. These were created with the Styles Palette and the Webdings alphabet. The Styles Palette offers you a vast variety of premade color systems designed specifically with Web-safe colors.

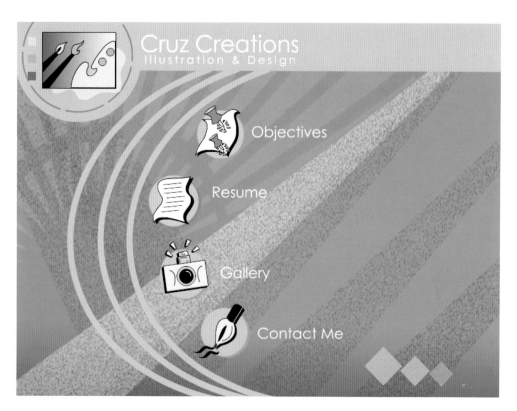

above • Sandra Cruz makes good use of a consistent color system. Notice that all of the colors harmonize together to form a cohesive design.

left • Barbara Gaterman created this whimsical interface, with the three primary colors set against a black background. The paintbrush animates by dancing around the screen in the opening sequence.

Primary Colors

Yellow

Blue

Red

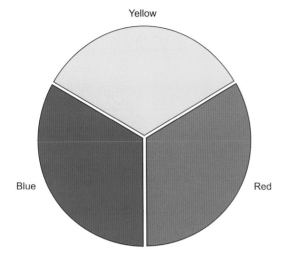

Complimentary Colors

Red

Violet

Orange

Blue

Yellow

Green

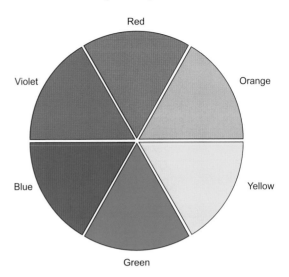

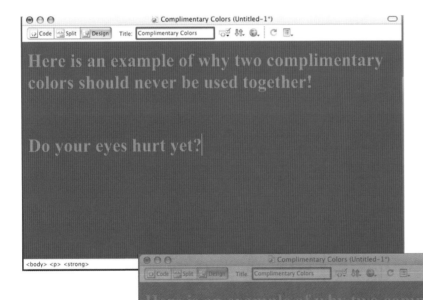

above left • Red, blue, and yellow are primary colors because they cannot be created by mixing any other colors together.

above right • As you can see on this color wheel, complementary colors are any two colors opposite one another.

left • Stay away from complementary colors in CD or Web design, where they cause type to vibrate, making it difficult for users to focus.

below • This is the layout shown above without color. A color-blind individual would have difficulty reading text under these conditions. Squint your eyes and look at the design. If the colors seem to blend into one mass of gray, you need to rethink your use of color.

Gino Vela

portfolio

above • Jair Dripnatik created this advanced Flash presentation. It has everything—great images, great sound, and an awesome interface.

left • This is one of my favorite interfaces, designed by Gino Vela. He uses the metaphor of the human body to represent his work.

left • Here is a great example of use of the global navigation system. While visiting each section of the interface, the top area always remains the same. This makes it easy to see where you are and where you can go.

below • Sandra Marcias used the grid provided in Flash to place all of the complicated elements you see here.

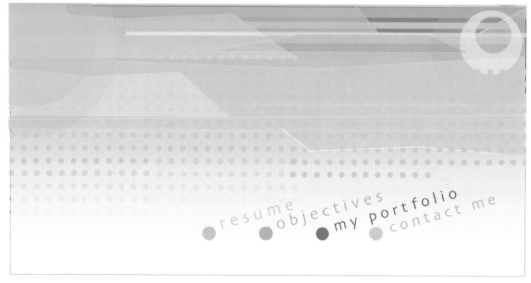

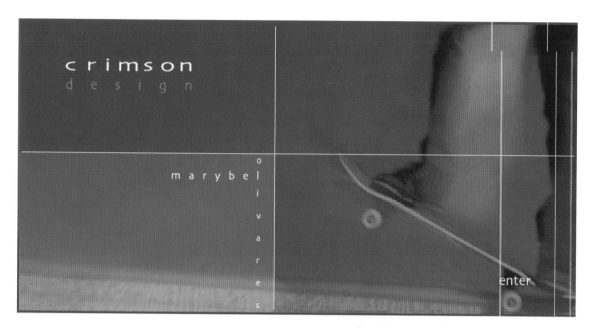

above • Marybel Olivares'
stylish interface shows that
even strong colors such as
red can be used to create an
amazing design interface.

right • Carolina Arcaya shows
that interface design does not
have to be boring. This one
features a high-tech look, but
is easy to understand and
navigate.

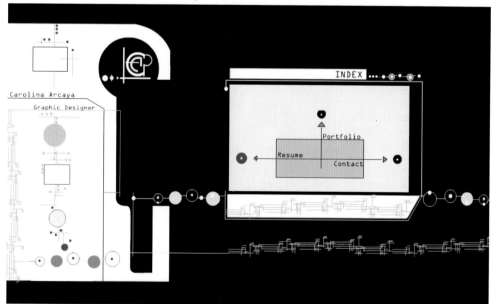

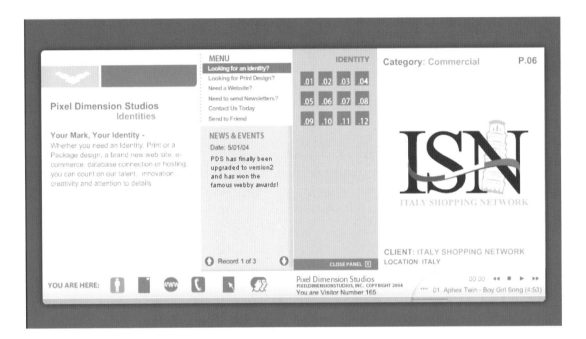

above • This fabulous interface is by Pixel Dimension Studios. It features both video and animation in a clean, easy-to-navigate site. Notice that you always know where you are in the interface thanks to multiple navigational devices.

right • Adriana Garcia designed this symphony in blue. The color system is a strong blue, and all of the graphics complement the chosen colors.

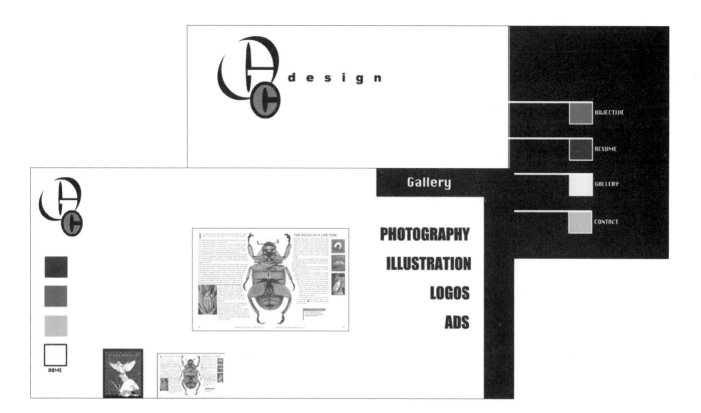

Guillermo Carvajal created this stylish interface. He used the three primary colors to create the buttons.

Therefore, it should be neutral and blend well with your art. Used correctly, the primary color sets the tone for the overall portfolio.

The secondary color supports the primary color of the design, and as such usually is similar to the primary color. Secondary colors are created by combining a primary color with a neighboring secondary color on the color wheel. They usually are analogous or next to one another on the wheel; for example, blue and blue-green (a tertiary color) are two analogous colors. They are related, but not the same. Whenever analogous colors are used, one color generally acts as the dominant color while the other colors are used as accents.

Tertiary colors are made of any primary and secondary color mixed together. They are usually expressed as blue-green or yellow-orange. When creating an analogous color system—one primary, one secondary, and one tertiary color are generally selected.

The highlight color is chosen to emphasize a particular section of the page. It is usually a color that *contrasts* with the primary and secondary colors, yet complements the others used in the rest of your portfolio. Here is an example of why complimentary colors can ruin a web page. Complimentary colors—two colors opposite one another on the color wheel make the page very difficult to read. Complimentary colors never look good in CD or Web design. The type will "vibrate" and the user will have difficulty focusing on the colors for any length of time. Highlight colors are pleasing to the eye when used in small amounts. On the color wheel, the complement of blue would be orange. Be careful not to get carried away when using contrasting colors. Orange type in a blue background, for example, will be extremely difficult for your viewer to read (see the color insert). What you want to do is contrast the complements. For example, use peach and sky-blue together to evoke an outdoorsy feeling. See the color insert for an example of good and bad use of complementary colors.

Another approach is to use split-complementary colors, that is, the color on either side of the complement. The colors are broken into two colors that are adjacent to the main complementary color. The split compliment of blue would be orange-yellow or orange-red. Split combinations tend to be less vibrant and add some variety to the page.

Jair Dripnatik uses an architectural approach to this interface. The overall effect is that of a floor plan coupled with a galaxy.

A word of warning before we leave this topic: Complementary colors are never effective in CD or Web design. They will cause type to "vibrate," and the user will have difficulty focusing on the colors for any length of time.

Think Soft and Monochromatic

Your color selections do not have to be bright. Softer versions of the colors you select generate subtlety, finesse, and readability to your site. Warm colors (yellows, reds, and oranges) will come forward on your page. Cool colors (blues and greens) will recede. Mix both together to build additional interest. Colors created with a light value (white added) tend to be viewed as contemporary or less serious colors.

A current trend is to use monochromatic color schemes in multimedia design. That means using a single color plus tints and shades of that same color. This creates unity in a design and can be very powerful when mixed with one accent color. And colors with black added can

impart drama to a Web site—but never place black on pure white, as this is very stressful on the eyes and will cause viewers to exit your project. Soften the contrast between the text, visuals, and background to solve this problem.

Use Web-Safe Colors

When creating your electronic your portfolio, always keep in mind that there are color limitations for projects destined for Web viewing. As you know, the human eye can perceive millions of colors. And, technically, you can produce millions of colors on your screen. But you'd be wise not to do so, because Macs and PCs use completely different color palettes.

To solve the problem of displaying color graphics on different monitors, Netscape invented the *browser-safe color palette*. This palette includes 216 "Web-safe" colors that are common to both Windows and Macintosh computers. By using these colors you can ensure that your Web site will display fairly consistently on different operating systems (Windows or Mac), as well as in different browsers such as Internet Explorer, Apple Safari, and Netscape Navigator.

All that said, this is less of a problem than it used to be, because today's state-of-the art monitors are set to thousands or millions of colors. What hasn't changed, however, is that the more colors you use, the slower the download speed of your Web pages.

Say No to Background Images

My rule of thumb is, don't use background images. Why not? They are distracting, and they take forever to load and make text nearly impossible to read over a "wallpaper-type" background image. And pictures used as backgrounds have to be created the full size of a Web page, which might be as large as 800 x 600. This makes the overall file size much larger. In addition, HTML documents that feature background images have formatting problems, as the image must be "sliced" into segments before insertion, which also mean extra work, more time.

One partial workaround is to use an image as a section of the overall page design. This keeps the file size small and insures a faster load time. A smaller image also leaves more negative space on the page. It "opens up" the layout and produces a very stylish solution.

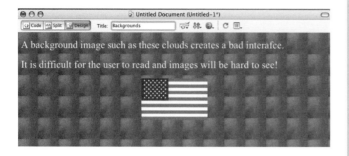

Backgrounds usually do more harm than good. This must have seemed like a good idea at the time, but it interferes with the image and makes it hard to read the type.

You could, for example, create a small seamless image file (that stays small) to be used as a wallpaper element. The image is created as a repeating pattern once imported to the layout. Just make sure that the pattern will not compete with the other elements on the page. Contrast is the key.

If you are determined to have a background, create one that is subtle and that almost disappears, well, into the background! And stick with solid colors. In short, make sure it doesn't overwhelm the main content of any pages.

Color Wrap-Up

In summary, let me reiterate the importance of considering the psychology and use of color *before* you construct your portfolio. A good way to do this is to find a Web page worth admiring (see the color inserts for good examples). Analyze the color and see if you can determine what makes the page so attractive. The more sensitivity you develop to color and its impact on interface design, the more professional your pages will look. In the next chapter, we turn our attention to the importance of typography. ∎

ANALOGOUS COLOR: Any three colors next to one another on the color wheel. An example of analogous colors would be red, red-orange, and orange.

COMPLEMENTARY COLOR: Two colors directly opposite one another on the color wheel. Red and green are complements of one another.

FLOWCHART: A diagram or visual mapping that shows "a step-by-step progression of a plan. It can be a simple drawing that maps out the way your portfolio will be navigated.

HOME PAGE: The top-level or main page of an electronic interface. This is the starting place of an individual or subject area.

HIGHLIGHT COLOR: A color chosen to emphasize a particular section of a design. It is usually a color selected to contrast with the primary and secondary colors.

HUE: The name of a distinct color of the spectrum—red, green, yellow, orange, blue, and so on. Hue refers to main attribute of a color that distinguishes it from other colors.

MONOCHROMATIC: Colors made from tints and shades of the same hue.

PRIMARY COLOR: A pure hue that cannot be reproduced by mixing other colors. The primary colors are red, yellow, and blue.

SATURATION: Saturation, also called chroma, is the amount of purity in the color. Saturation is usually coupled with hue and intensity to describe the physical sensitivity of a color.

SECONDARY COLOR: The color produced by mixing two of the primary colors from the color wheel. Red and yellow make orange. Blue and yellow make green. Blue and red make violet.

SPLIT COMPLEMENTARY: A color system that combines a color with the colors on either side of its complement. Red and green are complements, so red, blue-green, and yellow-green form a split-complementary combination.

TERTIARY COLOR: A color created by mixing one primary and one secondary color. Tertiary colors are also named for the two colors they are made from, with the primary color coming first, such as blue-green or yellow-green.

VALUE: Also known as brightness, value refers to the relative lightness or darkness of a color.

WEB-SAFE COLORS: The set of 216 colors common to most browsers. When used, Web-safe colors offer reliable results on different platforms and with different browsers.

glossary

8

Working with Type

The effectiveness of an innovative layout is dependent not just on your use of color, but typography as well. As in graphic design, typography is one of the foundations of good visual design. Setting, or placing, type involves the careful selection of a finely proportioned collection of lines and shapes, which reproductions of the original letterforms. The correct use of type is just as important on an electronic page as it is in any other medium. Type must always be pleasing to look at and easy to read. As with other areas of visual design, there are rules to follow and limitations to be aware of when it comes to working with typography for an electronic purpose. Which of these two paragraphs do you think would be more fun to read?

To work with typography successfully, you need to understand it. There is of course no "ideal type solution," but there are guidelines to follow to help you choose the right typography for any given situation. Legibility is the key.

Brief Lesson on Type

To begin, some terminology. There are *fonts*, there are type families, and there are *font classifications*. A font comprises a complete assortment of the letters, num-

Once upon a time there was a little girl named Katherine, who dreamed of living in a castle in a magical forest. The forest would be filled with animals that could sing happy songs and trees that could walk and talk. But alas, instead of living in a big castle with secret staircases and treasure chests filled with jewels, the little Katherine lived in an old rundown house with a leaky faucet.

Everyday the little girl would wish and wish for a magic wand. A" magic wand," Katherine would say, "will make all my wishes come true."

Once upon a time there was a little girl named Katherine, who dreamed of living in a castle in a magical forest. The forest would be filled with animals that could sing happy songs and trees that could walk and talk. But alas, instead of living in a big castle with secret staircases and treasure chests filled with jewels, the little Katherine lived in an old rundown house with a leaky faucet.

Everyday the little girl would wish and wish for a magic wand. A" magic wand," Katherine would say, "will make all my wishes come true."

ABCDEFGHIJKLMNOPQRSTUVWXYZ

abcdefghijklmnopqrstuvwxyz

above • **Which of these paragraphs do you think would be more fun to read?**

next page • **The Gill Sans font looks like this. Notice that it's a clean, modern-looking type.**

bers, and other characters of a design and sometimes one size. (Font is often confused with the word "type-face," which means literally "the face of printing type," or all type of a single design.) As an example of a font, here's one called Gill Sans.

A font family contains all of the variations of one font, perhaps, as many as 60 varieties. These variations might include italics, bold, extended, condensed, small

ABCDEFGHIJKLMNOPQRSTUVWXYZ
abcdefghijklmnopqrstuvwxyz

ABCDEFGHIJKLMNOPQRSTUVWXYZ
abcdefghijklmnopqrstuvwxyz

ABCDEFGHIJKLMNOPQRSTUVWXYZ

ABCDEFGHIJKLMNOPQRSTUVWXYZ

from top • **This is the font Gill Sans as a bold typeface.**
Gill Sans Light Italic gives a totally different look to the letters.
Here is a look at Gill Sans in large and small caps.

and large caps. Here again is Gill Sans presented in several different variations.

Fonts are generally grouped by category, based on common characteristics. Although there is some discrepancy among designers as to what should be considered a category, for our purposes, type will be broken down into the following categories.

- *Serif.* Serifs are thin short lines stemming from or at an angle to the upper and lower ends of the strokes of a letter. Serif fonts are used for primarily for body text because of their legibility. They are easy on the eyes, hence do not cause eyestrain.
- *Sans serif*. "Sans," in French, means "without," so a sans serif type is one that has none of the short lines stemming from or at an angle to the upper and lower ends of the strokes of a letter. According to most studies, sans serif fonts are more difficult to read. However, they are considered a good choice for headings and the Web.
- *Modern.* This category includes typefaces that feature strong contrast between thick and thin strokes of each letter. The typefaces of this category also feature strong vertical emphasis and fine hairlines on each letter.
- *Display, novelty, or decorative.* Typefaces in this category are designed to imitate brushstrokes or handwriting. Decorative or novelty types are most effective when used in larger point sizes for display. You often see them used as headlines and titles.

Using Type to Express Your Artistic Vision

If you have ever designed for print, you already know the power of type to express your ideas through the use of appropriate letterforms. In fact, type can be the focal point of your layout. Think of type as a kind of texture. This will help you to view type as a design element and allow you to focus on the visual representation of the words rather than the message. Just keep in mind that, like color, a typeface can either support or undermine your design, so you must choose wisely.

Display Type

Headlines, titles, subheads, and pull quotes are all examples of display, or novelty, type. Headlines are the most important. They direct the viewer what to focus on in the display. Open your favorite magazine and find an article. No doubt you will take note of the headline or title of the article first. As you scan down the page, you notice the body copy, the bulk of any printed piece. The headline tells you what is important about that article and why you should be reading it. Subheads and pull quotes also give visual emphasis to a page and help direct the reader's attention, as well as to divide the page into visually pleasing sections.

Here are a few guidelines for designing headlines.

- The size of your headline suggests its importance. Choose wisely.
- Leave some white space around the headline. It gives your page additional impact.
- In general, use heavy, condensed sans serif typefaces in headlines.
- Don't underline headlines (it will make them look like hyperlinks).
- Use slab serif typefaces (fonts in which the serifs are solid straight lines) to suggest strength.
- Use rounded typefaces to create a more relaxed and friendly mood.
- Use large modern typefaces to express sophistication.
- Use matching typefaces for headlines and subheads.
- Place pull quotes within paragraphs to break up long sections of type. And note that they work best when used in larger type sizes, and that contrast makes them stand out.

Times & Times New Roman

Garamond

Palatino

Caslon

Helvetica

Arial

GillSans

Mvriad

Bodoni

Ellington

Didot

Brush Script

Edwardian Script

STENCIL

Sand

from top • These are examples of serif typefaces.

These are examples of sans serif typefaces. Notice the absence of decorative line features.

Modern typefaces are designed to suggest a contemporary feeling.

Used in small quantities, display, novelty, or decorative typefaces offer interesting variations for your layouts.

Body Copy

Body copy is, of course, essential to page design because it comprises the bulk of your document. Thus it is important to choose your body type with care. As a general rule, stay away from heavy, decorative typefaces, as they are difficult to read in large amounts and cause eyestrain. As mentioned above, serif typefaces are generally best for body text.

Here are some other guidelines:

- Use sufficient leading (the space between lines of type) and paragraph breaks to improve the readability of the page.
- Use only one space at the end of a sentence. The two-space practice went out with typewriters.
- Justify (space so that the lines come out even in the margin) text in wider columns.
- Use hyphens and line-breaks to fine-tune line endings.
- Guard against "rivers" (gaps of white space gaps) in type. This problem is very common with justified text.
- Never allow more than two hyphenated lines in a row. It is considered bad design.
- Don't use double hyphens for em-dashes (the long dashes).

The Psychology of Type

Our reactions to type is similar in many ways to our responses to color. We are influenced by past experiences and associations. Most people have an expectation about what type should reflect, as shown here.

Which one of these examples does not look right? Only one of these says "dark and scary." Even those who don't understand the intricacies of type sense the correct usage of letterform.

Successful Use of Type in Multimedia: Readability

Many different factors contribute to the successful placement of type in multimedia. The first is size. Type must be larger on the screen than you might normally select for print, in order to improve the legibility of your carefully chosen words. The size you choose will then help to determine the amount and size of additional text elements you include. Color and contrast of the type will also have an impact on the readability of the page. Remember, type on the screen is much different from that used print media.

Type size, line length, and alignment all contribute to the well-designed electronic page. Whereas print-based type is measured in "points," on-screens type is measured in pixels. Individual screen characters as pixels require a different measurement system. In Web

Can Apples Really Save Your Life

By: Adrian Travis

The apple has taken on an almost mystical image as the miricle food of the new millenium. Donald Charp will tell you all about the amazing apple and its healing effects on the body.

Spreading his word

For a decade Donald Charp, 48, has been spreading the word that what you think, whether you are stressed or relaxed, furious or overjoyed, directly affects your health for good or ill.

That message has met growing acceptance. The National Institute of Health now funds mind-body research and has an Ad Hoc Panel on Alternative Medicine, to which Charp won appointment.

For doubters, Charp poses this: More people in this workaday world die at 9 a.m. Monday than any other hour of the week.

t s an extraordinary, stunning and unique accomplishment for which only the human species can take credit," Charp says.

What s the deadly difference between Sunday and Monday? "It s just an idea," he says.

Mind, body connected

The mind and the body, which Western medicine long treated as distinct entities, are inseparably linked, Charp explains. A thought can trigger release of toxic stress hormones (the fight - or - flight instinct handed down to us, genetically from primitive man) or soothing natural tranquilizers, depending on whether one perceives a situation as harrowing or happy.

Charp encourages people, including some of the biggest stars in Hollywood, to use the power of the mind to create health and, more controversial, to stop aging by changing their perceptions.

Actress Bobby Moore recently told a British magazine that she hoped Charp s teachings will help her live to 130 and conceive a son. Presumably, not in that order.

A one-man industry, Charp s message is so wildly popular that he has become a one-man, multimillion-dollar self-help industry. He has written 15 books and more than 30 audio and video series. He draws enthusiastic crowds at lectures and workshops nationwide and has ties to a company

"You don t have to believe what I m saying, but, I am as are many Americans, probably shortening my life with stress, fear and lousy living."

that sells ointments and herbal remedies associated with Ayurveda, an ancient medical system rooted in Indian Mysticism.

The spiritual key

Charp s latest book is entitled *The Way of the Land: Twenty-five Great Spiritual Lessonsfor Creating the Life*, promises nothing less than "the key to achieving love, personal fulfillment, and spiritual connectedness." WPBT

22

This demonstrates how type can improve a layout. Although this page features three different typefaces, the page has interest and texture. Notice that some of the typefaces are used in their individual variations.

design, HTML uses H1, H2, H3, and so on to designate type size. And a system called Cascading Style Sheets (CSS) is used to specify type by point size, percentage, or in relative units such as pixels, points, inches, centimeters, millimeters, and more.

I know you're probably confused at this point. Actually, it's quite easy, if you remember one simple rule:

Test often. Test wide.

By this I mean, test your project on your home computer. Then try loading the project on a machine at work, or on a friend's computer—and ideally on both a Mac and a PC. Look at the text on the screen. Is it readable on both operating systems? A mark of a successful digital portfolio is that it runs flawlessly on every computer and under every possible condition.

Here is a list of fonts that are considered to be cross-platform and Web-safe.

Windows	Macintosh
Arial	Bookman, Geneva
Verdana	Helvetica, Chicago
Tahoma	Helvetica
Symbol	Symbol
Courier	Courier, Monaco
Georgia	Palatino, Times

Type Limitations

You must always strive to use type to effectively convey your message in a clear and concise fashion—yet you want it to be original and attractive. This is a bit of a balancing act, I know. And you'll probably face limitations. Not all typefaces are available on every computer, and to a number of different companies produce type. For example, let's say you would like the text on your main page to be displayed using the Avant-Garde typeface. In

It was a dark and scary night...

It was a dark and scary night…

It was a dark and scary night...

No

above • Certain fonts are ideal for evoking emotions and responses. Which of these do you think best expresses "dark and scary?"

left • A classic typesetting exercise is to see how many ways you can express the word "no" in type. For example, you can scream no. You can say no, but mean yes. You can say no gently or whisper the word to intimidate someone. Combining color, type, and size are all ways to articulate the meaning of the word you intend to convey.

Let's grow old together... that's the way life is supposed to be. You meet the love of your life, and live happily ever after, but what if your spouse leaves you alone? Worse yet, what if you survive your children, your friends and all of your relatives. How can you take care of yourself and protect your assets? The government is supposed to protect you with laws. Checkpoints against any fraud that might be committed against you are supposed to be carefully regulated by law. But he law doesn't always work. Visit the case of Alice Martinez.

"The room was quiet, so quiet in fact, that I could hear the wine of the pipes of the apartment next door. I wanted to go there, to knock on that door, and ask for a little conversation- a little bit of life."

Martinez lives in Coral Ridge, Florida. She is now alone. Her two children, Robert and Mindy were killed in a freak car accident, in 1995. Her husband, Phil died several years earlier, in 1990. Martin always believed she would be looked after, "I thought that someone would always be there for me. Now, I go to bed at night and pray that I'll never wake up."

Here is an example of a typesetting error: two hyphens on top of each other at the ends of lines in body copy. Good typographers avoid too may hyphens in a row in a paragraph.

order for the text on your page to actually appear in this typeface, your viewers must have it installed on their computer, or it will default to some other typeface such a Courier (which looks like typewriter text). It may even cut off words or paragraphs.

Another factor to consider is that Macintosh and Windows computers display at different resolutions. The resolution for a Windows computer is 96 ppi, which stands for points per inch. On a Mac, it's 72 ppi. In general, Windows computers can display smaller type with more clarity. In fact, type displays about 2 points larger on a PC. Really small type, say 6 points, will be visible on a PC, but disappear on a Mac. As you can understand, these factors can have a major impact on your carefully designed layout.

There are two techniques that you can use to ensure that a typeface displays exactly as you intend it to on your page. The first is to turn the type into a graphic or bitmapped image. The second is to create a

vector-based outline of the type. Graphic designers, for example, typically use the "Create Outlines" function in Adobe Illustrator to turn type into simple vector-based objects. Macromedia Flash can perform this task as well using the "Break Apart" command. Once type has been modified to a raster-based or vector-based file, it no longer has to be installed on the viewer's computer to be seen. This solves most of problems just described. But it does not address loading time issues.

Speed

You know by now how important speed is in multimedia design. Type used in its original form will always create a smaller file size than type that has been converted to either vector- or raster-based graphics. If you must convert type, a vector-based file is the better solution, as they are always smaller than raster-based files. If you must have a special look for your font, bitmapping your text may be your only choice, but recognize that you do so at the expense of speed. The best solution is to use typefaces that are common to both Macs and PCs. These fonts are: Times, Times New Roman, Arial, Courier, Helvetica, and Verdana.

You now know that when it comes to type, there are resolution and size issues. So once again, the best solution is to test your pages on as many different computers, monitors, and internet browsers as possible. Correct any discrepancies you find and all will be well.

The Importance of Line Length

Many studies have been conducted to determine the ideal conditions for type and readability. Some of these have centered on the issue of eyestrain, which I have mentioned several times now. It turns out that the length of a line of type is a major contributing factor to this discomfort. It is caused because by the disruption to reading as your eyes move from the end of one line to the beginning of the next. As a designer, you want to minimize eyestrain for you viewers, so the best advice is to keep line length somewhere around 60 to 70 characters, although that is not a hard-and-fast number. A haiku on type by Professor Howard T. Katz, of the Art Institute of Fort Lauderdale, sums up the problem of eyestrain:

> Eyes are red and swollen.
> Watch out for the sharp serifs.
> Typography hurts.

Type Alignment

I remember how hard it was as a child to color inside the lines in my coloring books. Placing type in a layout for your portfolio is a little like that. You want the layout to look clean and neat, but you don't want to be constrained by "lines." Although type alignment is not a particularly difficult undertaking when it comes to CD design, it is for Web design, due to the limitations imposed by HTML requirements.

Frequently, for example, you must design with tables, whose layouts use rows, columns, and cells to display tabular, text, or image data (think of spread-

● ● ● **Using Type to Describe Oxymorons**

Oxymorons are fun! You hear them all the time—jumbo shrimp, alone together, half full. In fact, there are Web sites devoted to oxymorons. Take a look at how you might use type to express some of the more popular oxymorons.

sheets). When type is placed within a table, it can be aligned left, centered, or justified. As always, the readability factor comes into play. It is best to always to set type left-aligned, especially if you will be featuring large amounts of type.

Ten Rules for Good Type Design

To sum up this discussion, I leave you with 10 rules to follow to ensure you design effectively with type. By carefully choosing the typefaces you use, you can make your design say whatever you want, whether it's, "I'm playful," "I'm classic," or "I'm cutting edge."

- *Rule 1: Use sans serif typefaces when designing for the computer and low-resolution monitors.* They are

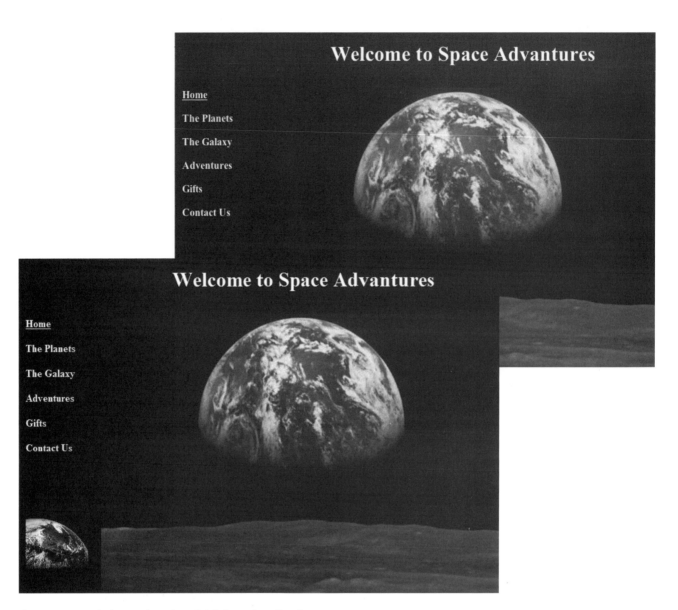

As you can see, the image above has slightly larger type than the version below. The screen shows a difference of about 2 points.

crisp, clean, and easy to read. Sans serif types include Helvetica, Arial, Avant-Garde, Officiana Sans, Gill Sans, and Eras. If you must use a serif typeface, stick to the tried and true: Times or Times New Roman, Palatino, or Garamond.

- *Rule 2: Resist the urge to use too many typefaces.* Just because you bought that CD with 10,000 fonts for $10 doesn't mean you have to use every one of them in your design. Limit yourself to three or four fonts per design. To achieve the most professional look, be consistent with font usage from page to page; and avoid using stylized typefaces as body copy. They are difficult to read and stress the eyes.

- *Rule 3: Bigger is better.* Small type is very much in vogue in print design, but it does not work for multimedia. The limitations of monitor resolutions make it almost impossible to display small body type effectively. The size you select will ultimately depend on the font you select. When it comes to display type, a large font definitely adds both ornament and drama.

Experience

| 2000 present | **Publication Specialist II, Broward County Cultural Affairs Division** |
| | **Fort Lauderdale, FL** |

a liaison between administrators, graphic designers and printers requiring strong communication skills and knowledge of industry terminology, responsible for concept development in all publications as well as supervising the distribution to the cultural organizations and the general public

| 2000 present | **Freelance Graphic Designer** |
| | **Fort Lauderdale, FL** |

experience in corporate id, promotional materials, program design, and holiday cards clients include Anchor Marketing, Great White Flying Service, Chef David's Kids, Hollywood Philharmonic Orchestra

| 1998 2000 | **Assistant Marketing Manager, Fort Lauderdale Jet Center** |
| | **Fort Lauderdale, FL** |

created a positive company image based upon marketing strategies and public relations, maintained the existing customer base, and develop new contacts through research

| 1996 1995 | **Store Manager, Culinary Creations** |
| | **North Miami Beach, FL** |

coordinated daily operations of the gourmet deli, booked catered events for up to 500 people, supervised a staff of 10 people

| 1995 1993 | **Customer Service Representative, Fort Lauderdale Jet Center** |
| | **Fort Lauderdale, FL** |

responsibilities included all travel requirements for crew and passengers flying into the facility ranging from catering, fuel, hotel accommodations, rental cars and limousine service, developed strong skills in multi-tasking and problem solving, there was a great deal of team coordinating to ensure the customers have all their needs met

Skills

photoshop, illustrator, quarkxpress, pagemaker, frontpage, flash, dreamweaver, conceptual development, layout, proofing, print production, marketing, public relations, sales, management

Honors

2003 Student Addy Award

Program Cover, Hollywood Philharmonic Orchestra
designed performances program for the season of 2001-2002

Christmas Cards, Chef David's Kids
design was chosen for their VIP list which then lead to other holiday card designs volunteered to do public relations work during the Christmas season

Education

Bachelor of Science in Graphic Design, The Art Institute of Fort Lauderdale
2003, CGPA 3.8 (A= 4.0)

Associate in Liberal Arts, Broward Community College
1989

Fluent in Spanish

yvette wasserman designs
2615 taylor street
hollywood, fl 33020
954.927.8495
ywgraphics@aol.com

above • Allow yourself to loosen up! Type is supposed to be fun! This little guy was created just to demonstrate the versatility of type as a design tool.

right • As you can see, this good-looking page, designed by Yvette Wasserman, demonstrates the best possible way to display large amounts of type. Notice the columns and flush-left type alignment.

below • Here is an illustration of different type sizes displayed on a Web page.

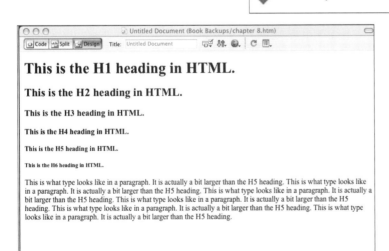

This is the H1 heading in HTML.

This is the H2 heading in HTML.

This is the H3 heading in HTML.

This is what type looks like in a paragraph. It is actually a bit larger than the H5 heading. This is what type looks like in a paragraph. It is actually a bit larger than the H5 heading. This is what type looks like in a paragraph. It is actually a bit larger than the H5 heading. This is what type looks like in a paragraph. It is actually a bit larger than the H5 heading. This is what type looks like in a paragraph. It is actually a bit larger than the H5 heading. This is what type looks like in a paragraph. It is actually a bit larger than the H5 heading.

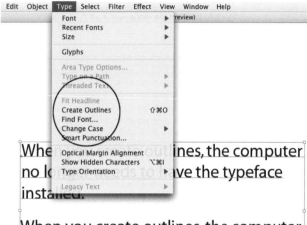

When you create outlines, the computer no longer needs to have the typeface installed.

When you create outlines, the computer no longer needs to have the typeface installed.

- *Rule 4: Don't create "false links" by underlining.* In Web design, an underlined word or phrase indicates a link to another page. It can frustrate the user when his or her mouse click leads nowhere. Instead to highlight type use attributes such as boldface, italics, or small caps.
- *Rule 5: Limit the amount of text on the screen.* It is considered bad design to force the viewer to scroll through pages and pages of type. Break up your text into small easy-to-read chucks of information. And keep lines of type short.
- *Rule 6: Don't use all caps.* In Web email, this is considered shouting. Moreover, all caps are difficult to read and hard on the eyes.
- *Rule 7: Use white, or negative, space to your advantage.* Include adequate breaks between paragraphs and major areas of text. Negative space is an artistic trick to guide your reader's eye from one point to another. Lack of it can actually cause the screen to flicker before a viewer's eyes.
- *Rule 8: Minimize load times.* Too many fonts that are defined as raster-based bitmaps will cause your

design to take forever to load. Whenever possible, use cross-platform system fonts.
- *Rule 9: Don't get carried away with font color.* When it comes to type, contrast is king. It is important that your message be easy to read, so make sure that your background and type are compatible. And while we're on the subject, stay away from reversed type—white on black type is very difficult to read.
- *Rule 10: Experiment and create your own style.* Just make sure the style does what you want and never detracts from the message.

Typography is an art form, no doubt about it. It can support your design, or even be your design, but always it must legible. If it's not, you've defeated the purpose. Be mysterious, be engaging, be outrageous, be whatever you want to be, but be a good type designer.

Now that you know a little more about how to use color a d typography effectively, we'll turn our attention to design and navigation issues. In the next chapter we will talk more about interface metaphors. ■

● ● ● Keep It Short and Simple

It is more difficult to read words on the screen than on a printed page, so when it comes to designing a digital interface, the rule of thumb is: Keep words to a minimum. Studies have shown that people will not spend large amounts of time reading online documents due to eye-strain. Keep your information concise, and limit the text on each page. If you feel you must include a lot of text in your digital portfolio, be sure to break it into small blocks or spread it over multiple pages.

Those of you who really enjoy the process of working with type should consider kerning (adjusting the space between individual characters in a line of type.) Kerning is especially important with large display type.

SKILLS

TECHNICAL/DESIGN

Logo Design
Editorial Design
Desktop Publishing
Corporate Image
Advertising Design
Annual Reports
Photography

SOFTWARE

Photoshop
QuarkXPress
Illustrator
Corel Draw
Basic Knowledge of HTML programming
Flash
Mac and PC oriented

COMMUNICATION

Bilingual, Spanish and English

back to resume

EXPERIENCE, FREELANCE

Art Institute of Fort Lauderdale
Department of Admissions
Part time
Work with the international admissions
representatives making phone calls to future
students
November 2002, present

Conexiones Magazine
Coral Spring, Florida
Internship
Advertising Design
2003

Elecsa S.A.
Valencia, Venezuela
Designed Corporate Image
2001

Sure Este
Valencia, Venezuela
Designed logo
2001

back to resume

Here is an attractive interface designed by Fabianna Diaz. Notice the use of white space between lines of type. Very clean. Very easy to read.

ADOBE TYPE 1 FONTS: Developed by Adobe in the early 1980s, Type 1 technology uses the PostScript page description language (PDL) to render fonts on the screen and in print. Type 1 fonts have two parts: the screen font and the printer font. Both must be present on the computer in order for a file to render (print) properly.

ALIGNMENT: Alignment refers to the shape of the text block in relation to the page margins. Type can be set to left alignment (sometimes called flush left), right alignment (sometimes called flush right), center alignment, justified alignment, and force justify alignment.

ASCENDER: The part of a lowercase letter that rises above the main part of the letter, such as on the letters b, f, and h.

CASCADING STYLE SHEETS (CSS): A complement system to HTML that allows style features (color, font size, spacing, and page layering) to be specified for certain elements. CSS is excellent for making a global change to multiple Web pages.

DESCENDER: The part of a lowercase letter (such as g, j, or p) that descends below the main body of a letter.

DISPLAY (ALSO, NOVELTY OR DECORATIVE TYPE): Large, bold, or special fonts typically used to command attention. Display type is designed to imitate brushstrokes or handwriting techniques. Decorative initial capital letters also fall into this category.

EM DASH: Width of a piece of type about as wide as it is tall.

EN DASH: Width of a piece of type that is half the width of an em.

FONT: A complete assortment of letters, numbers, and symbols of a specific size and design. For example, Times Roman Bold Italic 12 point.

FORCE JUSTIFY: Refers to type that stretches to fill the entire text block in relation to the page margins. Force justify text can be difficult to work with and cause awkward rivers of type on the page.

HEADLINE: The title of an article or a story; words used to introduce or categorize.

ITALIC: The slanted version of a typeface.

KERNING: The fine-tuning or adjustment of the space between individual characters in a line of type. Kerning is especially important with large display type. Without these adjustments, many letter combinations can poorly spaced.

LEADING: Leading is the vertical space between lines of type. It is measured from baseline to baseline. Generally the leading is at least the size of the type, although it is usually more generous. For example, 12-point type would be matched with 15-point leading. Type with a generous amount of space between lines is said to have "open leading," and type with relatively little space between lines is said to have "tight leading."

LINE LENGTH: The width of a typeset line, typically the area between the left and right margins. Longer line lengths are thought to be more difficult to read.

MARGIN: The white spaces that surrounds text blocks on all four sides of a page: top and bottom, left and right..

MODERN TYPE: More contemporary style of typography where the letters contain fine hairlines and the axis is vertical. Examples of Modern type include Didone and Bodoni.

NEGATIVE SPACE: The white space around type or an image. When a great deal of type is on a page, negative space creates a resting area for the eye.

PULL QUOTE: A phrase, sentence, or paragraph typically taken from text that serves generate interest and draw the attention to a specific piece of information. It is often used to emphasize an significant statistic or remark.

SANS SERIF TYPE: Type that does not utilize use serifs. Examples include: Helvetica, Avant-Garde, Arial, and Geneva. According to most studies, sans serif fonts are more difficult to read. For this reason, they are used most often for short text components such as headlines or captions.

SERIF TYPE: Typefaces whose letters have short lines stemming from and at an angle to the upper and lower ends of the strokes of a letter. Examples include Times, Baskerville, or Palatino.

SUBHEAD: A line of type subordinate to a headline, also used to break up long sections of type or to guide the reader as to content.

TRUETYPE FONTS: Fonts that use a single font file for each font. TrueType fonts are fully scalable and generate bitmaps (screen versions) as the user creates text in a layout or drawing program. Type 1 fonts were introduced by Microsoft in 1982.

TYPEFACE: All type of a single design. In contrast, a font is an implementation of a typeface.

TYPOGRAPHY: The style, arrangement, or appearance of typeset material. The primary function of typography is to present a page that is visually engaging and easy to read.

X-HEIGHT: The height of a lowercase character, minus any ascenders or descenders. The designation derives from the height of the letter x.

glossary

9

Maneuvering around Your Site
Navigation

Walk into any bookstore and look around at all the books. Now assume all those books are in no order at all—they're not divided by category or in alphabetical order. Then suppose I ask you to find a book about the life of Harry Houdini in that bookstore. Think how difficult it would be. Now transfer that concept to your digital portfolio. Without clear navigational clues someone visiting for the first time would be at a total loss as to where to go to find what he or she was looking for. It wouldn't take long for the visitor to leave—not what you want.

The home page of a Web site, as I've stated, is the all-important first impression for your visitors; the navigation system is the next most important element. Consequently, you must find a way to persuade your visitors to use the navigational device you create so that they become entranced with your portfolio. When you make it easy for viewers to become involved with your content, they will be more willing to explore your project thoroughly. For these reasons, learning to create a clear visual interface is the focus of this chapter

Getting There from Here

I recently looked at a digital portfolio whose content was fabulous. Unfortunately, it required patience and tenacity to find the series of hidden zones that revealed work only if you happened to pass your mouse over them. It was very frustrating. When asked about the confusing nature of the interface, the designer's attitude was that if the visitor didn't have the patience to find the work, then it wasn't meant to be seen by him or her. This is not the sort of user experience you would want to create.

You can feature every kind of cool effect you want in your project, but if your visitors can't figure out where to find them, after a while they will give up. It's as simple as that. By employing thoughtful and professional design, your visitors will always know where they are and where to go to see more—and how to get there. You must always strive to give the visitor a sense of place and a sense of context.

You need to give your viewers directions, a map of sorts, complete with landmarks for visual reference. The icons or labels you create for your interface comprise the map of your project. When they are clear and unmistakable, your viewers will always know where to go and where they have been. The following subsections contain guidelines for creating an effective navigational system for your digital portfolio.

Using Landmarks and Metaphors

Landmarks are easy-to-identify visual elements. Think about the times someone has given you directions for

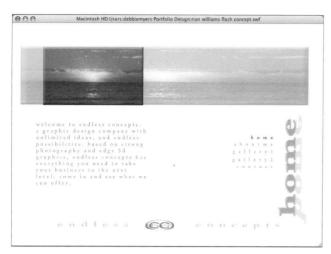

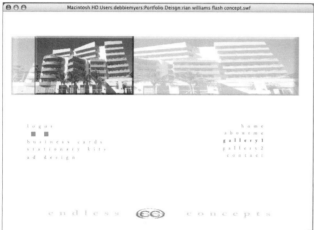

Rian Williams created this fresh and innovative digital portfolio. The important design element to observe is that the user always knows where to go within the interface.

Here is a selection of icons that that be created using the Wingdings or Webdings alphabet. Each letter creates a different picture. Holding down the Shift key while typing gives you even more choices.

getting somewhere you've never been before. In addition to street names and numbers, they say things like, "Look for the building with the red roof," or "There's a McDonald's on the corner, where you turn right." You can use landmarks similarly throughout your digital portfolio to ease the user's "journey."

Likewise, you can use metaphors as guides. You're no doubt familiar with the common computer interface metaphor of a trashcan to represent where to "throw" deleted files. All computer users now understand what that little trashcan icon represents. You can design metaphors that are straightforward or highly design-oriented. In the case of the former, for example, if you use the word "Home" on a page, your viewers will know

that selecting or clicking that word will return them to the home page of your portfolio. Or you may prefer to include a small icon of a house to represent "home." This is now a common visual metaphor for the home page. Certainly, you can choose more eclectic or personal icons as well. A photographer might, say, choose to represent his or her home page with a small roll of film or a flashbulb. A fashion designer might create an icon of a clothing button. As long as the viewer can understand the metaphor, the icons you use can be as creative as you wish.

Metaphors can also be thought of as extensions of the theme of your design serving to tie your project together. Some examples of metaphors you might use are: an art gallery, the rooms of a house, a futuristic world—really, just about anything you can imagine.

In the color insert, you'll see an example in which the user rolls over each area of the "brain" or "body" to produce color and text as navigational tools. The brain here symbolizes the artist, and each lobe represents the sections of the port. This is not only decorative and entertaining, but it works to help the viewer navigate the portfolio.

To help you decide on a metaphor to use, answer the following questions:

- *What structure does the metaphor offer the user?* The metaphor you develop has to make sense. Your portfolio will be divided up into a number of different sections. If , for example, you design a project that uses space-related images as the theme, they must be used consistently throughout the interface. In this case, you might design buttons as the planets of our solar system, with an icon of Earth serving to indicate "home." The metaphor you

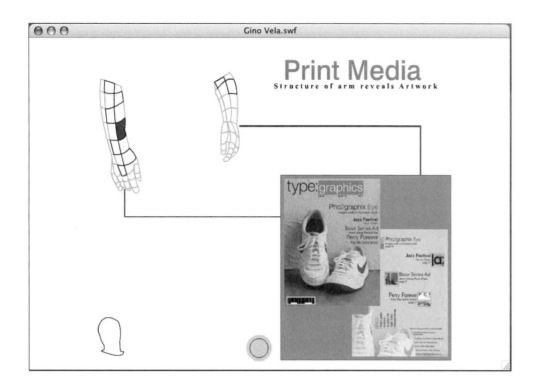

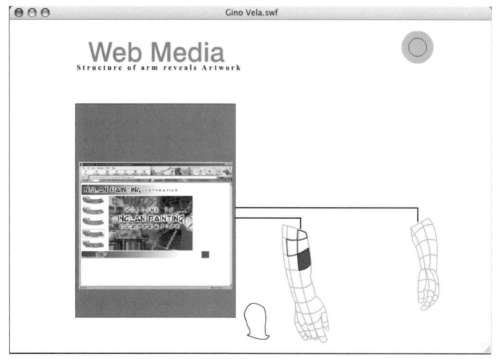

above • Here, whenever the viewer "rolls over" a darkened section of the arms with the mouse, various navigational options pop up on the screen. Uncolored areas indicate that there is nothing to find.

below • Once the viewer is in one of the sections, the option to examine individual pieces of art becomes available.

This interface by Robert Hough creates a concept that carries his illustrations from the images through to the chosen type. It all works together to form a beautiful interface.

select has to make sense in the greater context of the design.

- *Is the metaphor appropriate to the site?* I recently saw an interface that featured a series of pictures of the artist as a child. Good idea. The problem was that nothing else on the screen matched that idea. Bizarre buttons made of swirling suns and squiggly lines that morphed into odd shapes were out of place and did not support the central theme of a child and the creative process. A small series of childhood toys would have made a nice addition to the page and served to support the theme. As an example, a small plastic house from a Monopoly board would surely have pointed the way to the home page. Another site featured every possible cliché icon representing Italy. Certainly you can represent your cultural heritage, but it must make sense with your art. The most clever idea will be a lost cause if it doesn't support the art.

- *Does the metaphor make sense?* Metaphors can represent either a series of concrete physical objects or an abstract idea. Just be sure that they don't confuse the viewer. I once looked at a portfolio that was designed with skulls and daggers. That was one scary portfolio! You can certainly personalize your design, but always keep in mind that, in your design, you are giving bits of information (intentional or not) as to your personality and interests. If you cannot think of an appropriate theme for your design, opt instead to just use a beautiful set of colors. When in doubt, less is more.

- *Is the metaphor capable of being extended, expanded?* If you need to increase the size of your interface, can your metaphor grow with it? Consider again the space theme metaphor. There are nine planets: Mercury, Venus, Earth, Mars, Jupiter, Saturn, Uranus, Neptune, and Pluto. We also have one star: the sun. If each planet represents one section of your portfolio and you have nine sections, you're in great shape! If, however, you need to increase the number of sections, will you be able to devise additional metaphors to support the design and be

When in doubt, test it out! Once you have designed an interface, ask your friends and colleagues try it out. Better to find out there's a problem now than during an interview.

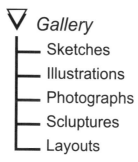

Gallery
- Sketches
- Illustrations
- Photographs
- Sculptures
- Layouts

left • This is an example of a hierarchical design system. Similar subject matter are grouped together under one "umbrella."

below • Even a basic flowchart like this one can be helpful in designing your initial layout, as it helps you to visualize the navigation system.

Main or Home Page

Resume | The Gallery | Contact Links | Honors and Awards

consistent? Nine sections may sound like a lot right now, but you may be surprised. Don't design yourself into a corner.

- *Can your metaphor stand up to testing?* Let's say you created an interface with icons that represent computer equipment. It makes perfect sense to you, because you're a technology whiz, but will all your viewers be able to understand them in relation to the interface. To find out, test, test, test. Ask your friends and colleagues to visit your digital portfolio. Don't assist them in any way. Watch how they work with it. Are they having any difficulties navigating the site? If they keep asking you where they should go next, you have a problem.

Navigation Techniques for Successful Interface Design

I've said it before, but it bears repeating: navigating your digital portfolio should be easy and intuitive. At all times, viewers should understand where they are, where they can go, and how they can return to the home page. The most successful interface is the one that causes no confusion, raises no questions.

Your interface, essentially, will consist of three main elements: the site identity, a way home, and the other sections. Designing an interface with five or six sections is easy; designing an interface with 25 or 30 pages is much

more difficult. Most digital designers agree that there are on three basic approaches to basic interface design:

- Hierarchical
- Global
- Local

Hierarchical

A hierarchical design system groups large amounts of information into major sections or under headings. Bookstores use this system. Books are shelved according to broad-based categories such as fiction, travel, self-help, crafts, biography, and so on. You enter the section you want and begin searching for your book. A digital interface can be designed using this system as well. Divide your pages up into major site sections that represent main areas such as Resume, Gallery, Contact Information, and Home. And within each section include a way to return to the home state.

Global

Global navigation is characterized by links or categories that appear on every page of the interface. This style of navigation features a common interface in which the same navigational elements always appear in the same location, such as the top or left side of the site (see the color insert for an example). This allows the user to jump to any section of the site at any time, wherever he or she may be.

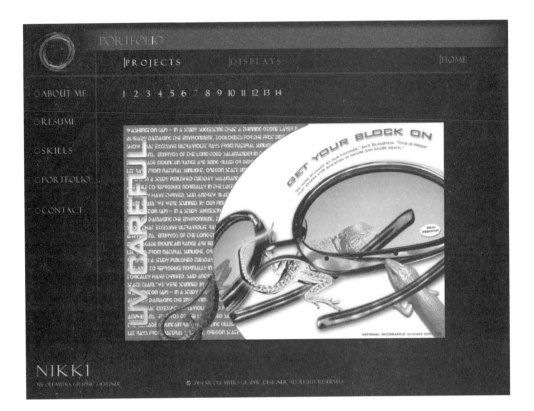

above • A global navigation system makes it easy to see where you are and where you can go.

right • This artistic interface was designed by Debbie Bostwick. Take a look at the links at the top and bottom of this page. The push pins indicate that the user can click to see more artwork, and the "main" text link at the top indicates how to return to the starting section of the site.

Local

Local navigation is a hybrid of the hierarchical and global systems. It is useful when you have a lot of information within broader categories. For example, say you have a major section entitled the Gallery. Within this section, there are subcategories called Photography, Fine Art, and Advertising. The user navigates all of the subsections of the Gallery, then back out to the main Gallery area, to return to the home page.

Strategizing Navigation

Before you can decide on the layout for your digital portfolio, you must design a strategy for navigation. This normally is done in the guise of a flowchart. The flowchart will help you to determine how to arrange the main elements of your digital port and how to link the pages. I recommend that you sketch more than one system, to help you to visualize which one will work best for your purposes. Trust me, flowcharting will save you a lot of time and frustration later on.

The sample flowcharts shown on pages 82 and 109 clearly demonstrate that visitors will be able to move seamlessly around the site. The connections are clear, so that, when implemented, content will be only a click or two away from the main page of the interface.

Common Navigation Elements

Once you have drawn a navigation flowchart, it's time to consider which navigation mechanisms you'll use to make the visitor's experience to your site clear and comprehensible. The most common devises used in navigational design are text (in this case, hypertext), buttons, image maps, and navigational bars.

Your goal in designing an interface device is to convey a distinctive visual style and identity. When properly applied, a cohesive interface device will hold together a series of related, or disjointed, sections. In addition, a well-designed set of navigation elements makes a positive statement about you, the individual who designed it.

Finding the Right Words: Using Hypertext Links

As I explained in an earlier chapter, on the Internet, a hypertext link (generated with HTML) is the most com-

Whenever you create a home page for the Web, always suffix the file name as either *index.htm* or index.html, to ensure that Web browsers such a Netscape, Explorer, or Safari can find it. But when you want people to find you online, be aware that most search engines such as Google, Yahoo, Northern Lights, and so on search on title names. A title name is the information you see at the top of a Web page such as Welcome to Robert Samuel's Creative Portfolio.

monly used form of Web navigation. As you also know by now, a hypertext link is indicated by an underlined word or phrase in text. When the link is clicked on by the user, it changes color, then transfers him or her to the linked content.

For digital interface design, however, a more sophisticated interface is in order. Why? Because an underlined word/phrase in a digital port would more than likely lead viewers to believe it to be an online link. Therefore, in digital design, navigational links are signified by color changes or quick animations. For example, when a user's mouse passes across link text, it might turn into a drop shadow. The best advice for these links is to use labels that clearly communicate the section the viewer will be visiting next, as shown here:

| Home | Resume | Gallery | Contact Me |

Buttons

I've already talked at some length about the importance of interface buttons. Simply put, it would be difficult to navigate even the most basic Web site without them. Buttons are created in two forms: as *HTML action buttons* and as graphical action buttons.

You will typically see HTML action buttons in forms. For example, say you are asked to provide some information to sign up to receive a newsletter. After you have filled in the blanks, you commonly are asked to click on a Submit button to transmit your data. The button code is generated by HTML (or programs such as Dreamweaver). This type of button is not necessarily attractive or interesting, but they are very practical.

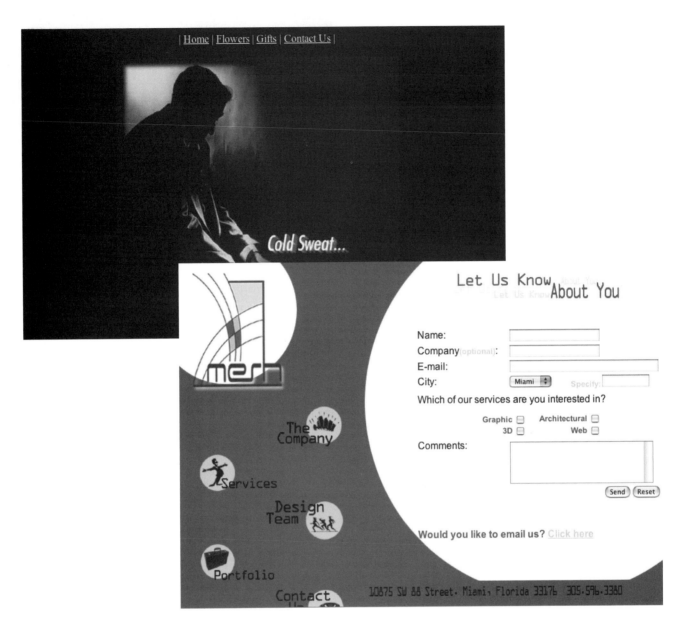

above • Here is a set of hypertext links in action. Notice that you can always tell where you are in the interface. The links change color to indicate when a section has already been visited.

below • Sometimes it's more fun to navigate with pictures! Have some fun when you design a page, just don't forget to design for the user.

Graphical action buttons, in contrast, are usually interesting and attractive. These are animated buttons that change in some way when the user passes the mouse across them. Although more difficult to create, graphical action buttons are more interactive, and give a clear visual clue to the user that some action will take place when clicked. The downsides to this type of button are that they take up more of your limited design space and generate larger files that take longer to download. Another problem is that they can be ambiguous and so may not communicate what you wish to every viewer. Therefore, I suggest that you never rely exclusively on such buttons for navigation.

Image Maps

I've talked about image maps before, too. Recall that an image map is a picture that has been divided into small

Here is an example of a graphical button that clearly indicates that a gallery can be visited.

regions, or "hotspots." When the user clicks on a hotspot, a new document begins to load. In the image map shown here, each of the links takes the user to a different part of the United States.

There are two types of image maps: *client-side* and *server-side*. A client-side image map is one designed using HTML. It runs directly from the user's browser, as opposed to a Web server. Server-side image maps, then, run from the server hosting the Web site. Server-side image maps speed up the Web display, but they require special software.

You can utilize image maps in interface design as well. You create hotspots on a page, which, when rolled over by a mouse, causes an action to occur. In a portfolio, you might, for example, create a series of squares. When one of the squares is touched by the mouse pointer, a piece of artwork appears.

One word of caution: Image maps will not appear if the user has turned off the picture function to make his or her browser run faster.

Navigational Bars

What is the most visually effective way to let the users know where they are in your interface? The navigation bar. You've no doubt seen them on the left side or perhaps at the top of most the popular Web sites. They are so common that most people understand how to use them, which makes it an easy choice for designers. The navigational bar, or "nav bar," as it is sometimes called, provides a visible link to every top-level page of your site, including the home page.

There is no hard-and-fast rule about where to place a navigational bar—though as you can see in the Art Institute of Fort Lauderdale's Web site (on the following page), and as just mentioned above, the left side is a common choice. Note here that the major areas of the AIFL's site are readily available to the user. As a selection is made, the page changes, but the nav bar remains in the same place to ease travel through the site. Other Web sites feature nav bars on the right, or even in the center. These are considered a little less intuitive, but can work in the right design.

Navigational bars can present information in a number of different ways. Text-only links, graphical links, highlights, animations, and drop-down lists are some of the ways the nav bar can tell your story. Nav bars do have one disadvantage: They can potentially take up a lot of your design space. To prevent that happening, keep them small and simple so that they don't get in the way of your work.

Choosing the Best Navigation System for You

At this point, you may be wondering, "Which navigation system should I use?" The answer is, as long as the person visiting your portfolio can move easily from section to section, it doesn't really matter. In fact, more than one than one approach may work. Sometimes the best thing to do is to mix and match them within the same interface. In fact, the more complex the site, the greater the need for multiple ways to navigate it.

● ● ● The Bread Crumb Approach to Navigation

The "bread crumb" approach to navigation is so called because it features a line of previously visited pages at the top or bottom of the page. The "crumbs," are intended to remind you of where you are in the site and how you got there and how you can get back to previously viewed areas. It looks like this:

Home > Gallery > Graphic Design > Logos

"Bread crumbs" are thought to improve the navigation experience because they lay a path back to the main part of the interface. In the example here, the user could click on any of the links to back out of the current section. Unfortunately, this particular approach is not of much benefit in a site that has a lot of information, because it does not give the viewer a clear sense of the amount of content available.

● ● ● Frame It

A quick note about frames. At some point you may decide to put your digital portfolio online. Some designers like to embed such projects in what are called framesets. I strongly advise against this, because framesets do not work in all browsers and therefore make it impossible for search engines to index their pages. If Google or Yahoo cannot index your site, no one will be able to find you! Frames cause other usability problems as well, and make it difficult to bookmark URLs. Frames also are difficult to print, take up a lot of page space, and do not make it easy to comply with section 508 of the Rehabilitation Act of 1973 for people with disabilities.

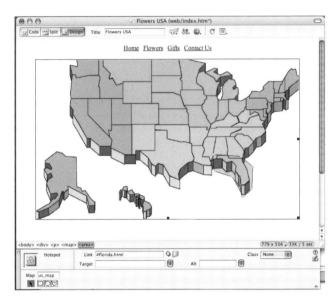

above • This image map shows the "hotspot" that has been created for the state of Florida. When the user rolls over the state, the mouse changes to indicate that this is a link to another part of the interface.

below • The Art Institute of Fort Lauderdale's Web page offers a wide range of navigational options. The visitor can visit the various sections from the right, left, or bottom of the site.

Navigation Review

The best approach to navigational system design is to follow these guidelines:

- Create a metaphor that represents you.
- Test the metaphor on people before you implement it.
- Map out your interface with a flowchart.
- Design a home page (you must have a home page).
- Decide a clear system of navigation, whether hierarchical, global, or local.
- Include buttons, which can be text, images, or a combination of both.
- Don't underline text unless you intend it as a link.
- Use graphics to help navigation, but include text links as well.
- Use buttons, nav bars, and/or image maps consistently.
- Provide more than one way to get to the home page.
- Use alternative labels for images (ALT=Name)
- Ensure that your interface works, so test, test, test!

    Other review points to remember include:

- Your portfolio must always offer a clear, visual, and understandable navigational system.
- Pages should be broken into a home state, small section headings, and smaller subsections, as needed.
- Navigation to other parts of your site should be obvious, either through buttons, text hyperlinks, nav bars, or bread crumbs.

Remember, by the time you show your portfolio, probably the potential employer will have already seen a lot of others. This means that the time he or she spend looking at your work will be minimal. So make it as easy for the employer as you can. Doing so will improve your chances of being chosen for the job. ∎

glossary

BROKEN LINK: A link or hyperlink that doesn't work when the user clicks on it. This generally occurs because the designer didn't properly establish the link. Broken links can also occur if the Web site is temporarily unavailable.

CACHE: The area of your computer's memory where temporary data is stored. The information stays as long as the computer is turned on. Cache memory allows you to hit the Back button to return to previously visited sites.

FLOWCHART: A diagram or visual mapping that shows a design setup. It may be a simple drawing that maps out the way your portfolio will be navigated.

GLOBAL DESIGN: A system of design that ensures links or categories appear on every page of the interface.

HIERARCHICAL DESIGN: A system of design that groups large amounts of information into major sections or headings.

LINK (ALSO, HYPERTEXT LINK): An association established between two Web pages. The connection is usually indicated by including a graphical icon to show that a connection is available. An accepted way to navigate digital interfaces.

IMAGE MAP: A graphic that contains several "hotspots," or invisible buttons, that link to other pages. For example, a world map might contain links to Europe, Asia, South America, and the United States.

LOCAL DESIGN: A hybrid of the hierarchical and global design systems. It groups a lot of information into broader categories.

METAPHOR: A symbol. An object, activity, or idea treated as a metaphor, such as a small picture of a house to represent the home page of a digital interface.

NAVIGATIONAL BAR: A list of options that from which a user can choose to move through the pages of a digital portfolio or Web site. A navigation bar is usually organized by topics, allowing users to jump to major areas of interest.

Advanced Design Techniques

10

With your interface goals, structure, and content worked out, you have all the information you need to start building your site. But before you click to open your authoring program, there's still one more vital question to answer: How exactly is this thing going to look? To answer that question, consider another: What attracts you to a Web site or digital interface? The color scheme? The layout? The music? The animation? You may add any or all of these components to your portfolio interface, but to do so effectively, you must understand both the positive impact and inherent limitations of each.

Each extra component you include in your interface will either add or subtract from the user experience. Too many bells and whistles will overwhelm the project. Too basic an interface will be boring. Your goal is to impress the viewers, so that they will spend quality time with your portfolio. The digital experience you create isn't just about readability and navigation; but about style. In short, your portfolio should encompass all facets of interface design. To that end, in this chapter, we'll examine a number of techniques for producing a successful interface.

Visual Organization

What do you see in this figure at right?

How does it compare with the figure below it, which is the same page with the information added? What is the most important section of the page?

Squint while you are looking at the first image. Did you notice the shades of grey and the values in the design? Did you see those same patterns in the full-text version? I'm guessing that you did. It has been proven that, on a subconscious level, humans are always looking for patterns in the everyday world. In Las Vegas, players around the roulette tables guess which color is "due" to come up next. In psychology, Rorschach inkblot tests are given to discover what a person "sees" in the "blot." Everywhere we look, we try to find patterns; and if we can't find one, we will create one.

When it comes to your portfolio interface, you can think of yourself as an information architect. Type and images form the masses of shapes and color of your design. Everything you place on a page has a weight. Although the viewer probably will not perceive this fact at first, its patterns will become noticeable after a brief period. Those patterns will then become distinct phrases and images. Once the page fully "emerges," the viewer will begin to pick out information that is relevant to him or her. Thus, the more difficult it is for the viewer to pick out what is important, the less successful will be your design.

above • Here is a Web page with all of the important information blocked over as gray bars so that you can see the visual emphasis of the layout.

below • Here is the same page designed by Umberto Abeja with all of the information in place. Notice how your eye travels around the page. This is known as "eye flow."

right • Humans always look for patterns. Here is an example. What do you see when you look at these drawings? Butterflies? Birds? Bats? It is natural for us to try to make sense out of everyday things. It is no different with digital interfaces.

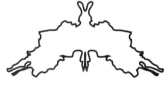

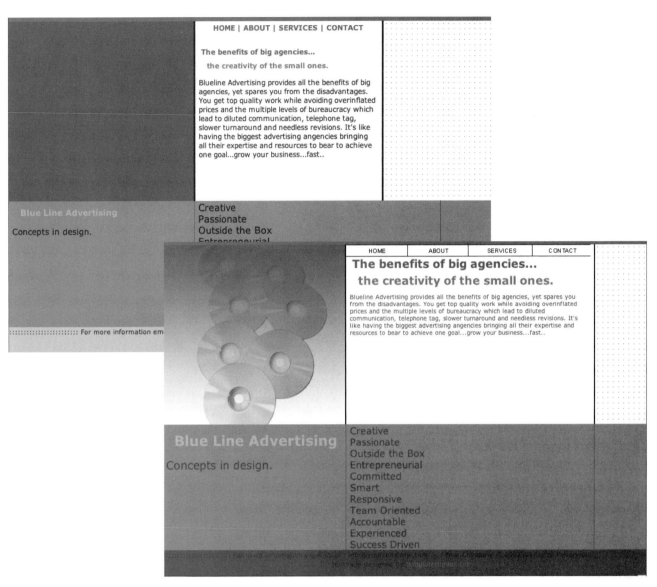

above • This is a dull Web page. The solid mass of undistinguished gray makes it almost impossible to find the content.

below • What is needed is contrast and balance. Splashes of color, large and small type, and images will prioritize the visual space.

This sequence is called the *visual hierarchy of design.* A visual hierarchy allows you to create a discernible system by arranging headings, subheadings, and images that give the page a structure. This then gives the viewer an understanding of the document's major structural characteristics at a glance. As a designer, you need to organize your menus, submenus, buttons, and text so that the appropriate elements receive the proper prominence you assign them in the hierarchy.

To clarify this concept, do this little exercise. Look at the picture above of an admittedly ineffective visual design. Think about how you might improve it. Now sketch your thoughts. How might you rearrange the different elements to make a more effective design? A word of caution: Don't allow the design to get in the way of the message. Here are a few other tips to get you started:

- If it's essential, make it bigger. A headline created in a larger font says, "I'm important!"
- The more important the content, the higher up on the page it should be placed.
- Divide your information into clearly defined areas.
- Break up long sentences or paragraphs into bulleted lists.

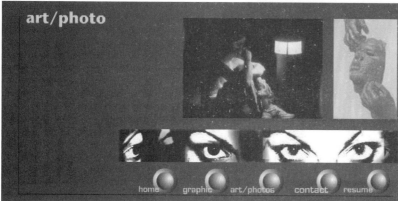

An intriguing interface designed by Hilda Vasquez. Notice that all of the design elements (such as the buttons and the titles) are consistently placed on each page.

The Importance of Consistency

Good navigation design is the first key to design success, as you learned in the previous chapter. Consistency is second. Consistency lays a solid foundation for visitor interaction with your interface, making the experience comfortable and seamless. Approach interface design with the objective of making it elegant and easier to use. This is largely a matter of balancing the layout.

Consistency is achieved a number of different ways. First and foremost, the person viewing your port should be able to understand the layout. You already know the value of a consistent navigational system. The same principles apply to backgrounds, page designs, and titles, as well as multimedia. The following subsections delve into some specifics of this important guideline.

Use Grids

Your interface must be functional as well as visually appealing. The idea is to draw the user into the material using a combination of words and pictures that all relate

to your theme. A poorly designed page will make it difficult for the viewer to understand how to find items of interest. Therefore, positioning graphical and text elements consistently throughout your project is a vital factor to your project's success (see the color insert for an example). It quickly increases the user's confidence in navigating your digital port.

Time for another exercise: Select three pages from three different Web sites. Try to determine whether a grid was used. How? Look for the placement of the different interface elements on each of the pages. What do you notice? An example of a consistent grid layout appears on the next page.

Put All Vital Elements "Above the Fold"

Most interfaces are designed for either a CD-ROM (800 ×600) or the Web (760 × 410). The 410-pixel height measurement is the space available, minus the browser window. Techies refer to this space as being "above the fold" (a carryover from newspaper lingo). This is where the most important information should always appear.

Sample layout boxes (left column design examples)

Introduction

I can distinctly remember the day, in 1976, when I told my boyfriend, that artists do not use computers. We were on our way to the University of Miami Computing Center to run a set of calculations for his Master's Thesis. He was carrying huge boxes of punch cards, encoded ōwith thousands of tiny holes. I was particularly adamant that day, that I would never use a computer to create art. "Artists," I said,"use paints and pencils." "Well, you really should think about it," he said. I made a mental note deciding never to think about it again.

Many years later, I found myself revisiting the subject of computers and artists. It was 1981 and I was sitting in a faculty meeting. I was teaching Color and Composition classes, along with Television Art and Television Production. The Director of Education, was discussing the future of computers and the College. He declared that computers would become an integral part of the curriculum at the Art Institute of Fort Lauderdale. He further stated that he was looking for volunteers, who would be willing to be trained on computers. These individuals would then bring the information back to t >he college and begin the development of a new curriculum. They would be "on the cutting edge of technology" and assume leadership rolls at the college.

At the time, I was heavily involved with television production classes. I was teaching the creation of artwork specifically for the television medium. It was during this time that I began to first acknowledge that the computer might possibly play a role in art. I had repeatedly asked for some computer equipment that could be utilized for this process, but had been turned down. I was told that the costs were just too great. If I could convince the College to allow me to participate in this computer training program, I would be able to find a way to take the computer to the production studio and accomplish my goal.

Shortly after the meeting, I was selected to participate in the computer training program. I was flown to Pittsburgh and given a lovely hotel room to stay in for two weeks. My partner in this endeavor was Paul Wol -lschleger, another instructor from the College. We met the evening before classes were to begin to discuss our anxieties as artists. We were both very skeptical about the future of art and the computer. We wondered about the artist being replaced by the computer. Would art evolve to become a mindless medium? We vowed that we would not allow that to happen.

(Additional overlapping sample layouts repeat portions of the above text, including passages such as:)

When all of the computers had been assembled, we were told that this would be the "big moment". We would insert the disks in their drives, turn on the monitor and finally, turn on the computer. When that was done, we would hear a happy little "beep" indicating that the computer was beginning its startup process. All around the room, there were happy little beeps as each machine was engaged. That is until I turned on mine. It ga´ve out a short "pop" and a little mushroom cloud of white smoke came wafting out from the back of the machine. Now I didn't want to seem like a hysterical female, so I casually raised my hand and called to Ver Hague, "Excuse me, Mr. Ver Hague, my machine is smoking... is that all right?"

From across the room, I could see Ver Hague's head pop up. He rushed through the maze of computers and people, shut down my computer, my monitor and pulled out my disk. As he did, Ver Hague took a deep breath and said, ?"No, generally computers do not smoke when you turn them on." The class erupted with laughter. I turned a deep shade of red and could feel the sweat starting to trickle down my neck. I thought to myself, "Please, God, just take me now!"

As can probably be imagined, at this point, you either run away from the whole thing, too embarrassed to continue; or

---

"Artists," I said,"use paints and pencils."

"Excuse me, Mr. Ver Hague, my machine is smoking... is that all right?"

---

from top • **It's very tiring on the eyes to read text across the full width of screen.**

Notice the difference when the type is set in narrower columns. Less left-to-right eye movement means less strain on the eyes.

Add negative space between the columns and breathing room to the page. Things don't seem so crowded now and nothing gets in the way of the message.

Subheadlines instill relaxed visual contrast and eye flow. HTML gives you six levels of headings, but that doesn't mean you should use all six in a single page.

Name of Web Site	Common Interface Elements
1.	1.
	2.
	3.
	4.
	5.
2.	1.
	2.
	3.
	4.
	5.
3.	1.
	2.
	3.
	4.
	5.

Find 3 websites and compare them for visual cohesiveness.

As a rule, that includes your name, the areas of the site you wish your visitors to visit, and major navigational icons. The idea is that the most important information should always be above the fold line or (in this case) fully on the screen, where it can be easily seen. Regardless of where the icons are placed (top, side or bottom) and as long as the critical information is available to the viewer, the navigational experience will be a good one.

Set Large Amounts of Type in Narrow Columns

As I've explained, large amounts of type that run across the entire screen can be really difficult to read. This restriction can present a design challenge if, say, your

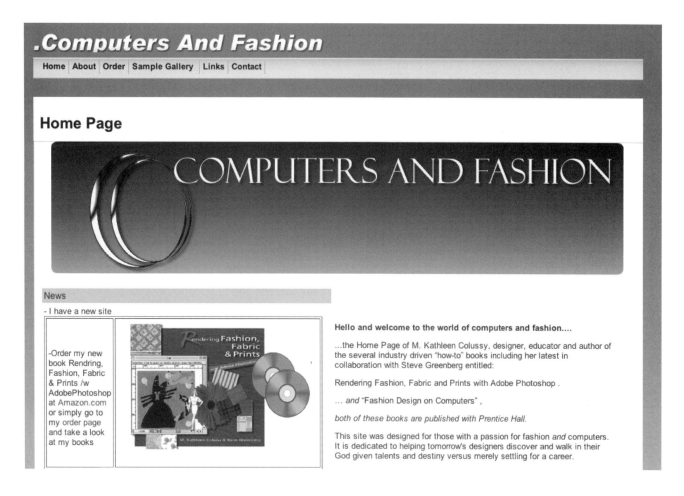

This amazing Web site, designed by M. Kathleen Colussy, is an excellent example of the use of white space and a grid. The site is easy to read and to navigate.

resume comprise a great deal of text. One way to solve this problem is to create a "resting place" for the eyes. Break up the text space into narrow columns. You see this technique commonly used in newspapers. Just be careful not to place two long columns of text side by side. That will make it even more difficult on the viewer.

Use Subheads to Break Up Information

Your pages will be more visually appealing to your visitors if you include in your design both headlines and subheadlines. Subheads break up large blocks of text and direct the reader to each section according to subject. This helps increase the overall legibility of the page. Without subheads, the user has more difficulty seeing

major patterns quickly and, therefore, interpreting information. Subheads are considered essential when a design page contains more than 500 words.

Five more tips to help you design text and subheads more effectively are:

- Use color to make your subheads stand out.
- Decide on a few important subheadings; don't use too many.
- Use headings and subheadings consistently.
- Don't boldface everything, because then nothing stands out.
- Split up large amounts of text into more easily digestible chunks.

Design to Scroll or Not to Scroll

Users say they don't like to scroll. Studies say otherwise. What's a designer to do? You have two choices:

Although the internet has made great strides since its humble beginnings in the 1960s, it is still a relatively young medium. In 1991, when the World Wide Web, (as it would be later be called) really started, a standardized language called HTML was invented by Tim Berners-Lee with assistance from Robert Caillau. The Web really caught on in the late 1990s and by this time, people were beginning to experience a compelling way to communicate ideas and information. With this new level of interaction, users came to expect a greater level of sophistication. Unfortunately, due to major telecommunication restrictions, it just wasn't possible to display the full range of media over the Web. Today, we are still experiencing many of these same technical limitations. Although faster access systems are beginning to become available, they are not in every community and the relative costs to the user are still relatively high.

All authoring programs allow you to import various forms of media, such as Flash and Director files, sound, and video.

- Create lots of short pages with smaller amounts of text on each page.
- Create longer pages with lots of type on each page.

Each approach has advantages and disadvantages. Small amounts of text and a few links mean little or no scrolling is required. There are many who endorse this strategy. The only problem is that it may take viewers several clicks through a number of pages before they find what they are looking for. The same is true backing out of the site. With fewer, but longer, pages, the user must scroll to see advance through the material, but there are fewer links, hence fewer ways to get lost. The important thing to remember is that the visitor will only scroll if there is something worth scrolling for! Whichever system you choose, make sure it is straightforward; don't add anything that isn't absolutely necessary.

Make Good Use of White Space

White space (also called negative space), as I explained in an earlier chapter, is the blank areas between the graphics and text in your design. White space is essential when large amounts of text are present, as it helps to guide the viewer's eye from one position to another.

As you might imagine, uncluttered pages make for a more relaxing and easy-to-follow experience. Some of the most effective magazine ads feature beautifully designed pages with plenty of negative space. White space is also a great navigational tool, as it can tell readers where one feature ends and another begins.

Too often, inexperienced designers try to cram in as much information as they can. This is a mistake. In short, think of the most stylish house you ever visited. Chances are it was that open space that really grabbed your attention. Now picture that same house with tons and tons of clutter—not a very attractive picture. White space is elegant and pure. Don't clutter up your design space with too many graphics. Keep the combined weight of the graphics down to about half of the available space. The Web page designed by M. Kathleen Colussy in this chapter, shows how white space helps the visitor find the information.

Multimedia and the Digital Portfolio

The term *multimedia* means, simply, using or including several types of media. These media may contain or transmit many kinds of material— text, graphics, drawings, video, animation, and audio. In the early days of the Internet, it was a "static" medium, capable only of displaying text to present information. Thanks to advances in technology, today, not only larger amounts, but all kinds of information can be transmitted in a matter of seconds, depending on the kind and speed of connection you have to the online community.

above • There are literally thousands of sites that offer free music and sound effects. Here is one such site, www.partnersinrhyme.com.

below • There are many Web sites that will help you to find copyright-free music. Go to your favorite Web search engine, type in "copyright-free music" and you will get innumerable pages to check out.

You are a multimedia artist; as such, you will most certainly want to include some form of multimedia as part of your project. What you choose to include will depend largely on the projected final output; I explained this at length in Chapter 5. For the purposes of this discussion, we're going to assume you will produce a project that is intended for both the Web and CD. And because the Internet has more limitations than CD output, we will consider lower specifications to make our multimedia selections.

I don't recommend using any of the popular multimedia editing programs that come with sample sounds and music. Too many others will be using the same thing. And, remember, your objective is to demonstrate your originality, your creativity.

As you might imagine, designing a basic Web site or CD PowerPoint presentation does not require as much time and effort as when they include audio and video files, so it's important to learn some techniques for optimizing the quality of the final product when you plan to include the more labor- and time-intensive audio and video components to your digital portfolio.

Adding Audio to Your Portfolio

In conjunction with other design elements, well-chosen audio can make your digital portfolio really stand out. Yet too many people treat music as an afterthought, rather than a focal point. Music should, in fact, be one of the first things you think of in the process of laying out your portfolio. Just as animation used well improves the narrative flow, the right music can enhance the story you are trying to tell. Think about how scary music adds to the experience of a horror movie.

Audio files are used for digital design in several different ways—audio tracks, sound effects, music, and voice files all can be embedded in digital projects. Music is probably the most common use of audio, although sound effects and speech are quite popular as well. Online instructors, for example, frequently use sound files to "speak" to their students in the same way they would in a lecture hall. And sound effects used to accompany button clicks can give effective clues as to the purpose of his navigational tool. Music can be used in the form of anything from a short recorded piece to an entire musical composition or album available for downloading. Pop musical groups have been using the web for several years to promote their work. Even the music industry has discovering the web as a promotion device.

Never assume that any music is out of copyright. Always double-check with the accredited author or current owner of the content. The last thing you want is to be sued for copyright infringement. The U.S. government clearly specifies what constitutes copyright, so take some time to find out the specifics of the law. Here are a few Web sites that will help you to learn more about copyright laws and music: www.reach.net/~scherer/p/copyrit1.htm; and the Library of Congress Web site at www.copyright.gov. In brief, you may use up to but not than four measures of any piece of copyright-protected music without being in violation. If you figure that there are four beats in a measure, that equals 16 beats of music.

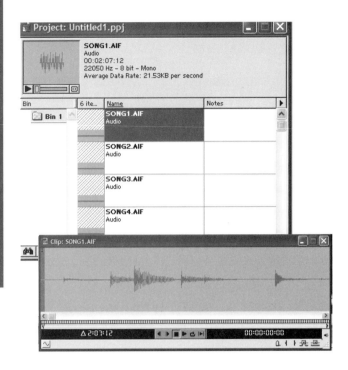

above • Adobe Premiere allows you import various types of audio files for use in your digital interface, and you can edit the music.

below • Once the music has been imported, you can edit the music to delete unwanted sound that may cause your files to become too large.

Preparing Sound for Multimedia

Adding sound to your site involves these basic steps:

Locate and acquire the audio.
Capture the audio.
Edit the audio.
Compress and encode the audio.
Add audio file to the multimedia project.
Inform users that appropriate players or plug-ins may be needed.

We'll go through these steps one at a time.

Locate and Acquire the Audio

Do you need audio? Would you have been as scared without the theme from Jaws? It's no longer a question of if you should add music to your project, what rather, what's the best way to accomplish it. However, before you can place anything on your Web page, you must first consider how you will obtain it. You can, if you're talented musically, create your own music; most people have to obtain it from a secondary source. I'll tell you about four ways here.

There are literally thousands of places on the Web to obtain free (or almost free) music. These sites feature every conceivable form of sounds and music (as well as textures and video). The quality can vary quite a bit, so take your time and shop around. Check out your local computer store as well; and consult the appendix for a couple of places to start your search.

You can also purchase, usually for a one-time license fee, CDs that come with special sound effects and all sorts of interesting sound tracks. These CDs can be purchased at the popular computers and online. To locate lots of music, type "free looped audio tracks" into your favorite Internet search engine. You'll be amazed at the number of free Web sites that offer inexpensive or free music. You make one small payment, usually about $30, and you can use these professional music recordings as many times as you like for any multimedia project you create. In addition, you can use this royalty-free music for other projects such as video, broadcast, stage, or live presentations. The only limitation is that you may not distribute the music to anyone else. Only you paid for, hence have the right, to use the music.

A third source of music is that which has reverted to the "public domain." All music produced by an American composer or lyricist before 1922 is now out of copyright and can be used without payment. No one can claim ownership of any music that has reverted to the public domain, and so these songs and/or compositions may be used without paying royalties to anyone. You

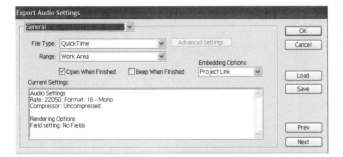

As you begin to think about the music you will use in your production, remember that music says as much about you as your art. Soft jazz, tension-driven trance beats, classical pieces all offer clues as to who you are. But think of your listeners, too. Rhythms that repeat over and over, for example, may be annoying to them. Remember, there's a subliminal message in everything you include as part of your production, so choose wisely—express yourself, yes, but include your audience in your decision-making process.

above • In this Adobe Premiere project window, the compressor is set to "uncompressed". The audio file will be adjusted first. The final compression system will be added as the file is exported to it final destination.

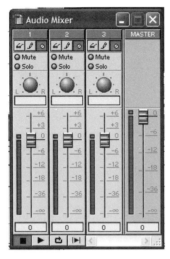

right • Most video editing programs, such as Adobe Premiere come with a sound mixer. Although not quite as complex as the professional mixers, these "mini" mixers offer a wide range of enhancement features for your sound files.

As long as you save your sound files in a compatible format, most multimedia programs will be able to import them.

never know, you just might find something that fits the look and feel of your project. Public domain music can be easily located by typing "free public domain music" into your Internet search engine of choice.

You can also hire a musician. And it may not be as expensive as you think. Why not barter for it? There are many fine musicians around who would be more than happy to cut some tracks for you in exchange for, say, your design skills to produce a poster announcing their upcoming gig. Or they may be willing to do it in exchange for receiving credit (and a contact number) somewhere in your project. Leave flyers in your school, neighborhood music store, coffee shop, or place of worship. Don't forget to check online forums. Chances are you'll find a few up-and-coming artists who would welcome the opportunity to have an audience to hear their work in a digital environment.

Capture the Audio

Once you have selected the audio you plan to include in your digital portfolio, you are ready to capture it into your computer. Capturing an audio file from a CD is a fairly simple process. Just open the audio editor you are using and hit "record" while the CD is playing in the CD-ROM drive. Some editors allow you to capture the file directly off the CD. (Note: If your editor can't "find" the audio, you may have to configure your computer to receive the audio signal. To do this, locate the internal sound manager and change its settings so that it knows to receive its audio input from the CD-ROM drive.

Edit the Audio

Music editing is a challenging and complicated task. Fortunately, there are dozens of programs on the market to help you with this, as well as several inexpensive shareware audio editors available online. Windows users can use SoundEdit Pro or GoldWave's Digital Audio Editor. Macintosh users have many choices as well. Two of many are Sound Studio and Audacity are shareware programs with many of the features of high-end editors. All offer

above • This awesome Web site by Jair Acevedo recognizes that the visitor may not have the latest Flash viewer. The visitor is informed that a new player may be needed, and then is given the Web address from which the player can be downloaded. Thoughtful and practical.

right • Here are a few of the many audio effects Adobe Premiere has to offer.

good, reliable ways to capture and edit sound. Full-blown audio editors, such as Adobe Audition (once known as CoolEdit Pro) or Sonic Foundry's Sound Forge XP, can be quite pricey, but they offer every conceivable effect and filter imaginable.

Compress and Encode the Audio

After you edit your sound, you will need to prepare it for the multimedia project. A number of settings that address the quality and size of your audio files can be adjusted. Digital audio files are large (the better the sound quality, the larger the file). Your favorite song, for example (44.1 kHz, 16-bit stereo), takes up about 10 megabytes per minute. Even with the fastest digital subscriber line (DSL) connection, it will take a while to download enough of the clip before it even begins to play. To speed up this process in your project (so as not to "lose" your viewers), save the audio clip in a format such as WAV, AIFF, or

MP3. AIFF is the standard for Mac computers; WAV files can play on both Windows and Mac platforms. For more compression, use MP3, which is great for reducing file size while maintaining acceptable standards of quality. Just keep in mind that music is generally enhanced and edited while still in an uncompressed format. Compression is usually done after the editing is complete.

The rule of thumb where audio compression is concerned is: Use the lowest possible setting to reduce file size without significantly reducing sound quality. As I have mentioned before, projects designed to go on the Web will be much smaller than those created for CD because the needs of the two platforms are so different. Most audio editing programs have a preview mode that allows you to hear the compressed music before you complete your final save. Experiment and find the audio level that is acceptable for your project. Here are some settings that can apply to both Web and CD audio usage:

- 22,050 Hz sample rate (also called *sampling frequency*)
- 16-bit resolution
- Mono channel setting

You will want to compress your sound files at some point in the editing process, although it is generally best

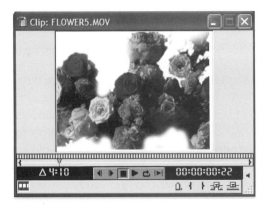

Clip: FLOWER5.MOV

△ 4:10 ◄ ► ■ ► ⟳ |◄ 00:00:00:22 ◄

Video can be opened and previewed in small window before it is added to the timeline of the video editing program.

Once upon a time, video was shot in sequence and the clips were edited in the order in which they were shot. This was known as "linear editing," because the finished product was built as edit decisions were made. That meant if a mistake was made in the early part of the edit, the entire video had to be rebuilt. Today, with digital "non-linear" editing, all edit decisions can made as the project is built. Nonlinear editing allows you to test edits and preview the finished product before exporting to more permanent media.

to leave your sound uncompressed as you work with it. You never want to compress a file twice. It makes the sound muddy. So complete every little special effect first, then compress at the very end.

Here are some additional guidelines on creating quality sound:

- *Normalize your files.* Most audio editors have a "normalize" command, which lets you equalize your sound files. This keeps the file from being too loud or too soft in certain spots, by creating a steady, stable signal.
- *Purchase and use a good set of headphones or speakers.* How can you tell if the sound quality is good if it's coming from that three-and-a-half-inch computer speaker? You don't have to spend a fortune to be able to filter out the ambient noise in your room.
- *Test your audio on different computers.* Run sound files on different platforms just you do text files. Play them through the big speakers (if available) and on the built-in computer speaker. Make sure the sound quality is acceptable to you in both environments.
- *Never work on the original file.* Experiment, play around, make changes, go crazy, but don't accidentally mess up or erase your original file! Save frequently under different file names.
- *Keep it simple.* Just because you can add major sound effects and bizarre sounds doesn't mean you should! A good piece of music always stands alone.

Add Audio Files to the Multimedia Project

As I've said before, the type multimedia program you select will determine the method of audio implementation. Generally, audio files are imported to the authoring program, where they are added at key points throughout the production. As an example, theme music might play throughout the project and sound effects might be added to buttons. Audio files can be set up to play using two systems: *nonstreaming* and streaming.

Nonstreaming, or static, audio files are fully embedded in the project. These files (and all other parts of the production) must be fully loaded before they can begin to play or be heard. And, again, audio files can be quite large, meaning that download times on the Web and spin-up times on a CD can be lengthy, make these files as small as possible.

Streaming audio files are not attached to the project file. They are *referenced* via programming scripts. Once "called," the audio file is downloaded to a player, where it begins to play. Probably you figured out that the main disadvantage to using streaming audio files is that you need to know some programming to use the technology. Additionally, the user may need to have a special player to hear the audio.

Inform That Players or Plug-ins May Be Needed

The final step in this process is to inform your users if they will need an additional program to hear your audio. Nothing is more frustrating than waiting for a file to load only to have nothing happen once the file is on the screen. If you created a Web site, supply a link to download the missing player. If you are offering your project on CD, include the file as part of the disk. You won't be sorry.

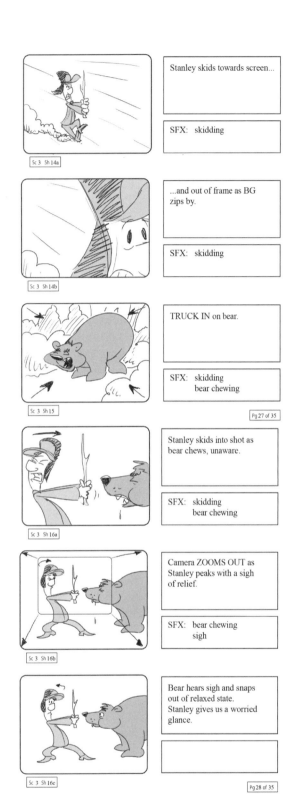

Randy Gossman conceptualized this entertaining storyboard. Notice that the descriptions clearly indicate the movement of the actors within each frame. The camera action (such as a zoom-in or a pan) is indicated as well. A good storyboard leaves nothing to chance.

The Effect of Sound Effects

Sound effects enhance a visual or textual experience. Think about the text example I used in a previous chapter: "It was a dark stormy evening. The wind was howling through the trees. Occasionally, a branch would whip against my window, and I could hear the distant sound of thunder. I knew a storm was coming." How many sounds would it take to create the audio track for this little scene? Would the scene be effective without them? Doubtful.

Even special-effects button sounds can really add to your production. They're kind of like sprinkles on top of ice cream: You don't need them, but they sure add a lot! Just be sure you select sounds that will enhance the button and not "overstay its welcome." For instance, the famous Homer Simpson "Duh!" sound was used in one production I viewed. It was funny the first time, but after about 20 clicks, it became annoying.

Meeting the Video Challenge

What's your favorite type of television show? News? Reality? Talk? Drama? Sitcom? Do you know why? Because you are entertained or informed. When it comes to making a decision regarding the use of video in your digital portfolio, you must do the same, either inform or entertain. We live in a video-oriented society, so it's only natural that you would want to include video in your multimedia project. Unfortunately, video is the most challenging of all forms of multimedia content to deliver digitally. One second of uncompressed video requires 27 megabytes of disk space—a huge amount. Needless to say, this takes careful preparation, which I'll explain here.

Preparing Video for Multimedia

Let's say that you have decided to make a short video to display one of your 3-D sculptures; or perhaps to explain your personal thoughts on design. Here are the basic steps involved in producing video files for your multimedia project:

Shoot and capture the video.
Edit the video.
Compress the video.
Add the video file to the multimedia project.

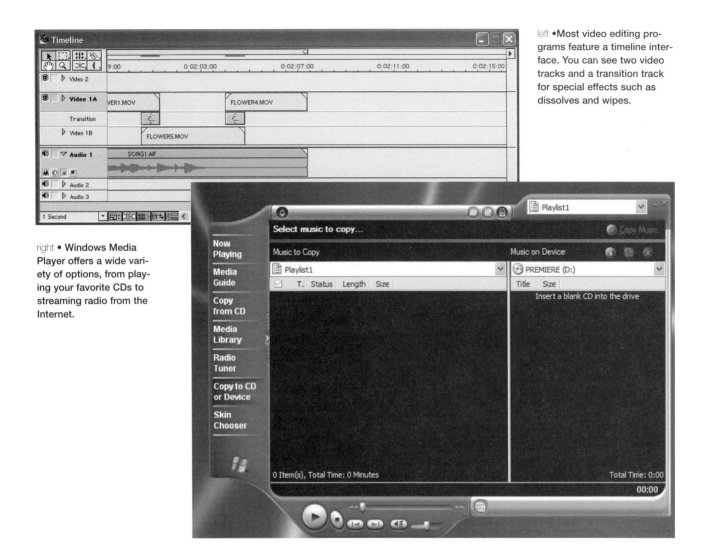

left •Most video editing programs feature a timeline interface. You can see two video tracks and a transition track for special effects such as dissolves and wipes.

right • Windows Media Player offers a wide variety of options, from playing your favorite CDs to streaming radio from the Internet.

Inform users that appropriate players or plug-ins may be necessary.

Shoot and Capture the Video

You may think of yourself as a budding Stanley Kubrick or Francis Ford Coppola, and you may want to produce the next great video masterpiece, but that takes time and lots of money, so for the purposes of your digital portfolio, let's discuss a more practical (and cost-effective) approach to video production. We'll start with a good, basic production recommendation: Use a tripod for your camera. You want your camera to be as stable as possible. This will really improve the quality of your video footage. In addition, minimizing the differences between frames contributes to a better overall video compression. A shaky camera doesn't allow the video

program compression algorithms to effectively reduce the size of the file. More movement equals more information, and more information makes the file larger.

Because the size of your final video will be small (most Web-based videos are no larger than 320 x 240) you need to be aware of a number of basic shooting strategies:

- *When shooting a close-up, leave a little breathing room around your subject.* Close-up shots are very important when the format is small, where a large group of people will look like ants. An extreme close-up will look like an image in a horror movie.
- *Keep backgrounds simple and neutral.* A video camera will try to compensate for too-white or black-saturated colors. Again, be on the alert for

anything that might distract from your message. Move the camera movement slowly and steadily. On a tiny screen, even the smallest movements become exaggerated.

- *Don't forget to turn off the timecode function on your camera.* Tape one shot, rewind the camera, and review the shot in the viewfinder. An extra 10 minutes here might save you an entire day of reshooting.
- *Create a storyboard and use it.* The clear mark of a video amateur is someone who shoots and shoots with no concept in mind.
- *Avoid starting and stopping the camera dozens of times.* This will result in a lot of jump cuts or shots that have no continuity. The overall look of the shots should clean and simple. And remember, sometimes a still shot can tell your story as effectively as a moving shot. Again, the screen is small, so a busy shot will difficult to focus on.
- *Leave a little extra time at the beginning and end of each shot.* It takes video a couple of seconds to get "up to speed." If, for example, you want the image of a dog to run across the view screen of the camera, turn on the camera early. It's difficult to control exactly when the pup will decide to run, so you want to be ready and the camera to be rolling. Believe me, this will make your editing a lot easier.
- *Follow your storyboard and keep track of your shots.* There's nothing worse than completing your shoot only to discover that you forgot one shot and have to go back out and shoot again.
- *Avoid excess adjustments to the camera.* Zooming in and out or panning left and right can make low-frame-rate movies difficult to view.
- *Don't forget lighting.* The camera sets the iris in the lens according to the brightest light in the environment. It's important to play back the video and look closely at the quality of the shots.
- *Consider all the angles.* A creative videographer examines the various visual elements in the viewfinder frame and determines the best possible shot. For example, an unbalanced asymmetrical composition can give a sense of motion. Even a lamp can look visually exciting under the right conditions.
- *Create the illusion of depth.* We see the world in three dimensions, but video flattens out any sub-

ject matter. To minimize this effect, always place your camera at an angle so you can see at least two sides of the person or object in your viewfinder.

Once the shooting is completed, you are ready to capture in the video, which means converting it into digital format. If you are converting video from an analog device, such as a VCR, you will need to purchase a video capture card (a different type of card from the one you use for gaming). If you own one of the newer digital camcorders, you will not need the card, as the incoming signal is already digital. You will also need a program that captures video, along with the necessary cables to connect the camera to the computer. In most cases, you then simply hit Play on your VCR or video camera and select Record in the video capture software program. Video footage appears in a viewing area, and once saved, becomes available to be edited.

You'll have two options for capturing video. The first is to simply record the uncompressed video as-is, that is, with no compression. The video is edited and compressed at the end. This is a good plan, as long as you're aware that the uncompressed video will take up huge amounts of space on your hard drive. The second is to encode "on the fly" (for example to MPEG). The disadvantage of this method is that there is a gap in the processing between the time the video comes into the computer and the time it takes to compress it. This sometimes leads to dropped frames and a "jerky" video. So, if you have enough space on your hard drive, I recommend you capture your video without compression.

Here are a few more video capture suggestions:

- Give your computer as much available RAM as possible. If 512 megs of RAM is good, 1 GIG is better.
- Don't run any other programs while capturing video. They take up valuable computer resources.
- Only record what you need, unless you have extra hard drives.
- Select a low frame rate for the capture. Use 8 to 15 frames per second. You may need to tinker around with this one. The lower the frame rate, the faster the load, but at a cost. You don't want to totally forgo the illusion of motion. Try to find a happy medium. Remember that the quality of each frame is more important than the number of frames per second.

- Make sure the video window size is no larger than 320 x 240 pixels. Currently, this is really the most the Web can handle.
- Purchase a good video capture board. And remember the adage "you get what you pay for": A $199-dollar board does not have the capability to capture full-motion, fullframe video.
- Experiment with your capture settings before doing the actual work. Get the settings right now and you won't have so much work to do later.

Edit the Video

If you want to add a movie to your digital portfolio, a video editor is essential. Several video editors are available for both PCs and Macs, but all are somewhat feature-limited. That said, the two leading products are Adobe's Premiere and Apple's Final Cut Pro. They aren't cheap but they are the best, and as I just said above, you get what you pay for. Both products allow you to take all of your movies clips and assemble them on a timeline. You can add audio and innumerable special effects. And, if you can afford it, Adobe's After Effects is another excellent addition to your multimedia toolbox. It can animate your titles and move objects along motion paths; plus it offers many filters and effects, such as scaling, color enhancements, and masks.

Here are my guidelines on editing:

- Don't clutter the screen with too many words. Remember, content rules.
- When in doubt, use a basic transition, such as a "cut," the quick change from one shot to another. A cut is the cleanest form of editing.
- Don't use transitional effects such as slow dissolves. Leave that for the mushy, sentimental movies. Too many dissolves will put your viewer to sleep.
- Wipes are passé. Remember *Batman* or *Charlie's Angles*? Wipes were fun back then, but are considered old hat today.
- Always fade in from black at the beginning. Always fade out to black at the end of your production.
- Review the video. This is the most important guideline. You don't want to overlook a misspelled word, for example, which will jeopardize the impression your port makes on the viewer—people always remember the errors.

● ● ● Video and Audio Review Guidelines

- Don't shoot a minute of video until you have a clear concept of the project. A storyboard of the shots will help you to determine how many shots you will need and the length of each shot.
- Shoot three to five times the amount of video you think you will need for the project.
- Negotiate permission for any audio or video material that you will include in your portfolio.
- Obtain releases from every person who gives you material to use in your project. This includes video, images, and audio material.
- Consider using a commercial "voice" if you need a "voiceover" (a narrator). Strong regional accents will detract from the professional effect you are trying to achieve. If you can't afford a professional voice, ask your friends to audition for the job. You might be surprised! Just make sure your audio talent knows how to pronounce difficult or technical words and acronyms.
- Listen carefully to the ambient sounds during a recording session. Do you hear planes flying by or cars honking? Such sounds will distract from the professionalism of your production.
- Don't overwhelm the viewer with sound effects just because they are available. Remember what I said earlier, they get old fast.

Compress the Video

After you have edited your movie clips, you're ready to convert your video project into its final form, as a movie that can be played on a CD or Web site. This involves the process of compression, which as you know from earlier discussions, reduces the size of your video while maintaining acceptable quality. There are many different compression systems, or codecs, (compression/decompression) on the market today. The two most widely used ones are:

- Sorenson
- Cinepak

Which you'll choose is driven primarily by platform. Sorenson is most widely used by Macintosh users, although Cinepak is available for both Macs and PCs. Cinepak is widely used on both digital-video and

This interface, by Jair Acevedo, has embedded audio and video yet takes only moments to download. The trick? Small video files and even smaller audio files.

CD-ROMs. It has decent output quality and is included free with the QuickTime software. Its only drawback is that it has a very lengthy compression time.

Once the file is compressed, it can be saved and exported in one of several different formats. The most common are:

- Windows Media Player for Windows and Mac
- MPEG (Motion Picture Experts Group) for all platforms (including UNIX)
- RealNetworks RealOne for Mac and Windows
- QuickTime MOV for Mac and Windows

The first, Microsoft Windows Media Player, comes free with Windows (and a special Mac version can be downloaded). It is a universal player that supports more than 20 different file formats, including WAV, AVI, MPEG1, MPEG2, MIDI, MOV, MP3, QuickTime, and RealVideo. The player also supports Web-based streaming media, which enables the user to play back audio and video content without having to download the file from the Web. Once at the Web site, Windows Media Player instantaneously plays back the content that the viewer wants to see or hear.

Motion JPEG (M-JPEG, Joint Photographic Experts Group standard), or MPEG (Motion Photographic Experts Group standard), was introduced in QuickTime 2.5. It is considered a lossy (which, remember, means it degrades the information if used and resaved repeatedly) compression system codec. It produces bulky file sizes at 100 percent quality, but creates smaller file sizes than Cinepak. MPEG is a good choice for files intended for the Internet. MPEG compresses individual frames, which can then be played back. Compressing large amounts of video is a daunting task, so video capture boards that use the M-JPEG technique usually rely on dedicated encoder chips. The MPEG codec is included in most popular digital camcorders.

RealNetworks RealPlayer is a program that can transmit audio, video, text, and animation directly to your desktop. It uses streaming technology, which requires special server software, although some versions of the player are free. The user selects a file based on the connection speed, and the program optimizes the file for that speed. RealPlayer offers full-screen video capacity and enhanced sound quality.

QuickTime (movies saved with a .MOV file extension) is a popular cross-platform player that runs on Macintosh, Unix, and PC computers. This product has been around for quite a while, in many versions. On newer versions, the video starts playing before the entire file downloads. And, importantly, QuickTime is free, which naturally makes it very attractive. No other application currently allows you to view a movie without first loading drivers. QuickTime offers high-quality video and audio/video.

An understanding of codecs and players is essential to the creation of video for multimedia. Regardless of which you choose, recognize that delivery will not be instantaneous; but by using the appropriate codecs and players, you'll deliver high-quality video that your audience won't mind waiting for. For most video projects, QuickTime is probably your best choice. It is an industry standard, and most computers have the necessary plug-in.

Add the Video File to the Multimedia Project

Once you have edited and compressed your video, it is ready to be placed in its final application. If you creat-

ed the video for a CD, it will be transferred to a multimedia program such as PowerPoint or Flash. You can create a button that loads the video for the enjoyment of the user. If the movie is being uploaded to the Web, you will embed it in an HTML document. On the Web page will be an invitation to the user to play the video; and, if accepted, the file will be streamed to the user's computer.

Inform Users That Appropriate Players or Plug-Ins May Be Necessary

This, you'll note, is the final step in all the procedures described in this chapter. It's important, so don't overlook it. In this case, offer more than one way to watch your video. For example, make the movie available in both QuickTime and RealPlayer formats. You never know what software the viewer will have, so cover your bases. Also, as a courtesy, offer your visitors the opportunity to load any plug-ins necessary to play the video by supplying links to the sites that have the required software players.

As CD and Web technologies continue to evolve, there will be new ways to bring multimedia to life. As a multimedia developer, your goal is to track the most popular types of players in order to attract the widest possible audience. ■

ANALOG SIGNAL: A signal based on an alternating current. The current is then modified in some way, usually by varying the frequency, in order to add information. Broadcast and telephone transmission have conventionally used analog technology.

CAPTURE VIDEO: To convert video from standard analog signal into digital format.

CD-RW (REWRITEABLE COMPACT DISK): Similar to a CD, except that a CD-RW disc can be written and erased up to 1,000 times.

COMPACT DISC (CD): A relatively small optical disc on which text, data, sounds, and visual images can be recorded with laser technology. The discs themselves can only be "burned" one time.

COMPRESSION: A system that reduces the size of multimedia files while attempting to maintain acceptable quality. There are many different compression systems, or codecs (compression/ decompression) on the market; the most widely used are Sorenson and Cinepak.

COPYRIGHT: The rights to an original literary, artistic, or musical work held by an individual or corporation. Additional rights may be gained in such areas as film, broadcasting, computer programs, trademarks, and many other materials. Unauthorized use of copyrighted materials is punishable by law, and can include fines and/or imprisonment.

CUT: A quick shift from one video shot to the other.

DISSOLVE: The slow transition from one video shot to another. Both shots are blended together for a brief period of time.

ENCODE AUDIO: Compress and prepare the audio for final output.

GRID: A system of horizontal and vertical lines that provides coordinates for designing a page layout.

NORMALIZE: In the context of audio, to equalize sound files. Most audio editors have a "normalize" command, to prevent audio from being too loud or too soft in certain areas, by creating a steady, stable signal.

STREAMING AUDIO: Audio files that are not embedded in the final production, but are referenced via programming scripts.

STORYBOARD (OR FLOWCHART): A diagram or visual device that shows a step-by-step progression. It can a simple drawing that maps out the way your portfolio will be navigated.

TIMECODE: A signal that contains a chronological record of the absolute time in a recording. Most video camera have a timecode feature that should be turned off before beginning a shoot.

TRIPOD: A three-legged stand used to steady a camera or video camera.

VIDEOGRAPHER: A person who engages in the profession of video production.

VISUAL HIERARCHY: A method of page design that organizes and prioritizes the contents of a page using size, prominence, and content relationships.

WIPE: The transition from video shot to another. One shot appears to "push" the other shot off the page. Wipes can appear from the left, right, top, or bottom of the screen.

11

Designer Checklists

Before we move on to the final topic in this book, presenting your portfolio, I want to review the many factors we've discussed that go into the design of a successful your digital portfolio. In this chapter, you'll find lists of questions that you can use as checklists, to ensure you have covered all that you need to before you put your portfolio "out there." Before we begin, though, I want you to recognize that your first (and probably second or third) multimedia design project will not be perfect. No one's is. Expect to make mistakes. Expect crazy things to happen. That's how you learn. Eventually, you will get it right.

Designer Checklist for Digital Portfolios

☐ *Did you define specific objectives for your project?* Quick! In 100 words or less, describe your design philosophy for your project interface. If you can't, then you're not ready to begin. This project is intended as a reflection of your design sensibilities and conception skills. To be seen as a cutting-edge designer, you must have a concept.

☐ *Is your project innovative?* What sets you apart from everyone else? What do you offer that is different from every other job applicant? Maybe it's your sense of humor. Or perhaps you use a clever animated character to introduce your work. Whatever style of interface you develop, try to bring something new and unique into the project (see the color insert for an example).

☐ *Do your pages have a consistent look and feel?* Most people do not navigate projects in a linear way. That is to say, you can't control the way your project will be viewed. Therefore, it is very important that all of your pages reflect a cohesive look. Potential employers should always be aware of who you are and where they are while viewing the project. Use logos, colors, or design elements, but use them consistently. A lack of consistency communicates an unprofessional image.

☐ *Have you included all of the necessary information in your interface?* Does your interface include:
   A statement of philosophy or career objective?
   A "gallery" of your work?
   Enough pieces to give a complete picture of you as an artist?
   A "where to contact me" page?

☐ *Did you give credit to contributors, such as musical talent?* Include a credits page in your presentation, if necessary. This acknowledges that you under-

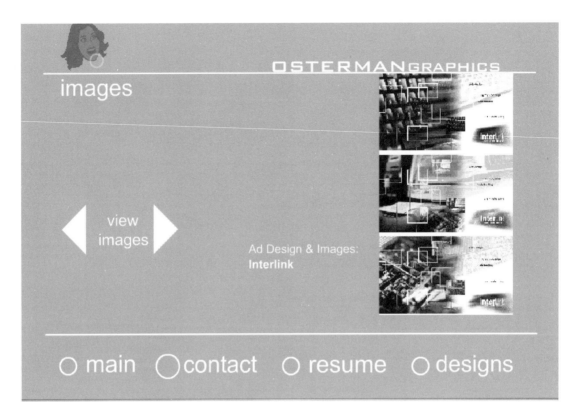

images

OSTERMANGRAPHICS

view
images

Ad Design & Images:
Interlink

○ main　○ contact　○ resume　○ designs

This playful interface was developed by Jessica Osterman. It has a
clear navigation system, yet establishes her sense of humor.

stand copyright laws, as well as protecting you
against lawsuits.

☐ *Are your pages designed so they are easy to read?*
Create a menu so the reader does not have to scroll
down the page to locate important information.
Start with a clever animated opening, but keep
your home page simple. You want to engage the
viewer right off the bat. A well-organized, easy-to-
comprehend home page will encourage the user to
explore your site further.

☐ *Are your links clearly labeled?* Don't make the user
guess what a button does. Go ahead and use a cute
icon in place of a word; just make sure it clearly represents that section of the port, such as. The same goes
for text links: Make them clearly descriptive, such as
Objectives, Resume, Gallery, Personal Philosophy,
Resume, Technical Skills, Contact Me. Links should
always reflect the skills you are marketing and the
field in which you are seeking employment.

☐ *Did you showcase your best work?* If you have 25
pieces of art, determine which are the weakest and

pull them out. There are two related reasons for
this. First, by including too many, chances are
viewers won't take the time to go them all; second,
that means they might miss your best selections—
meaning you might miss out on being the candidate of choice. Choose only your most pertinent
work for inclusion in the port.

☐ *Did you use text in a creative way?* Vary your text
styles to emphasize the most important parts of
your interface. Utilize different sizes, different
fonts, and different attributes (italics, color, and
bold) to highlight information and create a site
that is pleasing to the eye.

☐ *Did you include thumbnails of your work?* One of
the best ways to display a digital gallery is to use
small thumbnails as links to larger versions of
your art. Thumbnails can be created as either
rollovers (where the image pops up on the screen)
or as links (where a mouse click opens the image
in a separate window). This is especially effective
if you have six or more images.

☐ *Did you exercise restraint in your use of sound and
animation?* Don't clutter up your beautiful interface with a lot of pointless distractions. If an

image, animation, or sound doesn't enhance your design, don't use it. Aside from slowing download times, not all animations will work in all browsers.

☐ *Have you tested your site to ensure it works properly before posting it?* Take the time necessary to test your links. Do it often; occasionally, links get lost or damaged so verify they are in working order. And don't forget to update address and telephone changes when they occur.

☐ *Do you maintain a flowchart that represents where the project links are located?* Fancy or simple, on computer file or napkin, it doesn't really matter as long as you keep a well-developed mapping of your interface. Nonlinear programs allow you to adjust if you change your mind along the way, but linear programs can be very unforgiving, so the more completely you track your interface, the less likely you will experience problems.

☐ *Do the icons and images artistically and logically reflect the look and feel of the project?* Let's say you decide to create an interface around a travel theme. While creating your buttons, you choose an image map of the United States to act as your Gallery button. Will that make sense to the user? Probably not. Again, test your ideas on several people to get feedback.

☐ *Do you provide regular visual guidance?* Do you give visual clues to viewers that they are where they meant to be? That is, if after they click the Gallery button, will it be clear that they are indeed in the gallery area? Does text or graphics indicate that the transfer has been successful? Would a sound clip help?

☐ Have you decided between vector- or raster-based graphics as the primary element of the interface? If you want to increase the speed (and download time) of your project, always use vector-based graphics. But if you have lots of pictures that must be displayed, using raster-based images is your only option.

Design Elements Checklist

☐ *Do you have (or need) a grid?* Grids help to organize your material into a logical sequence. Design one and try placing your objects on the page. Do you like the results?

● ● ● **Link Lookup**

There are a number of different online companies that will check your site links for free. (But if you like the result, the company asks you to purchase the service.) Here are a couple of sites to check out for this purpose:

LinkCheck v4: www.poisontooth.com/linkcheck
Link Validation Spider: www.dead-links.com
HTML Toolbox: www.netmechanic.com/index.htm
Web Page Purifier: www.delorie.com/web/purify.html
Web Page Backward Compatibility Viewer: www.delorie.com/web/wpbcv.html

☐ *Have you made good color connections?* You've made the home page background color a deep emerald green. Should the gallery section be vivid yellow? Number one, that's not a very uniform color system, but more importantly, yellow may not be the best choice to feature your designs. Is there adequate contrast between the type, images, and background? Unusual colors may be fine for certain projects, but good design is the name of the game where your art is concerned. Is the on-screen text readable?

☐ *Is text laid out effectively?* Can the viewer tell the difference between body text and text that act as links to another area of the portfolio? Did you check for spelling errors?

☐ *Is there an understandable navigational menu?* Don't leave your viewers wondering how to get there from here.

☐ *Is your galley properly "curated?"* The gallery can feature a self-timed art show, a series of forward and back buttons that navigate the viewer through the work, or a series of clever rollovers. Whatever method you use, make sure it shows the work to its best advantage.

☐ *Are interface buttons logical and in good working order?* Most people understand that a button with an arrow pointing to the right means forward, and that a button with a little house on it usually indicates the homepage. The point is, make your interface buttons intuitive. Don't ever make the user guess what they signify. Do all of your buttons all work? When's the last time you checked?

☐ Are common interface design elements used consistently? Rules, borders, dots, and type all contribute to the overall look and feel of your design. Make sure that any elements you use support your message.

Technical Design Checklist

☐ *Did you test the project on multiple platforms?* Will the project play on both PCs and Macs? In the Macintosh world alone, there are G3s, G4s, and G5s. Different speeds may cause your project to run at different speeds. Will it play on multiple operating systems? There's more than one version of Windows on the market today, and Apple has at least four. Will your project work on all of them?

☐ *Will the project open on multiple Web browsers?* Netscape, Safari, Internet Explorer, and others each of them will treat your files somewhat differently. Make sure the project works with at least the most popular.

☐ *Are loading times reasonable?* No one is going to wait more than several seconds for your project to load. Keep your visitor in mind and don't try their patience.

☐ *Did you have someone "beta test" the project for you?* Before a play is opened to the public, the actors always rehearse their scenes. Think of the beta test as your project rehearsal. You certainly don't want to go on a job interview and find then that your file refuses to open. Despite what looks like a long loading time, the interface designed by Marybel Olivares (in the color insert), is cleverly created with the help of compressed images.

☐ *Have you prepared for the worst?* Never undervalue the power of the computer gods to trip you up. Do you have a backup file? Better yet, have two. Do you have a battery backup USP system?

Miscellaneous Designer Checklist

☐ *Do you keep a record of all your ideas and designs?* Don't discard any of your ideas. Even if not appropriate for the project at hand, they may be right for another somewhere down the road. Keep all of your thumbnail sketches—you never know...

☐ *Do you have a support system in place?* Things always seem to go wrong when you least expect it. Where are you going to go for help? Books? The Internet? Friends and colleagues? Know in advance where to turn for help. And don't be embarrassed to ask questions.

☐ *Do you allot enough time to produce the project?* Never underestimate how long it's going take to construct the digital portfolio. No matter how long you think it's going to take, it will always take longer. There will always be some little problem that stops you dead in your tracks as you near the deadline. Once, without realizing it, I used a program that contained corrupt data. After several frustrating hours of watching the program randomly crash, I decided to reinstall it. As it turned out, I had to install an early version first, then reinstall each incremental upgrade until I had the program running again at its current version. Three hours later, everything was fine (except my nerves).

☐ *Do you make it easy on your viewers?* I've said this before, but it bears repeating: Offer links in your project to places where software players can be downloaded, if necessary to experience your site. Make it as easy on your viewers to experience your project; this is a simple act of consideration—and one that will pay big benefits for you.

☐ *Do you stretch your limits?* I say, always bite off more than you can chew! You'll never grow as an artist if you don't push beyond what you already know. Just don't do it when you're on a hard deadline.

An excellent example of elegence in action can be found in the colors insert. This interface designed by Pixel Dimension Studios shows a clean interface, yet features a complete navigational system. There is music and video, but the files are small and the Web page loads almost immediately. Yes, it took a lot of time to design, but the results are seamless to the viewer.

above • Here is a colorful and clean interface designed by Marybel Olivares. As the visitor's mouse approaches each square and rectangle, the linked section is revealed.

right • Joel Tunon shows why he is an illustrator. He wisely uses the white backdrop to showcase his beautiful drawings.

below • Although these is a lot of information on this Web page, the clean interface makes it easy to see everything. The links are clearly labeled and the icons act as additional references.

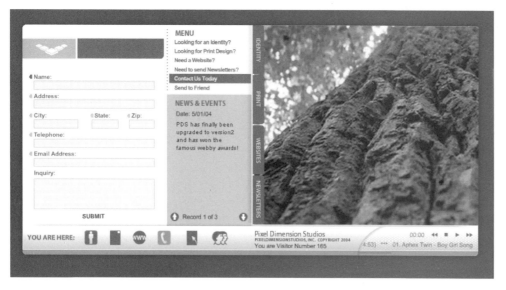

Final Thoughts

Let me close this chapter with some suggestions about what to do when things go wrong—as they inevitably will. First, don't panic; don't lose your cool. Don't become so frustrated that you behave in a way you'll regret later. I witnessed one student yank a keyboard from its cable and hurl it across the room, where it slammed into a wall. Aside from the embarrassment factor, the incident earned him a suspension and cost him the price of a replacement keyboard. If you feel yourself getting that worked up, *get up,* walk around, clear your mind, get something to drink, breathe some fresh air—in short, chill out. Then sit down again when you feel up to it and have another go. It will do you no good to try to work when you are not up to the task. I know I don't have to tell you that creativity comes in spurts. When you are truly in the mood, the project will come together in a meaningful way.

And keep in mind, as I mentioned early in the chapter, probably you won't be happy with your first effort. You wouldn't be a true artist if you were. Besides, you don't ever want to tell yourself "it's good enough." You want to keep improving. So make that second or third effort. You'll get there.

Visit the color insert to see a beautiful interface designed by Adriana Garcia. Adriana spent many hours tinkering with the design, trying out ideas. Although frustrated at times, Adriana was finally happy with the results. It is important to give yourself some time to "live with the design." You will want to use it for a long time, so it's best to like what you have created.

Don't forget to have fun! The process of building a portfolio is supposed to be enjoyable as well as hard work. So relax and enjoy the experience. When you need inspiration, explore Web sites devoted to digital portfolios. As yourself: What works? What doesn't?

Finally, be creative, but be practical. Make sure your portfolio is professional, but don't be afraid to cut loose. Here are some web sites to help you in your creative quest:

Portfolios.com: www.portfolios.com
Artspan: www.artspan.com/become_mbr.php
A 2 Z Web Design:
   http://a2zwebdesignsource.com/Graphic_Design_
   Artists
Stickysource.com: www.stickysauce.com/pixelpeo-
   ple/portfolios1.html ■

 12

Taking Interviews and Presenting Your Portfolio

The telephone rings. It's someone from the human resources department at a company you're interested in working for calling to set up a job interview. You've done it! You've landed the job interview of your dreams. Your resume has done its work; now it's up to you, to the first impression you make personally and to your portfolio. Showing your port is your big chance to demonstrate your accomplishments. But before you take that all-important interview, you must prepare. This chapter tells you how.

Preparing for a Job Interview

Preparation is the key to successful job search. The more information you have about the potential company, the more you can articulate your message. In addition, your knowledge about the company demonstrates that you are resourceful and have a genuine interest in the position.

Research the Company

No doubt about it, being called on an interview is cause for celebration. You're one of a select few to "make the first cut." But now you must distinguish yourself fur-

ther. The first way to do this is to conduct research, to give you knowledge that places you ahead of the pack. You want to find out as much about the company as you possibly can, about it goals and fiscal outlook. Here are some recommendations for successfully researching your potential employer.

Visit the Library

Everything you need to know about the company is there. Research librarians can help you to find all about the relevant information. They can direct you to business journals such as Hoover's Inc. Reports, which provide valuable business information on the top 750 companies, both public and private, in this country, as well as on over 40,000 of the world's top business enterprises. In addition, they detail events, strategies, and people that have impacted the company. Other business journals such as Moody's Company Data, or Morningstar also are available to help you on your information quest.

Request a Copy of the Company's Annual Report

Larger companies will provide an annual report upon request, free of charge. Get it for the company you're interested in and read it. The report provides information about the direction of the company and any current

How badly do you want that interview, that job? Taking an unconventional approach might just do the trick. You want to stand out from the crowd, right? One student I know volunteered to work for a company for no pay for two weeks. She told them that if they didn't like her, then they didn't have to hire her. She got the job! Don't be afraid to offer something a little off the wall when applying for the job. Send a small box of paint and brushes when applying for that gallery position. Include a miniature floor plan or a toy house when applying for an interior design position.

I won a job using this approach myself once. While on a job interview, the prospective employer informed me that he wouldn't be making a decision for some time because he intended to interview other applicants. I informed him that there would be no additional applicants because I had removed the job ad from the wall in the employment office at my college. He hired me the next day!

For other ideas, check out books on self-promotion. You can find them in both the business and art sections of your local bookstore.

Kwesi Williams exhibits a superb package he has designed.

media coverage. It also gives details about the financial condition of the company and offers insight into its management philosophy.

You may be able to find the annual report online, typically in PDF format. These Web sites are a great place to start your research:

Report Gallery: www.reportgallery.com
Annual Report Service:
    www.annualreportservice.com
The Public Register's Annual Report Service:
    www.prars.com
Financial Times (for European companies):
    http://ft.ar.wilink.com/asp/P003_search_ENG.asp

Visit Standard & Poor's Online

The Standard & Poor's Web site (www.netadvantage.standardandpoors.com/NASApp/NetAdvantage/login.jsp?url=/NASApp/NetAdvantage/index.do) is a valuable research tool, especially for checking out private businesses, those that are not publicly traded on the open market. You'll also find biographies of thousands of corporate executives and directors, to help you identify the movers and shakers (and if you're lucky, your eventual boss). There may even be information available on the company's customers and vendors.

Tailor Your Portfolio for Each Interview

I don't need to tell you that every job you apply for is different. So each item you place in your portfolio should reflect the requirements of the job at hand. If the position calls for someone with Web design skills, arriving with a selection of printed brochures will not impress.

Turn a critical eye toward your work. Don't forget what I said earlier in the book: You will always be remembered by the weakest piece in your case, so pull anything that you think won't "carry its weight" for the

Interviews are stressful. Stay alert. Talk about your work and try to have fun!

● ● ● **Finding Your Way**

If you are unsure of the address of the interviewing firm, go online to Mapquest (www.mapquest.com). Here you will find exact directions to any location in any city. Then take a test drive to the location ahead of time. Getting lost on the day of the interview will make you late, not to mention, very nervous and anxious—both of which will not help you make that important good first impression. You want to be calm, cool, collected, and on time.

● ● ● **Relocation Resources**

Thinking of relocating to another city? The Chamber of Commerce (www.uschamber.com/default) is the first place to visit. Need to know a little more about a new area? Each city Web link offers information about the city, its restaurants, entertainment, cost of living, jobs in the area, and just about anything you can think of. A great resource!

And if are a parent with schoolage children, you'll want to know what schools are like in a new area. One of my favorite Web sites for learning more about kindergarten through twelfth grade schools is www.greatschools.net. You can find detailed information about public, private, and charter schools throughout the United States.

upcoming interview. Seriously outdated work may cast doubt about your current talents and skills, and this is no time to be sentimental about an old favorite piece. A polished and current portfolio is what you want. The more pieces you have to choose from, the more you can customize your port to make an impact on the interviewer.

How to Take a Successful Interview

Start with a positive attitude. Don't forget, you were chosen from a pool of many applicants. The job is yours to win. The secret to your success lies in careful preparation and effective communication. Believe in yourself and your abilities. Try to relax. An interview is an opportunity to present yourself and your work, not an interrogation. In this section, I'll walk you through a plan to help you get that great job.

Dress Appropriately

It is said that a job is won in the first six minutes of the interview. The point is, impressions are formed almost immediately. Therefore, your choice of clothing can make the difference. Always dress appropriate for the organization. You want to convey an image of profes-

sionalism, confidence, and ability. I have heard job candidates comment, "Why should I dress up? They're all artists and everyone wears jeans." True, but they already have a job! Dress correctly now, and later, after you have the job, you may dress casually if that's accepted in the company. In general, "correctly" means conservatively. Men should wear a jacket and tie, or a suit. Women should a wear skirt or pants suit, or a dress, or some other well-coordinated outfit. Neutral colors are the safest. And, ladies, take off wild nail polish, and leave the trendy shoes in the closet. Be conservative with accessories, your fragrance, and cosmetics. Don't wear jewelry that makes noise. It's distracting during an interview.

Lay out what you plan to wear the night before. Make sure your portfolio is ready to go. Then get a good night's rest.

Be prepared to talk about your work. You will be asked why you created a piece. Clearly articulate your creative vision.

Put Yourself in a Positive Frame of Mind

Plan your journey so that you can be sure to arrive 10 to 15 minutes before the interview. This gives you time to gather your thoughts, check out your surroundings, and to relax. Look around for any literature available that might provide a little more information about the company. Greet the receptionist with courtesy and respect. You never know, he or she may report your behavior to the employer. This is where you make your first impression.

While you are waiting, paint a positive mental picture, or a mental movie, in which the interview goes perfectly. Imagine the interviewer asking questions that you answer with clarity and insight. For the ending of your "movie," imagine the interviewer telling you that you are the perfect person for the job. These are the types of visual images that you want going through your mind before the interview.

Make a Good First Impression

The employer reaches out to shake your hand. Stand up straight and offer a firm, full-handed handshake to men and women alike. Don't go to either extreme: neither light and demure handshakes nor overpowering, knuckle-cracking handshakes are appropriate. The interviewer knows you are nervous, but you want to give the impression you aren't.

Address the interviewer(s) by title (Ms., Mr., Dr.) and last name. If you are unsure of the pronunciation, ask the receptionist to pronounce the employer's name before going into the interview. (Better yet, you should call in advance of your interview date to find out.) Do not sit down until you are offered a chair. Sit up straight and make and maintain eye contact with the interviewer.

In addition to your portfolio, bring additional resumes and letters of reference with you to the interview. Include extra CDs of your digital port to give out. may wish to carry a notebook with your questions written in advance (more on this later in the chapter). This adds to your professional demeanor.

Interviews often begin with what's called an "open-ended icebreaker" question, such as "tell me about yourself." Anticipate this and have an answer at the ready. Don't ramble on about your childhood. Practice an appropriate answer that, ideally, reveals your intelligence and sense of humor. Once you get past the first question, you'll find yourself beginning to relax.

Types of Interviews

Most interviews are either *directive* or nondirective. In a directive (or structured) interview, the employer asks a predetermined set of situational questions designed to gather specific information about your ability to handle the job. Nondirective interviews are unstructured in nature, using probing, open-ended questions designed to have you do most of the talking. You will generally be exposed to a mixture of both types of questions in an interview. Both types are designed to help the interviewer to learn more about your skills and personalities.

Other interview methods include the *stress-style* interaction, used to determine how you react under pressure. You may, for example, be asked to role-play a client conflict or to take a timed test. Or you may find yourself in a group interview, which pits you against

Nothing more stressful than an impromptu interview! You have to be prepared to think fast and get your point across before the interviewer moves on to someone else.

your competition. This type is often used to determine how you interact as a team member, hence can be very intimidating. A third type, the *team interview,* involves more than one interviewer questioning you. In this case, you will have to find a way to establish a link with each person, so in this style of interview, direct eye contact is especially important.

Be aware that not all employers are adept at conducting interviews; sometimes, they are quite inexperienced at it or are just as uncomfortable as you are. When you find yourself in this situation, maintain your professionalism and practice effective interviewing techniques. You'll be rewarded with positive feedback and a good job offer. Here are a few more insights on interviewing successfully:

- Smile. Banish negative thoughts. Don't let the phrase "what if they don't like me?" enter your mind.
- Take time to think before you answering a question.
- Exude confidence.
- Avoid single-word responses such as "Yes" or "No."
- Acknowledge that you understand the questions you are being asked.
- Show enthusiasm.
- Don't use slang expressions. You are in the business of communication. Use professional language—not, "like, you know" or "uh."
- Don't fidget.

- Refrain from nervous habits such as playing with your hair.
- Say nothing negative about past jobs, employers, or coworkers.
- Always present yourself in the best possible light.
- Never offer personal information.
- If you don't understand a question, say so. Ask the employer to please rephrase the question.

Presenting Your Portfolio

During the interview, you'll probably start to wonder when is the best time to present your portfolio. Most likely, the opportunity will arise naturally during the course of the interview. You might, for instance, be asked, "What did you do at your last job?" You could answer by saying, "Let me show you some of the projects I worked on while I was at XYZ Company." Or the potential employer might ask you directly to show your work, by saying for example, "Have you brought work along today to show me?" or "Show me a sample of the projects you've worked on." Now's your chance! Open your case and begin explaining some of the pieces. If you have heeded the advice of this book, you are prepared with a detailed explanation for each of your pieces.

In other situations, the opportunity to display your work may come in a more subtle way. The interviewer may start discussing some of the company's current projects. At this point, you can say, "I have a couple of

above • A good interview involves a lot of give and take between you and the employer. Don't monopolize the conversation, but do make your case.

right • How would you describe this piece during an interview? What would you say about the color choices? The type selected or the layout? (This beautiful brochure was designed by Paul Kane.)

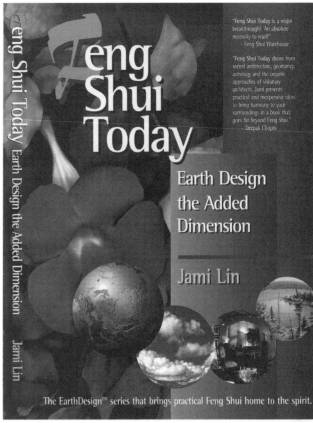

similar projects that I was involved in that I'd like to show you," or "I solved similar problems at my firm, and I'd like to show you how." And while you are showing your work, pay attention to the body language of the interviewer. If he or she seems uninterested or shifts around a lot, it's time to move on to another piece. Do not feel that you must show every piece in the case.

One of the keys to negotiating a successful interview is to listen very carefully to the questions you are asked. If queried as to how you arrived at a solution for a piece, don't explain how it was made. That's not what you were asked. You may be asked if the piece was successful and satisfied the client. You might be questioned as to why you selected the colors you used. Whatever the question, answer it appropriately.

A word of warning: You won't be asked in every interview to show your portfolio. When this happens, don't take it personally. Some employers would rather hear you talk about your ideas or what you can do for the company.

Length and Breakdown of Interviews

First interviews normally take about an hour, although they can last much longer. Generally, you can expect

approximately 30 percent of the interview to be spent discussing you and your qualifications and 70 percent discussing the company and the vacant position. Though this may seem an unbalanced breakdown, studies bear it out. The first interview is generally regarded as a screening process, and your objective should be to leave the interviewer with the unmistakable impression that you want and can do the job.

Assuming you were successful at the first interview and are invited back for a second, in this one, you can expect to spend 50 percent of the time discussing yourself and your qualifications and 50 percent on the vacant position. This session will be clearly focused on you. Generally, the second interview is the final step before a job offer is made or not, and is generally conducted with the person you will be working for directly—your immediate supervisor.

The second interview frequently last longer, an entire day. You may be given a tour of the work environment. You may also have an opportunity to talk with future fellow workers. Be very careful speaking to these

people—you never know who has the ear of the your boss. More on the second interview later in the chapter.

Listen closely, and indicate by gestures and facial expressions that you understand each of the interviewer's remarks and questions. Questions being asked at this stage are for very specific reasons. So think about why each question is being asked before you formulate a response. If you have trouble formulating an answer, try a second approach. And make sure your message has been understood. It's perfectly acceptable to refer to your notes in answering questions.

The employer will set the tone of the interview, but you should never miss an opportunity to sell yourself. It is your responsibility to make sure that anything important about your qualifications is covered during the interview!

Your Turn to Ask

At some point during the interview (generally, near the end), you will be asked if you have any questions. Be

above ● **This is a great interview in progress. There is good interaction between the employer and potential employee. You can tell by the body language that both parties are engaged and interested in the conversation.**

top left ● **Everything looks great! So be proud of your work and be ready to take the interview. It could happen when you least expect it.**

Once the interview is completed, promptly send a thank-you letter. Send it by snail-mail or by email, but send that letter. It shows interest and respect.

- Why is this position open? Is it an existing post or a newly created position?
- Can you describe your company's corporate culture?
- Please describe a typical workday.
- What would you like done differently by the next person who fills this position?
- If chosen to fill this job, what kind of projects can I expect to be involved in the next three to six months?
- What gives your company the competitive edge over other firms in this field?
- What promotional opportunities are available within your company?
- Do you provide professional development and continuing education programs?
- Will I work independently or as part of a team?
- How many more candidates do you expect to interview?
- When would you need me to start work?
- Why did you come to work here?
- What particular computer equipment and software will be made available for my use?

Close the Interview and Follow Up

It's time for your big finish. If it hasn't already come up in the question-and-answer period of the interview, ask when the employer expects to make his or her decision. Then, as the interview concludes, make one last positive statement about your future with the company, such as one of the following:

"I am really looking forward to working here."
"May I contact you or would you prefer to call me?"
"Your company offers the kind of creative environment I would very much like to work in .

Be upbeat; never sound desperate. Stand, shake the interviewer's hand, and make your exit. Don't forget to thank the secretary or assistant on your way out.

Send a Thank-You Letter—Promptly

You had a great interview! To expand on that success, take the time to say thank you and remind the interviewer that you're the perfect person for the job. As soon

ready. This is your chance to show that you've done your homework. You want to sound intelligent, sincere, and interested. It is important that you have prepared some well-thought-out questions. The questions you ask can reveal as much about you as those asked by the interviewer. You may, of course, ask about salary and benefits during this time, but never first. Never ask about money issues early in the interview. Be careful not to ask something the interviewer answered earlier. This will indicate you weren't paying attention during the interview; that said, don't hesitate to ask for clarification on anything you're not sure you understood earlier.

This is your last chance to point out any of your strengths not covered earlier, or to stress important qualifications mentioned earlier. But don't go and on. Make your points once and clearly; then state again that you are very interested in the job. Finally, ask when you can contact the interviewer to follow up.

Here's a list of questions you may want to ask when given the opportunity in an interview. Also, use it to trigger ideas for other questions you may want to ask.

as possible, sit down and make some notes about the interview. These first few thoughts will become the basis for your thank-you letter. This letter is one more way to promote yourself to the company. It's also another opportunity to add any important information that you might have forgotten to mention. If you were interviewed by a team, send individual letters to each member. The letters can be essentially the same, but personalize them in some small way. If you do not hear from the company in a week or so, call the firm and ask about the status of your application.

Here are a few more interview follow-up tips:

- Don't procrastinate. Send your thank-you letter within one day.
- Print the letter on matching paper and envelope.
- Verify the correct spellings of names and titles of each person who interviewed you.
- Express your appreciation for the opportunity to meet with the company, but don't gush.
- Tailor the letter to the company. Don't send a generic letter. If you noticed something that was particularly interesting about the company during your visit—point it out.

Here is a sample thank you letter. Notice that it has been created in a standard business format, with name, address, and the date at the top, and the addressee's name and address on the left just above the salutation.

Alan Courtland
2710 3rd Court
Glenwood, FL 32722
305-555-1234
Courtland@yahoo.com

Mr. Robert Samuels
All Design, Inc.
3720 S.W. 12th Street
Altamonte Springs, FL 32716
May 18, 2005

Dear Mr. Samuels,

Thank you for taking the time to meet with me to discuss the graphic designer position at All Design, Inc. I was very impressed by the quality of service your company provides. I am convinced that my design abilities will fit well with your current needs.

I appreciate that you spent so much of your time with me. Now that I have met you and some of your colleagues, and know more about the activities of All Design, Inc., I am even more excited about the possibility of working with you and your team of designers. The high level of creative energy among your artists, as well as their personal pride in the company, was evident in all of them. I feel that I would definitely be a worthwhile addition to your company.

Again, thank you for your time and consideration, and I look forward to hearing from you.

Sincerely,

Alan Courtland

Second Interview Structure

If you have been invited for a second interview, it's a clear indication that the employer believes you have all the skills and credentials necessary to fill the open position. The second interview is conducted to determine more specifically how good a "fit" you are on a more personal basis. You can expect the second interview to last significantly longer than the first. During this time you may be introduced to many of the upper management people and other coworkers and be given a tour of the premises. This is a great opportunity to ask any questions that you didn't raise the first time or that occurred to you after you left.

As during the first, you want to be relaxed during the second interview, but keep your energy level high and your attention focused for the duration. And be prepared to discuss salary during the second interview, if it was not discussed during the first interview.

Bring extra resumes with your for the second interview, in case you are asked to give one to other management-level staff you meet (only hand it out when asked, however). Probably your resume has already been given to the key staff, but it's always a good idea to come prepared. You will look professional and considerate.

Interviewing: A Two-Way Street

Getting a job is a lot like getting married. You and your new company want to be productive, work well together, and grow together. So before you take that "walk down the aisle," it is critical that both of you find out as much as possible about one another. However, whereas in a personal relationship no holds are barred when it comes to the kinds of questions people ask each other, in a professional environment, there are restrictions as to what an employer can ask a job candidate, and you need to be aware of those.

Handling Inappropriate Questions

The interview is going so smoothly that you are starting to think that the job may be yours. Then in the middle of the process comes the question, "Are you planning on getting pregnant anytime soon?" or "Will your religion prevent you from working weekends or holidays?" These types of questions, and many others, though perhaps asked innocuously enough, are prohibited by law in interview situations. These are spelled out in the Equal Employment Opportunity Commission (EEOC) guidelines, which you can learn about online at www.eeoc.gov/abouteeo/overview_practices.html.

If this happens to you, be aware that usually illegal questions are asked in ignorance; that is, the person isn't aware he or she has ventured into "protected areas." In this case, probably the best approach is to change the subject as delicately as you can, perhaps by saying something along the lines of, "I'd like to review the subject of office hours." This is not the time to assert your constitutional rights. By changing the subject, you give the interviewer the chance to realize that he or she said something incorrect and will let the matter drop.

If, however, you feel that the question was asked with intent (unfortunately, as we all know, discrimination still exists) you have every right to terminate the interview. Here are examples of topics that, if asked about, might be interpreted as discriminatory:

- Race, creed, color, religion, sexual orientation, or national origin
- Marital status
- Disabilities of any kind
- Health or medical history
- Age or date of birth (unless you are under 16)
- Date and type of military service
- Pregnancy, birth control, and child care
- Psychiatric treatment, drug addiction, or alcoholism
- Arrest record (You may however be asked about a conviction if it is accompanied by a statement saying that a conviction will not necessarily disqualify you for employment.)

Questions You Must Be Prepared to Answer

Your resume offers information, and your portfolio speaks volumes, about your professional qualifications, but the bottom-line reason a company conducts personal interviews is to find out which candidate is a good match for the company. To determine that, employers typically ask a number of similar questions, some serious and others that might seem quirky to you. But when you know the intent behind these questions, you can better prepare how to answer them.

Here you'll find a sampling of questions in this arena, along with possible responses. The point is not to memorize these answers, but to jump-start your thoughts as to how you might respond during your interview.

Tell me about yourself. Take a couple of minutes to discuss your education, work experience, and recent accomplishments. Don't ramble on about unrelated subject matter.

Where do you want to be five years from now? When I was asked this during an interview, my response was, "I want to be president of NBC." This is question begs a more unconventional response. Resist the temptation to say, "I want your job," which will not be taken well.

What are your weaknesses? For this tough question, it always best to turn a negative into a positive, responding, for example, "I sometimes expect too much of myself" or "I am too hardworking."

What did you dislike about your last job? Under no circumstances, complain about former bosses or coworkers. Rather say something along the lines of, "The job was not challenging enough" or "There was not enough opportunity for advancement."

What was the last book you read? What was the last movie you saw? The point here is to demonstrate that you know the importance of striking a balance between your professional and personal life. Don't be afraid to reveal that you like scary movies or mushy romantic novels.

Why do you want to work for this company? "Because I've done my research, and yours is the best company, and I want to work for the best!" Then describe the positive attributes of the firm. (You have done your research, right?)

What can you offer us that no one else can? This is no time to be modest. Tell the employer about your successful projects, your triumphs, and your leadership roles. Make it clear to the employer that you have healthy self-esteem and confidence in your abilities.

What kind of working environment are you looking for? Your answer should reflect your research on the company. If the company is a small one, your answer might be, "I prefer to work for smaller companies where my skills can really impact the company directly. A larger company requires a different answer, such as, "I want to work for a larger company where I have plenty of opportunities for advancement."

What other companies have you interviewed with? Be aware that you do not have to divulge any specifics about your job search. You can say that you have been on several other interviews and are still waiting to hear the results. If you have been offered a job and didn't accept it, you can reveal this as well, but be prepared to say why you turned it down. Don't be critical, just say that you believe that this company would be much better for you. By the way, if you have been on a lot of interviews, do not divulge that, as it might be interpreted that no one is interested in you.

If you could start over what would you do differently? This is a trick question. Do not answer with a negative comment such as, "I would have never gone to work at ABC Graphics if I had known they were going to fire me. Focus on some minor event that will have no reflection on the job you area applying for, such as "I wish I had decided to study art earlier," or "Actually, I'm pretty happy with my decisions so far."

above • Polished and sophisticated dress is important. Conservative outfits will make you appear professional.

below • It's always hard to decide which piece to put at the front of your portfolio. It is an important decision, as it sets the direction for everything to come. Take your time and choose carefully.

Other Questions You Should Know How to Answer.

Many common interview questions are designed to get you to reveal aspects of yourself or your personality that you might not be expecting. Here is a list of some very popular questions that might come up and for which you should be prepared to answer:

- What are your goals in life?
- What are you good at? What are you bad at?
- What kind of person are you?
- Why did you leave your last job?
- How do you work with others?
- Do you prefer to work in teams or alone?
- What motivates you?
- How have you changed as an artist in the last couple of years?

- How do you deal with stress?
- What would you do if a coworker didn't like you?
- What would your friends say about you?
- What would your coworkers say about you?
- What to you constitutes the ideal work environment?
- What has been your biggest problem at work and how have you handled it?
- What would you like to make as a salary?
- If you weren't doing this, what you like to do?
- How are you at dealing with people?
- What additional training would you like to receive?
- What do you most look forward to in a job?
- What makes you think you can succeed in this job?
- Why should we employ you, instead of someone else?
- We sometimes have difficult deadlines. Are you available to work after hours?
- Do you have any hobbies?
- Are you a member of any clubs or charitable organizations?
- What do you do when you're not working?
- How would you describe your management skills?
- Do you consider yourself a leader or a follower?
- Where else have you applied for a job? (You don't have to answer this)
- Have you taken any other interviews?
- If we offer this job to you, how much notice would you have to give your current employer?
- Have you ever traveled outside this country?
- What other languages do you speak?
- Do you have any questions at this time?
- How would you describe yourself?
- What subjects did you like best (or least) in college?
- What do you know about our company?
- What three things are most important to you in your job?
- How do you determine success?
- What is your philosophy of design?
- How would you describe success?

Interviews sometimes happen by committee. This is doubly stressful, but there is more opportunity for you to mix with the company's movers and shakers. Look at it as a way to show how well you interact within groups.

Responding to a Job Offer

The phone rings. You pick it up and say, "Hello." The voice at the other end says, "Ms. Radford, we like to offer you the position at Creative Design." Now the job is yours—if you want it. Not all offers are made over the telephone, however; some are made in writing or during the second interview. By this time, you should know if this is the job you want. Unless you are waiting to hear from another (possibly better) job, it's time to make a commitment. If you are holding out for another job you prefer over this one, don't act in haste or you may regret it later. It's perfectly acceptable to ask for time to think about the offer—in which case, ask when you need to get back to the company with your answer.

If you decide you want the job, and salary was not discussed in a previous meeting, now is the time to express your desire to negotiate your salary. Whatever you decide to do, respond in writing to the offer as soon as possible. If you accept the offer over the telephone, a letter of acceptance is still in order. If you are no longer interested in the job, say so. Don't say, "I'll get back to you" and not do it. Not only is this very rude, it may come back to "bite" you, as you might want to work for this firm in the future.

Preventing Portfolio Presentation Problems—and Dealing with the Inevitable Glitches

You are so ready for this interview! You are appropriately dressed and are standing tall and confident; your

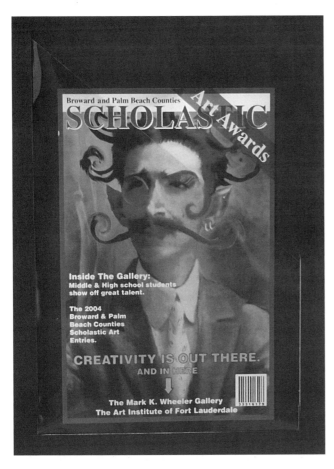

This illustration and portfolio pocket was created by Kwesi Williams.

portfolio is in hand, and you feel ready to meet the challenge. The interview begins. Everything is going splendidly when you are asked to open your design portfolio. You lift up the case on to the employer's desk, and as you unzip it, several of the pieces slip out of their sleeves and slide (in slow motion) to the floor. You are mortified.

Think this can't happen to you? Think again!

An important aspect of preparing for the interview is to prepare for what can go wrong. You never know what kind of situation you will face when you step into an employer's office, so let's take a few minutes to design a game plan for handling possible problems.

If you have put your artwork in a sleeve-style portfolio, make sure the pieces are securely bound. Use small pieces of tape to keep them from sliding around in their sleeves. Don't use big pieces of tape or heavy-duty adhesive. You want to be able to replace older pieces with newer pieces to freshen up the work as necessary. If you have pieces that must be removed during the interview (such as slides or folders), create holding sleeves or pockets that will hold the work in place until needed.

If any of your work is mounted on boards and placed in a portfolio box, you face additional challenges. Ideally, you hope to be provided a fairly large table on which to display the work to the interviewer. But what you find instead is that the interviewer asks you to show the work on top of his or her desk, which is already spilling over with papers and materials. So practice beforehand handling the boards under such awkward conditions, so you don't fumble around. In addition to looking unprofessional, you risk damaging your work. (In any case, you should plan to occasionally reprint and remount your work to keep it looking fresh.)

What about an electronic portfolio? What equipment should you bring to an interview for display purposes? In theory, you only need the CD; in actuality, that may not be the case. As I explained in Chapter 6, there are many issues to consider—monitor size, computer speed and memory, spin-up time of the CD, fonts, and colors. Some or all of these things may contribute to the success—or failure—of your presentation. Another problem to consider is software compatibility. You may have created your project in the latest version of the software, but will it run if the interviewer's computer has an earlier version, or doesn't have the same software at all? It's a good idea to save the project in a backward-compatible version that is designed to play on older systems, especially true if you use a program not in widespread use. I once created for an interview a neat little multimedia show to describe my philosophy of education. To save money, I had used a shareware program. The project contained about 50 slides, which took quite a lot of time to run because the program embedded the slides in a way that consumed a great deal of computer memory. When I arrived at the interview (early, to make sure my program would run), I discovered that the machine the committee had set up for me to use was too old to work at all. I had to ask them to locate another computer. This delayed my interview, as well as all subsequent interviews that day.

Even when you believe you've thought of everything, you may still run into problems. For example, a presentation designed to be backward-compatible can do weird things to your file. For example, a presentation created in the newest version of Flash may not open at all in a previous version of the same program. In some cases, files may open, but formatting problems may occur (such as strange-looking bullets or misaligned paragraphs or tabs); program scripts may not run, fonts may not appear—you get the idea.

Even if you decide to bring a laptop computer with you to the interview, you can't be careful enough. Test your project on the machine well in advance, especially if it's not your computer. There may not be enough memory, or fonts may be missing. Don't take any chances. And don't forget about power. I once left for an interview, grabbed my laptop, forgot to check the battery, only to discover that the computer had no power when I arrived at the interview; *and* I had forgotten to bring along my power cord. I had to ask the interviewer to find one for me. Not the best way to begin an interview.

Marketing Yourself: Distributing Your Portfolio

I don't have to tell you, the competition for jobs is intense. There are only a limited number of available positions and many people vying to fill them. How do you distinguish yourself from the masses? By marketing yourself. In today's extremely competitive job-hunting environment, the most successful job seekers are those who understand the value of reaching out to the job market; and one of the best ways to accomplish that is to launch a Web site.

A Web site will enable you to show your design work to potential employers throughout the world. By doing so, you also demonstrate that you're a cutting-edge designer. Everything about your site—your artwork, your text, the fonts, the colors, the download time, and much more—contributes to your image, and to your eventual success.

Your goal is to get a job. A Web site will help you make this happen. This section will tell you how.

Do-It-Yourself Web Site Development

Chapter 6 explained how to build a Web-based portfolio. Now you need to know how to get it online. You will require the following elements:

Domain name
Web "host"
Method to "publish" your pages
Strategy to promote your site

Domain Name

You're familiar with the zip code in so-called snail-mail addresses. A zip code helps direct the correspondence directly to your neighborhood. Think of a domain name as your zip code on the Internet. A domain name directs a request for a Web page or an e-mail to its final destination. It is always composed of two words or phrases, separated by periods, or dots. Here are a couple of examples of domain names:

www.aii.edu
www.google.com
www.netscape.net

All Web pages use a series of numbers that make up the location of the page (they are not generally visible to the user). But so that you don't have to type a long string of numbers (such as http://64.236.24.28) every time you want to visit a Web site, domain names are used

Here is a more complete explanation of domain names, using the following imaginary Web site:

www.mywebsite.thehost.com

The domain name breaks up into three parts:

Top-level domain
Second-level domain
Third-level domain

For www.mywebsite.thehost.com, the top-level domain (or TLD) is .com, located at the right of a Web address. These letters identify the Internet Protocol address and point you at the correct address of the site (like a zip code). The letters represent a series of numbers that make up a computer running on a network. Every computer connected to the Internet is assigned a unique number, known as the IP address. (For example, if you typed http://64.236.24.28/, you would arrive at www.cnn.com). Every Web site has a top-level domain name (or suffix) that identifies the category of the site. Sties are broadly defined as either generic or by country. Generic domain names are used to classify many different types of environments, such as commercial business, educational institutions, and personal Web pages. Their suffixes are as follows:

com, for commercial business
gov, for government agencies
edu, for educational institutions
org, for nonprofit organizations
mil, for military
net, for network organizations

Country domain names specify the Web page's country of origin, for example:

uk, for United Kingdom/Great Britain
th, for Thailand
fr, for France
dk, for Denmark

The second part (or second level) of the domain name (in our example name, "thehost") is the unique name that identifies the site. The two parts together make up the overall domain name. Second-level domain names are what you submit to register your Web site. Domain names can be registered through many different companies (known as "registrars"), which compete with one another. A listing of these companies can be found at the ICANN Web site (www.internic.net/regist.html).

To continue with the zip code analogy, as you know, these numbers now come with a second set of four numbers (known as the Delivery Point numbers), such as 33316-1234. These add on-numbers identify a particular area within a larger geographic region (such as a city block or a large building complex). Web names may have secondary addresses as well. Third-level domain names includes both the first- and second-level portion of the domain, plus a third part, to further define where a file may be found on the server. The most popular is "www" (the abbreviation for World Wide Web), but it can also stand for other areas of a Web site. For example, our fictional Web site, www.mywebsite.thehost.com might have greatart.thehost.com or, in our example, www.mywebsite.thehost.com. "Greatart" and "mywebsite" are the third-level names.

---

instead. A domain name directs your request for a Web page to the appropriate host or IP (Internet Protocol) address. A more complete explanation is provided in the sidebar below.

Selecting a domain name is a little like grocery shopping. If I tell you to buy a can of tomato soup, you'll head to the soup aisle of the supermarket, not the juice section. Picking out a domain name should use a similar logic. Your domain name should always reflect the service you provide.

The problem is that many good domain names are already taken. So it's a good idea to make a list of domain names you like and then do some research online to find out if they're still available. Two sites you can use for this purpose are Register.com (www.register.com/index.cgi?1|3851936627) and Dotster (www.dotster.com/?AID=514796&PID=530493).

Be aware that you might not be able to "own" your domain name. If someone has already registered the name you want, known as the "registrant," you may have to "rent" the name. You can research the owner of a domain name on the Internet using Whois.net (www.whois.net/). You pay a monthly fee for the right to use it.

If you already have a design or company name, you may find some difficulties acquiring the rights to a related domain name. The cost to secure the rights to a domain name are usually based on the popularity or ease-of-use of the name. You may find that the price is just too high for someone just starting out.

If you want to create a domain name from scratch, you have lots of options and lots of things to consider. First, think about how you will be marketing your site. (We will discuss this more in a bit.) Printed materials such as brochures and business cards will have your Web address on them. User will then have to type the Web address in order to visit your site. A long name makes it more likely they will make typing mistakes, so keep it short and simple. Stay away from characters such as dashes and underscores. Avoid having double letters in the name, such as www.designnexis.com. And if you find yourself having to spell the name over and over for your clients and interviews, you should rethink your domain name, and modify it as soon as possible.

Here are a few suggestions to assist you as you choose your domain name:

- Use words that represent your design services.
- Choose words that imply quality and value.
- Stay away from cutesy names that pun, but are impossible to spell, such as www.I-luv-2-design.com.
- Make the name memorable.
- Use words that are short and easy to type.
- Refrain from including words that can be easily misspelled.
- Stay away from hyphenated words.
- Don't create abbreviations for your domain name. No one will remember them.

- Use the plural form of a word if it seems natural. A domain name may be taken, but you may be offered the option of using the plural form; for example, instead of www.mydesign.com, www.mydesigns.com.
- Be careful not to infringe on trademarks.

Finding a Web Host

Once you have designed and named your Web site, you will have to decide where it will reside, or as it is known in the Internet community, be hosted. Your files must be placed on a Web server (which you can think of as a giant hard drive) that is connected to the Internet 24 hours a day. The server might actually be a dedicated computer located in your home or office. Most designers, however, prefer to use a Web hosting service, which provides the server where your Web pages reside. When you register your domain name, you point it to the host server. The hosting service takes care of all the technical details, allowing you to concentrate on designing your beautiful site. There are two types of hosting services: free and fee-based. Before you get all excited about the free service, remember the famous cliché, "You get what you pay for." Let's break down the pros and cons of both.

Free Hosting

There are many Web-hosting services available that will host your personal site for free. But you don't actually get something for nothing. What they frequently ask for in return is the right to runs advertisements on your site. If you feel that your carefully designed and constructed site will be marred by ads that appear at the top and sides of your pages, and over which you have no control, then this is not the option for you.

Free services are generally used by those with small Web sites. So if you can get by with fewer than 5 megs of space, and you don't mind the ads, then check out one of the following hosting sites. (Note: This is a small selection of free-service sites. New ones become available all the time.)

http://angelfire.lycos.com/
http://www.esmartstart.com/
http://www.freehomepages.com/
http://geocities.yahoo.com/home/
http://www.sapphiresoft.co.uk/

http://www.tripod.lycos.com/
http://www.zingto.com/

These site are particularly great for artists:
http://www.onetalentsource.com/
http://www.artistportfolio.net/
http://www.onart.com/
http://www.portfolios.com/

If you connect to the Internet with a provider such as Bellsouth, AOL, CompuServe, or Earthlink, chances are very good that you are entitled to free (although limited) server space. (In truth, the host service is not free. You are already paying Internet access fees.) Still if you do not need a lot of space, this is an excellent option. Best of all, generally no ads will be posted on your site. Check with your service provider for details about space allocation.

Paid Hosting

With a paid service, you get all the bells and whistles—fast Internet access and the ability to upload huge amounts of files. Web hosting prices range from the ridiculously low prices to extremely high, depending on your requirements. It is possible to get a complete Web hosting package for a little as $5. Web sites such as http://www.ourinternet.us/ offer plans for every budget (they host my web site: www.debbierosemyers.com.) For as little as $3.95 per month, you have 150 megs of storage space, free email, and a "guest book" where the potential employer can sign in and leave a telephone number. Paid services offer additional perks such as promotional tools to help you announce to the world that your site has arrived.

It is important to do your research before deciding on a paid service. Quality can vary from one provider to the next. How long have they been in business? You don't want to be the guinea pig for a startup company. Make sure that the provider offers 24/7 service and support. Having problems uploading your files at 3:00 in the morning is one thing; not being able to reach someone to find out the cause is another. Make sure that support staff is made up of professional programmers or network specialists. Establish that the provider has the facilities to keep its server running on full backup systems.

Finally, determine whether security issues have been addressed. You need to be reassured that your page infor-

On this Web page designed by Mario Ayerbe, the interface is uncomplicated but effective—and it loads fast.

mation will be safe and secure. Ask if a security expert is on staff at the company. There is no such thing as perfect security on the Internet, but if the company is not forthcoming on its capability to protect your files, then it is not for you. Inquire about its methods used to keep hackers (malicious computer experts) from invading the site.

Find a service provider that offers at least 50 megs of storage space (especially if you are thinking of running a business). Ask what extra charges there are for using more than the allotted space. High-volume sites need a lot of speed. Does the provider offer high-speed Internet access?

What kind of domain names will it offer you—www.mywebsite.thehost.com looks professional; www.thehost.com/mywebsite does not. It is too long to type and way too long to fit on a business card. Some service providers do not want to spend the money necessary to create full path names for their clients. The /mywebsite naming system does not take as much time to create.

Does the company provide a way for you to upload and test your pages? Will you have full file transfer protocol (FTP) access? (We'll discuss this in more detail in the next section.) Does the company offer support for advanced languages such as Common Gateway Interface (CGI) so you can use forms, data-

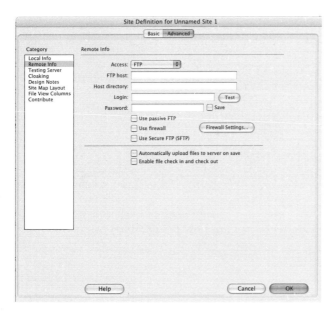

This dialog box in Dreamweaver makes it easy to connect to a remote server. Once you have all of your information assembled, you simply type the information into the appropriate boxes. When the Web design is done, you drag the files from your computer to the host computer.

base searches, and image maps? Does it support FrontPage, Dreamweaver, and Cold Fusion? Larger hosting services do.

Publishing Your Pages

Once you have selected a service provider, you are ready to get your files online for all the world to see. Moving files from your computer to the service provider's computer is know as *publishing* or uploading. This process may be accomplished in a number of ways.

The easiest way to move your files is using a "drag and drop" method. Programs such as Dreamweaver offer a visual way to see both your files and the remote location to which you will be moving them. You simply drag files from one side of the window to the other. This copies your Web pages to the remote site. Dreamweaver accomplishes this effortless file movement with a built-in FTP method, which makes getting your files online very easy.

You can also transfer your files using free programs such as Fetch (for the Mac) or WS_FTP LE (for Windows). They allow you to move your files much in the same way as Dreamweaver. They are not quite as intuitive as Dreamweaver, but they do the job just the same.

Promoting Your Site

Your Web site is finally online! Now you have to make sure people can find you. It's time to discuss marketing techniques. Your domain name is the starting point of Web promotion. Position your domain name on your business cards, letterhead, and resume. If you have developed any promotional materials, be sure to include it there as well. Tell all your friends and coworkers.

Make sure you have your Web site listed as part of your signature at the bottom of every email you send. Email potential employers and announce your site. Don't just email your resume, email your Web site as well. Here is a sample letter to show you how:

DEAR MR. THOMPSON,

Are you presently looking for a creative designer? I am seeking a position with an up-and-coming design house such as yours. I am including my resume for your consideration. I have also just created a Web page to manage and promote my career, and I hope you'll to be one of the first to see it. Go to http://designsthatwork.com. I hope you will take a moment to visit my site. I would really appreciate your critique or any comments you might offer.

Sincerely,

Your name

Print out some of your best Web pages to include in your portfolio. Carry printed samples of the Web site, just as you would your resume. If you are marketing yourself using postcards as promotional material, be sure to include your Web address on the postcard. If your school has job boards, be sure to include your Web address on any applications you fill out. Also incorporate it in any bios you create for professional organizations, clubs, museum shows, volunteer work, or workshops you attend. If you do anything for your local community, send a press release to the local newspaper and include your Web site address. The business desk of the newspaper will provide you with some guidelines on the proper procedure. You can also use a Web news release service such as PR Web (www.prweb.com/), free of charge—but don't post a press release unless you have something to say.

Don't forget to show your Web site to your current employer. It will serve to remind them how talented you are; and don't forget any companies you do freelance work for. You never know to whom they might mention your site!

Design a cool freebie. Generate a contest. Who doesn't like free stuff? If your budget will allow, head to the dollar store in your area and pick up some items that might make nice giveaways. Send the promotion to anyone you think might be beneficial to your career. (Just don't purchase anything you deem to be questionable in terms of taste.) Personalize the subject line of your email to attract their attention.

Never overlook the power of newsgroups. Find one that interests you and jump in! Let's say you enjoy sports. Find the newsgroup for your favorite team and become a member. Contribute to the discussion, and when you "sign off, include a "signature" under your name at the bottom of your message. This is a subtle way to send your message without offending anyone.

If you know anyone who creates newsletters in your area of expertise, offer to write an article. With your name and Web address at the bottom, you will effectively get your name out there for others to see.

You will also want to attract potential employers to your site via search engines. There's nothing quite so thrilling as typing your name (or the name of your company) into a search engine such as Google, Dogpile, Ask Jeeves, AltaVista, or Yahoo! and seeing your Web site appear on the very first page of "hits." How do you make that happen? The trick is to have your Web pages examined by the different search engines. It doesn't have to cost a dime, but it is a little complicated. First, you have to announce to the various companies that you wish to be included in their pages. It may take as long as four to six weeks (and longer) before you see yourself listed. So

many Web sites are now being added on a daily basis that the search companies are behind in their evaluation schedules. You may even have to resubmit several times before you get results. Have patience. You can also pay a service to list your site for you, but if you are persistent you can so it yourself.

All the search engines will list you for free, although for a fee, they will "express" list you. This is a fast-track process designed to get your site out there faster. The cost varies from a low of $30 at Ask Jeeves to $299 (for one year) at Yahoo! It's not cheap, but it may be worth it if you are in a hurry to get your site noticed.

The best strategy to explore is directly at your Web site. Insert special words that will help the search engines locate you more easily. These words, called *meta tags*, are embedded in your Web page coding. Your software package will offer helpful information on how and where to place meta tags. Also write a short descriptive title that will appear at the top of every one of your Web pages. Once your site is online, the search engines will send out special robots (called spiders) to evaluate your site. The spider will look at your meta tags in order to index the content on your site. This, in part, determines your site's ranking when someone tries to find you using a search engine.

How does a Web site get ranked in the number-one position in a search engine? No one really knows all of the formulas that are used to select the first site from a search. Some think that it is a combination of meta tags, content tags, title descriptions, relevancy of Web pages to the aforementioned items, and just good plain luck. There are products designed to help you better position your Web pages. WebPosition Gold (www.webposition-gold-2.net) is one such product. It analyzes your existing Web pages and gives

above • Carefully observe the body language of the interviewer. Look for nonverbal clues as to their interest level. People who are involved in what you have to say generally sit up straight or lean in toward you. This young man is obviously quite engrossed in the artwork. The job is practically yours!

right • It may seem as if it will take forever, but you will find the job of your dreams! Keep working on your digital and traditional portfolio. Practice job interviews, network, and hang in there.

advice on how to improve them. It comes with a simple HTML editor and even submits your pages to the major search engines.

Another way to get people to your site is by linking it to others. This not only helps your traffic, it has the added benefit of making your site look more attractive to the search engines, and will help raise your overall ranking. The first step to do this is to contact Open Directory Project (www.dmoz.com), a dedicated to helping you get your site out to the major engines. A volunteer group of people there provide directory services for the most popular search engines and portals, including Netscape Search, AOL, Google, Lycos, HotBot, DirectHit, and hundreds of others.

Do you belong to any professional organizations that maintain Web sites? Ask for a link to your site from their main page. Does your local community have a

Web site? How about your local chamber of commerce? Ask if you might include a link in its pages as well.

Addressing the Long-Term Needs of Your Portfolio

Your portfolio is a work in progress. As such, it will never be finished. You are a designer; you should and will always be making new art. Therefore, you will always be updating your portfolio to reflect your advancement in your career[md]replacing student work with professional pieces, for example. Furthermore, you should always have extra pieces that you can rotate into the port as the job potential changes.

Electronic portfolios, too, should be updated on a regular basis. Software is upgraded almost every year and a half, and each version change brings greater sophistication. Your digital port should reflect the newest techniques available. This always means a little extra work, but that's what being a professional is all about. ■

ANNUAL REPORT: A corporate document that provides important information to the stockholders about the company. This information includes details about the financial status of the company, and offers insight into the management philosophy.

BACKGROUND CHECK: A procedure used by companies to verify the information provided by an applicant on his or her application form. These items can include: employment verification, educational background, and references.

BENEFITS: Your compensation package. The medical benefits, life insurance, sick leave, holidays, vacation, stock options, and retirement plan are all of your salary negotiation. A good benefits package can add up to 40 percent of your salary.

CAREER FAIR: Special events in which employers from many different companies come to interview candidates and fill positions. There are many types of job and career fairs, from generalized ones that a city might hold to an industry-specific one for professionals.

CAREER OBJECTIVE/JOB OBJECTIVE: A concise statement about your accomplishments or job goals. This is not a required part of the resume, but used wisely, it can focus the employer's attention on the specifics of your focus.

CAREER PLANNING: The process of appraising your skills, personality, and career path in order to make informed decisions about future employment.

COLD CALL: Contacting a potential company without first sending a cover letter and/or a resume. This is one way of uncovering jobs that might not be otherwise advertised.

CORPORATE CULTURE: The behaviors, routines, and regulations dictated by company policy and adhered to by employees. Corporate culture can refer to both formal and informal company policies concerning every-

thing from dress code and employee relationships to breaks, social interactions, and professional hierarchy. It is important to learn about a company's culture before you accept a position, to make sure you will fit in and be happy.

COUNTEROFFER/COUNTERPROPOSAL: An offer made by a potential employer that counters an offer you have proposed. The negotiations begin with the employer's first offer. If you wish, you may make a counter offer in the hopes of securing a higher salary or more benefits. The employer then counters that to make yet one more offer. This is generally used to arrive at a compromise when the employer and employee are far apart in salary range. It can involve money, benefits, or special job perks (such as a company car).

DECLINING LETTER: A letter sent to an employer to turn down a job offer. It is considered a courtesy to submit a formal refusal when a job is offered that you are not accepting. You never know when you might want to work for them in the future!

DEGREES AND CERTIFICATIONS: Official recognition bestowed upon a student upon completion of a program of study. These may come from workshops, trade schools, colleges, and universities.

DIRECTIVE (OR STRUCTURED) INTERVIEW: Interview in which a predetermined set of situational questions are asked. These questions are designed to gather specific information about your ability to handle the job.

DOMAIN NAME: The "zip code" in a Web address. A domain name directs a request for a Web site or an email to its final destination. A domain name is always composed of two words or phrases, separated by dots; for example, yahoo.com.

DRESS FOR SUCCESS: The idea that what you wear should reflect a professional attention to detail. Dressing properly will give you a competitive

edge by making a positive first impression.

HIDDEN JOB MARKET: Job openings that are not publicized. Experts believe that as many as 20 percent of all jobs are never advertised. You can learn about such jobs by making cold calls to employers, networking, or just checking the company's job board (see Job boards).

JOB BOARDS: A place within an organization where positions are listed. It might within a company or in a general area such as at the job placement office of the local college. Jobs are generally sorted by profession. Job boards may also be posted at the specific Web site of the organization.

LETTER OF ACCEPTANCE: A document you provide that states you approve in writing of a job offer. It's very important that you answer a job offer in writing, to restate the dates, conditions, and salary structure of the offer.

LETTER OF AGREEMENT: A document provided by the employer offering you a job. It details the dates, conditions, and salary structure of the offer.

LETTER OF RECOMMENDATION: A document written on your behalf in support your statement of job skills and work ethic. It is usually written by a former boss, coworker, or friend.

META TAG: Special words that will help the search engines locate Web sites. These tags are embedded in Web page coding.

NONDIRECTIVE INTERVIEW: An unstructured interview, comprised of probing open-ended questions to encourage the job candidate to do most of the talking.

RECRUITERS: (Also known as "headhunters" or "executive search firms.") Professionals whose job it is to identify and prequalify candidates for specific positions. They usually specialize in specific industries or geographic regions, work for corporations, and typically are paid on a commission basis for successfully placing the applicant.

RESIGNATION: A formal letter declaring that you will be leaving the present job within a specified period of time (usually two weeks). It's very important to leave any job under the best of terms. You never know when you might need that contact.

RESUME: A short descriptive summary of your educational and work history. It lists your primary skills and strengths. Your resume and portfolio are your most important job hunting tools.

SALARY: Typically, a fixed and agreed-on amount of compensation paid to an employee over a specified period of time, usually annually. Salary may also include additional monies in the form of overtime, bonuses, and other benefits.

SALARY HISTORY: Documentation of the compensation you have received at each of your previous jobs. This information is never revealed to a prospective employer unless absolutely necessary. If you admit to making too little, you may not be offered what you are currently worth. If you made too much, the new company may not feel that it can afford you. This issue is best skirted, if possible.

SALARY NEGOTIATION: The act of discussing salary in order to arrive at a satisfactory result for both the employer and employee. The goal is to obtain the best possible salary for your skills and years of experience. However, salary to some degree is based on industry standards, which can vary from region to region.

TEMPING: Working part-time for a specified period. Some companies use temps to prequalify people for full-time employment. Occasionally, companies just need extra help on a big job or to fill in for permanent employees who are on vacation or leave. Many temp workers enjoy moving from position to position because they offer new challenges, flexibility, and variety. Numerous agencies specialize in placing people into part-time or short-term positions.

TESTING: An in-house exercise designed to test your ability and skill for a given position. Job tests can be nerve-wracking, but can be useful to the employer. They prove that you really can perform as you state on your resume. You may, for example, be asked to create something on the spot, under timed conditions. Another form of testing is for drugs.

THANK-YOU LETTERS: A follow-up note written to express thanks for the opportunity to interview with a prospective employer. A thank-you letter is considered a common courtesy and should always be sent after an interview. Only a small percentage of job seekers actually complete this task, and by doing so you separate yourself positively from the crowd.

WEB HOST: A company responsible for keeping your Web site up and running

Bibliography

Baron, Cynthia L. *Designing a Digital Portfolio.* Indianapolis, IN:: - New Riders Publishing, 2003.

Berryman, Gregg. *Designing Creative Portfolios.* Menlo Park: Crisp Publications, Inc., 1994.

Cox, Mary. *Artist's & Graphic Designer's Market.* Palm Coast, FL: Writers Digest Books, 2004.

Fleishman, Michael. *Starting Your Career as a Freelance Illustrator or Graphic Designer.* New York: Watson-Guptill Publications, 2001.

Heron, Michael, and David MacTavish. *Pricing Photography: The Complete Guide to Assignment & Stock Prices.* New York: Allworth Press, 1997.

Hungerland, Buff. *Marketing your Creative Portfolio.* Ci Upper Saddle River, NJ: Prentice Hall, 2003.

Linton, Harold. *Portfolio Design, 2nd ed.* New York: W.W. Norton & Company, 2000.

Marquand, Ed. *How to Prepare Your Portfolio, 3rd ed.* New York: Art Direction Book Company, 1995.

McKenna, Anne T. *Digital Portfolio: 26 Design Portfolios Unzipped.* Gloucester, MA: Rockport Publishers, 2000.

Metzdorf, Martha. *The Ultimate Portfolio.* Cincinnati, OH: North Light Books. 1991.

Romaniello, Stephen. *The Perfect Digital Portfolio.* New York: Sterling Publishing Company, 2003.

Scher, Paula. *The Graphic Design Portfolio.* New York: Watson-Guptill Publications, 1992.

Supon Design Group. *The Right Portfolio for the Right Job.* New York: Madison Square Press, 1999.

Tain, Linda. *Portfolio Presentation for Fashion Designers.* New York: Fairchild Publications, 1998.

Williams, Anna Graf. *Creating Your Career Portfolio.* Upper Saddle River, NJ: Prentice Hall, 2001.

Appendix: Internet Resources

Drost, Herman. 2002. "How to Prepare Images for Your Web Site, Part 2." Available online at www.isitebuild.com/imageoptimization2.htm.

Holzschlag, Molly. 2000. "Color My World." Available online at www.molly.com/articles/webdesign/2000-09-colormyworld.php.

ICANN. 2004. "Building a Website." Available online at www.icann.org/new.html.

Johansson, Donald. 2002. "Colors on the Web." Available online at www.webwhirlers.com/colors/combining.asp.

Kimball, Trevor. 2003. "My Design Studio." Available online at www.mydesignprimer.com/index.html.

Lerner, Michael. 2004. "Building a Website." Available online at www.learnthenet.com/english/html/51server.htm.

Litt, Judy. 2004. "Graphic Design." Available online at http://graphicdesign.about.com/.

Lynch, Patrick J., and Sarah Horton. 2002. "Web Style Guide," 2nd ed. Available online at www.webstyleguide.com.

Monster Interview Center. 2004. Available online at interview.monster.com/archives/attheinterview.

National Association of Colleges and Employers. Jobweb. 2004. Available online at www.jobweb.com/Resumes_Interviews/default.htm.

Black, Jillian. "Primary Colors." 2004. Available online at www.netwrite-publish.com/color4.htm.

"Psychology of Color." 2004. Available online at www.tamingthebeast.net/articles/colour.htm.

Hege, Ståle, and Jan Egil Refsnes. Refsnes Data. 2004. W3 Schools. Available online at www.w3schools.com.

So You Wanna Design Your Own Web Page? 2000. Available online at www.soyouwanna.com/site/syws/designpage/designpage.html.

Timberlake, Sean. 2004. "The Basics of Navigation." Available online at www.sitenavigation.net/snguide.html.

Williams, Robin. 2004. "Type Talk." Available online at www.eyewire.com/index.htm.

Index